UNEMPLOYED YOUTH AND SOCIAL EXCLUSION IN EUROPE

Unemployed Youth and Social Exclusion in Europe

Learning for Inclusion?

SUSAN WARNER WEIL
SOLAR, University of the West of England, UK
DANNY WILDEMEERSCH
University of Leuven, Belgium
THEO JANSEN
University of Nijmegen, The Netherlands

with

BARRY PERCY-SMITH
SOLAR, University of the West of England, UK

Routledge
Taylor & Francis Group

LONDON AND NEW YORK

First published 2005 by Ashgate Publishing

2 Park Square, Milton Park, Abingdon, Oxon OX14 4RN
711 Third Avenue, New York, NY 10017, USA

Routledge is an imprint of the Taylor & Francis Group, an informa business

First issued in paperback 2016

British Library Cataloguing in Publication Data
Weil, Susan Warner
  Unemployed youth and social exclusion in Europe : learning
  for inclusion?
  1.Unemployed youth - Europe 2.Unemployment - Government
  policy - Europe 3.Youth - Employment - Government policy -
  Europe 4. Marginality, Social - Europe 5.Young adults -
  Europe - Social conditions
  I.Title II.Wildemeersch, Danny III.Jansen, Theo
  331.3'4137'7'094

Library of Congress Cataloging-in-Publication Data
Weil, Susan Warner.
  Unemployed youth and social exclusion in Europe : learning for inclusion? / by Susan
Warner Weil, Danny Wildemeersch, and Theo Jansen with Barry Percy-Smith.
     p. cm.
  Includes bibliographical references and index.

  1. Unemployed youth--Europe--Social conditions. 2. Unemployed youth--Services for--
Europe. 3. Unemployed youth--Services for--Research. 4. Youth with social
disabilities--Europe. 5. Marginality, Social--Europe. I. Wildemeersch, Danny. II.
Jansen, Theo. III. Title.

  HQ799.E85W45 2004
  305.235'094--dc22
                                                                    2004021036

ISBN 978-0-7546-4130-8 (hbk)
ISBN 978-1-138-25897-6 (pbk)

Contents

Foreword

Susan Warner Weil and the writing team have, in this book, produced a new and challenging analysis of the situation of young European citizens aged between 18 and 25 who are unemployed. Drawing on evidence from six countries from Western Europe, they have problematized the dominant discourses that drive policy and practice in this field. Many have done this before them, but few have extended beyond critique to provide a sustained and systematic elaboration of ideas and frameworks that offer fundamentally different ways of approaching the 'activation' of young people at an international level.

I first met Susan Warner Weil and Barry Percy-Smith at a series of research seminars and conferences associated with the Economic and Social Research Council's *Youth Citizenship and Social Change* program, and subsequently met Danny Wildemeersch for the first time at the Learning Lab, Denmark. They were generous enough to say on those occasions that they had been inspired by my advocacy that we need to get into the 'espoused, enacted and experienced' levels when researching youth 'measures' at international level. I was greatly honored when later they invited me to write the foreword to this excellent product of their own original thinking and research.

In recent years, youth transitions theory has been developed beyond the established but oversimplified structure/agency framework to an approach that relates macro-structural influences to individual level motivation and action. Much better understandings of 'transitions' are emerging as researchers seek to elaborate and investigate concepts of the socially located subject, bounded agency and social-cultural capital as mediated through practices in the family and community. This has owed much to the efforts of researchers who have risen to the challenges of working at international level. At this level, it has been possible to learn from the best of the rich youth research traditions of western Europe: from the structural analysis tradition of British youth research, to the philosophical underpinnings of continental approaches; from the Nordic life course research to Southern European socio-cultural traditions.

The 3-year, EU-funded research project on which this volume is based has investigated the situation of young European citizens aged between 18 and 25 who are unemployed in: Flanders, Belgium; Denmark; Germany; the Netherlands; Portugal; and England, the UK. The researchers explore schemes and programs that are meant to 'activate' young people, encountering an array of practices that are 'manifestations of dominant activation policies and discourses'. They uncover, at the 'espoused' level, the 'obsession' of policy makers with activation, comparing neo-liberal approaches with the various social democratic stances. At the levels at which policy is enacted and experienced, the voices of the actors –

young people and practitioners – come through as insightful, illuminating and diverse.

The most important, original and central idea of this book is to contrast 'restricting activation' with 'reflexive activation'. In reflexive activation, problematizing the excluded becomes problematizing exclusion; limited responsibilities become extending responsibilities; and de-contextualized practices become contextualized. Reflexive activation addresses paradox and contradiction, and focuses on reforming the 'action space' of activation as the authors lead the reader through the themes of changing labor market identities, transforming competencies and shifting pedagogies. Arguing that 'alternative visions of what may be possible in reconciling social and economic tensions remain under-explored', the authors propose a new approach to interventions in the lives of young unemployed adults. Any review of the history of 'initiatives' and pilot projects in this field tells us that the 'managing by projects' approach is not serving us very well. Continuous re-invention without systemic learning reproduces closed loops and serious errors. Impediments to public learning and failures of policy memory are seen as perverse consequences of the instruments of reform that are being used. But the authors do not 'throw out the baby with the bathwater'. They offer the reader 'performance management and accountability in a different key' – *participatory* monitoring and evaluation as a reaction against the uni-linear flow of accountability demands, creating 'ripple effects' instead of 'roll-outs', and permeable boundaries which allow for continuing review of new horizons or lines of inquiry that may have opened up.

Finally, the authors aim to practice what they preach. The activation of youth in research and policy domains is complex and difficult territory; yet the authors offer examples and analysis that go well beyond the statements of worthy intent about the importance of the 'voice' of young people. Discussing what is appropriate and what is not appropriate in 'involvement' strategies, they bring us full circle to the question of leadership, asking whether the EU is capable of exerting the kinds of leadership that will enable participatory public learning without becoming colonized by dominant technocratic discourses?

A tall order, indeed, but in the chapters which follow the authors convince us it is a question worth asking and a challenge worth pursuing. In Noam Chomsky's words, 'if you act like there is no possibility of change for the better, you guarantee that there will be no change for the better. The choice is ours, the choice is yours…'.

Karen Evans[1]
May 2004

---

[1] Karen Evans is Professor/Chair in Education (Lifelong Learning) and Head of School of the School of Lifelong Education and International Development, Institute of Education, University of London, UK.

Preface

The publication of book is the final product of the *Balancing Competencies* project, which was conceived in 1997. It has been the result of intensive and creative work that began with the writing of a project proposal for the *Targeted Socio-Economic Research Programme* of the *4th EU Framework on Research and Development*. As you will see, we conducted research in six European countries (Flanders, Belgium; Denmark; Germany; the Netherlands; Portugal; the United Kingdom, England), on the limitations and opportunities of education, training employment, and guidance practices and policies for 18-25 year olds. The research started in 1998 and finished in 2002. In 2001 we published a final research report that is available on the web.[1] In 2002 we submitted to the European Commission an additional report called 'Refocusing Balancing Competencies'.[2]

After the report was completed, the authors of this book embarked on an intensive study project. This involved wide reading, extensive reworking of earlier presentations of research findings, the addition and deepening of insights from our empirical work, and further development of new ideas, concepts and theorizations concerning activation practices and policies, at the level of practice and the wider system. The key themes of both the research and this publication are, all over Europe, acknowledged as main issues for concern and for joint effort. We present them here as questions with which we engage throughout this book:

- How does and might the EU intervene to help to reconcile high rates of unemployment *and* social exclusion of youth and young adults?

  - What strategies can support learning for inclusion and learning from diversity, in ways that give rise to greater social and economic empowerment amongst young Europeans, both as individuals and as members of communities?

  - Is 'activation' as currently espoused, enacted and monitored, through existing policies, an appropriate remedy?

  - What other strategies are required, beyond those currently developed in the field of education, training, employment, and guidance, which might help to redress inequalities now growing across Europe?

The empirical findings from our research were extensive, but at its core are descriptions and analyses of specific projects, that, in the above mentioned countries, aim at facilitating the economic and social participation for young adults who are at risk of being excluded. The inevitable tensions arising from EU aspirations to this dual objective (in the context of a globalizing economy) are placed at the core of our inquiry and this book. As importantly, throughout the research, we were aware that notions such as (un)employment, employability, exclusion, inclusion, and activation are social constructions, reflecting in different ways specific interpretations of social and economic conditions by different actors. This insight became the leading thread of the conversations and studies that finally resulted in this book publication.

Our starting point is that each actor involved – policy makers, professionals, young adults, and researchers – operates on the basis of specific yet often contradictory and diverse perspectives. These are intended to control and order the complicated and messy phenomena of unemployment and social exclusion. Policy makers tend to be dominated by managerial and economic concerns; professionals by pedagogical questions. Young adults are experiencing the condition of unemployment and social exclusion as an existential affliction. Researchers tend to privilege the discourse of logic and rationality. Yet, none of these perspectives tells us what (un)employment and social exclusion really are, nor what the correct remedies should be – they are just different, and always restricted, ways of looking at the world and coping with its unbearable complexity.

Elaborating on this assumption, we organized the book around tensions and possibilities at the interfaces between the voices of these different actors, while remaining alert to global discourses, such as neo-liberal economics, 'modernization', and so called 'progressive learning strategies' in the field of unemployment. We focused on the interstices and impediments that arise, when different and, by definition, limited perspectives are negotiated in specific practices of education, training, employment, and guidance for young unemployed. The paradoxes, contradictions, and dilemmas that arise when different perspectives meet; the irreconcilability and unintended consequences, as well as the possibilities – that is what we illuminate through this book.

As such, we do not present 'solutions' in a traditional sense. What we learnt from our research and study is the vanity of approaches that pretend to 'know' how to generate 'learning for inclusion' for youth-at-risk. We explore the paradoxes arising from failures across different groups of actors trying to remain critically reflexive. And thus, we too have been confronted with the paradox of how to represent our perspective on the multi-facetted nature of (un)employment and social exclusion, recognizing always its potential narrowness, and the scope for simplification and technocratic exploitation of what we offer here.

We have engaged with this project knowing that, if there are any imaginable solutions at all to the dilemmas of social exclusion and unemployment, they cannot reside in education, training, employment, and guidance activities alone. We concur with findings reported in a recent summary of EU research on such issues: namely, that 'education measures need to be reinforced by wider social and economic reforms when addressing social exclusion' (PJB, 2003). At the same time, we believe that policy and practice choices must become more connected to dialogues that are critical, creative, and respectful, and that support all actors in finding a voice helping them to be taken seriously. We need new forms of inquiry and research that help us – in the real time of initiatives – to become more alert to the unintended effects of policy intentions and everyday choices, and that challenge us to move beyond mere advocacy from diverse perspectives.

As a consequence of our attempt to deal with such challenges induced by conditions of late modernity, readers will notice the interweaving of different styles in this book. The very nature of the complexity with which we have engaged, and the research approach we have adopted, encouraged us to develop a text that is itself an aesthetic contribution. This reflects the idea that form and content need not be separated, and that research can be communicated through a wider set of discourses than usually expressed in academic texts. This is important to us, if research is to generate dialogues and learning in the wider world. Our various voices and the styles we use (analytical, empirical, propositional, metaphorical, ironic, narrative, and imaginative) are unfolded gradually through the text. It was our intention to create a sense of insight as emerging questions from our research are gradually 'layered in' more and more deeply, thereby mirroring key aspects of our own research journey. We hope that these more and less familiar forms of representing research can support readers through different forms of co-inquiry and engagement with this material, while staying reflexive about their own assumptions and choices. All of us can, all too easily, presume to know all about the issues explored here – and all too easily, cease to be humble about our individual and collective blindness. Such learning, also, has had to become integral to our own story as a research and writing team. More specifically, the book develops as follows:

Part I is written in mostly a storytelling and multi-voiced narrative style that invites readers to engage with this text in various ways. This section sets out the research intentions and questions that preoccupied us at the beginning of this project. It introduces the research approach that enabled us to learn from each other and our various findings as we went along. We then open up the main contours of European conversations about employability and activation that we encountered through our case studies, and their often not too clear connections with the lives and projects experienced by young Europeans. Three multi-voiced narratives invite readers to imagine themselves as unemployed, and to consider the choices that are open to young Europeans in this situation. Each narrative is followed by ironic and reflexive questioning that encourages readers to enter into a co-inquiry alongside us, and to suspend, temporarily, their fixed positions. Through these interweaving styles, we are able to foreground the main paradoxes, contradictions and dilemmas which we further grapple with in the following chapters.

In Part II we adopt a more traditional academic and qualitative research style to describe and analyze the empirical findings. Firstly, we unfold more contours in the landscape of projects that we studied, thereby developing issues introduced in Part I. We then look at this landscape through different lenses:

- that of the 'inner logics' of participants in activation projects and the notion of changing working identities;

- that of agency and empowerment, with a view to the impact of different understandings of competency-in-action;
- that of professionals' dilemmas of action and choice in projects that are increasingly being impacted upon by wider systemic discourses, including those relating to performance management and audit.

In each chapter of Part II, the perspectives of youth and professionals are played off against each other in the context of various projects. Pedagogical interventions and existential practices are interpreted and discussed, using conceptual and theoretical languages that characterize much academic discourse. However, throughout, this discourse remains grounded in the voices of young adults and professionals, and the range of empirical material on which this book draws.

Part III is tuned in a related, but different key. We address European ideologies and national policies and strategies related to 'activation'. Giving due attention to the political nature of this topic, the style develops more into a critical investigation of the (untested) assumptions and consequences of mainstream strategies, and the vastly unexplored options for alternative interventions that might better support 'learning for inclusion'. We develop in some depth discourses of restrictive and reflexive activation. We then consider how principles of, for example, connective inquiry and valuing diversity might support less restrictive activation through new forms of policy learning and inquiry across the EU context. We consider in practice what it may mean to involve different groups of social actors in such processes, with particular attention to the participation of young adults in nontokenistic ways.

We, the authors, hope that the enthusiasm and excitement that have sustained us throughout this project, from its start in 1998 through to the finishing of this book, will inspire readers. Now, more than ever, as we expand the EU, we need to punctuate advocacy of solutions to 'learning for inclusion' with the humility of a permanent question mark. The greatest reward for the effort we have invested in this book will derive from conversations about whether and how we have helped to validate and spark creative practices and more reflexive discourses of education, training, employment, and guidance across the EU.

Susan Warner Weil, Danny Wildemeersch and Theo Jansen
with Barry Percy-Smith
2004.

---

[1] http://www.improving-ser.jrc.it/.
[2] Wildemeersch (2002).

Acknowledgements

We are well aware that this book would not have been possible without the creative input of all the researchers and practitioners who have been involved in it over the years. The authors also want to express their gratitude to all the young participants in the projects we visited and observed, as well as their coaches, teachers and trainers, and other professionals and policy makers. This includes all those who were willing to engage in the focus groups and in reflections on the intermediate and final findings and interpretations. Everywhere, with no exception, we were welcomed very warmly and without reservation by everyone. Such collaboration and support is vital to a project like this, in which we attempt to reflect deeply on the everyday experiences of the actors involved and to explore wider significations of this. Certainly, without this, what has resulted here just would not have been possible.

We are also well aware that thanks to the active participation of these partners, a larger number of diverse communities of practitioners, policy makers, and researchers will now have access to very interesting, relevant, and lively material. We hope this will generate various opportunities to develop a more informed and critical understanding of policies and practices of activation, and the courage to recognize and act on what else is possible.

And now we turn to our European team of co-researchers. This project required us all to meet for regular 3-day intensive seminars. Together, we would refine and further develop the emergent research design approach that the TSER program had, to our delight, approved. We would debate and agree research methods, revising these as we learned what was possible and where further research was demanded by what had emerged thus far. We would risk re-framing and re-focusing our research questions, tracking throughout convergences and divergences across our research findings. We found the right balance of challenge and support, as we struggled to make sense of the cumulative nature of our research cycles, and with how best to give our findings expression. Gradually, theorizations emerged without becoming disconnected from the voices and practices of those who were also participating in this project back in our respective countries. We gradually discovered that in this kind of research, we too were the field. What was happening between us 'in our seminars' was generating as much data and insight as that which we were gathering 'out there', in that wider field in which we were all too a part.

Everyone who has been involved in this kind of European research knows how intensive and sometimes chaotic it can be, and how much extra time and energy it takes to bring such an adventure to a good end. If such a project is successful, how rewarding it can be for those involved.

Through what has been a truly rewarding project, our research team has created a base and a network, which has been fruitful at various other occasions and sustains collaborations until this day, including the preparation of this book by ourselves as members of this original team. Therefore, in addition to reiterating our expression of thanks above to all participants in our research, we extend our deepest gratitude to our co-researchers. It is you who contributed to the very exciting research experience from which we have been able to 'grow' this book:

Ines Amaro (Lisbon), Carine Ex (Nijmegen), Wiltrud Gieseke (Berlin), Knud Illeris (Roskilde), Marc Jans (Leuven), Christin Janssens (Leuven), Elke Roex (Leuven), Annette Karseras (SOLAR, UK) Bernd Käpplinger (Berlin), Noemi Katznelson (Roskilde), Manuela Marinho (Lisbon), Barry Percy-Smith (SOLAR, UK), Birgitte Simonsen (Roskilde). Furthermore, we wish to offer a special thanks to Lieve Van Den Brande and Angelos Agalianos of DG Research of the European Commission who very much supported us as researchers in keeping the complexities and uncertainties of such a project under control.

With regard to this major book project, we wish to thank:

Marc Vlecken (Leuven) for your patient and excellent administrative support whenever called upon, electronically and otherwise;
Hans De Greve (Leuven) for the careful composition of the index;
Veronica Dunning (SOLAR, UK) for how you held, so graciously and skillfully, the crucial organizational and logistical threads that enabled us to work across four countries without too much stress;
Madeleine Munro for your superb support throughout this book journey, but especially for coming to my rescue at the end with the proofing, alongside Dianne;
Dianne Walsh for your moral support, generosity of spirit and significant investment of time and skill in searching out relevant literature, and finalizing the references, when you were juggling so many other commitments too – and again, for coming to the rescue at the end with the proofing – brilliant work, so valuable and timely, so much appreciated;
Naomi Katznelson for allowing us to re-develop the core of your fine chapter on young adults' inner logics (published in our final report, EU, 2001 and now part of a completing PHD project at the University of Roskilde);
Marc Jans, Christin Janssens and Barry Percy-Smith for allowing the same liberty with your excellent chapter on Interpretive Professionals, also published in our final EU report;
Bernd Käpplinger and Wiltrud Gieseke, for letting us make use of your original chapter on 'learning cultures' in the 2001 report as the springboard for Chapter 5;
Barry Percy-Smith for offering literature, time and invaluable insights throughout this project, and for offering and checking text related to involving young adults as co-researchers;
Liz Hayes and Alan Taylor for your timely encouragement and advice at the end;
Annette Karseras for your support with our original proposal to the EU and the TSER project when with SOLAR, UK and, from your new base in Japan, for

seeing us through so valiantly to this book's end. Your editing and invaluable help with the text went well beyond your brief to produce camera ready copy. Thank you for investing so much of yourself in this project and such high quality work, as ever. We could not have done it without you.

We would also like to extend our thanks to everyone at Ashgate who found the right blend of patience and determination to see us through to publication.

Finally, we wish to thank all of our colleagues, friends, and families who kept believing that this was truly a worthwhile endeavor that deserved our time and energy. As importantly, you and everyone above trusted throughout that we would see this through to an end some day.

And so, has this venture come to an end? That now, is a matter for you, our readers, as you engage with the unfolding of this book. We hope it will awaken some fresh thinking and practice, give you courage, and catalyze new dialogues and inquiry about the many challenging matters we open up herein. These will long continue to concern us and we hope, many others: policy makers, practitioners, professionals, and researchers. A failure to learn from diversity and for inclusion as we enter into a newly expanded and more diverse Europe will have many social and economic costs, of that we are quite certain.

But it is the young adults who are so often labeled 'socially excluded', and who are perceived as 'unemployable', who have to live with the worst consequences of our failing to learn about 'learning for inclusion'; our resistances to understanding more fully the unintended consequences of often well meant interventions – at different levels of the EU. It is to them that we dedicate this book, in the hope that it will help give rise to less restrictive, and more reflexive, opportunities for social and economic participation in a newly expanded EU.

Susan Warner Weil, Danny Wildemeersch and Theo Jansen
with Barry Percy-Smith

PART I
ENCOUNTERS

Chapter 1

Orientations

Increasing Employability and Decreasing Social Exclusion: The Defining Tension

This book considers the situation of young European citizens, aged between 18 and 25, who are unemployed. Many, whose stories we open up here, are currently labeled 'socially excluded'. This term first came from UNESCO and the EU as an attempt to direct,

> attention to the social mechanisms that produce or sustain deprivation. Some of these are new, such as the declining demand for male unskilled or semi-skilled workers. Others derive from the welfare state itself (like poverty traps) or from social engineering that went wrong. The most notable example of these are 'estates on the edge' – housing estates built to alleviate poverty, but which have instead become areas of social and economic desolation... Exclusion refers to circumstances that affect more or less the entire life of the individual, not just a few aspects of it (Giddens, 2002, pp. 104-105; see also Power, 1997).

At its core is an exploration of various vocational education, training, guidance and employment schemes across Europe that are meant to 'activate' these young adults, through their narratives as well as those of the professionals who are meant to help them. This book opens up insights into their joint and painful entanglement in a difficult – if not impossible – 'policy–practice dance'. On the one hand, these schemes are meant to ring-fence young adults from official unemployment statistics and to keep them gainfully 'active', either in work or some form of preparation for work. Such schemes are also meant to 'deliver' on social exclusion objectives and somehow, simultaneously, contribute to the 'integration' of these young adults.

A myriad of paradoxes and contradictions inevitably arise for those involved in navigating – much less trying to reconcile – such a difficult cusp. Two different kinds of policy and practice objectives meet in the 'encounter space' of 'activation schemes'. Yet these objectives are inherently in tension, and often in direct conflict.

This book is based on a 3-year, EU-funded research project that involved six countries. At the beginning of our study in 1998, we characterized these economically as follows:

3

- Denmark (a 'post-welfare' state).

- The Netherlands and Flanders, Belgium (where the welfare state is being redefined in the perspective of social processes of individualization).

- Germany (and particularly, the former GDR at the stage of de-industrialization).

- Portugal (at the stage of primary industrialization).

- England, the UK (a post-welfare and post-industrial market oriented society).

We began our work by acknowledging the risks of focusing policy exclusively on the economic objectives that had guided the formation of the EU. Debate has been widening to consider how to maintain economic competitiveness in a globalizing market, without sacrificing social objectives (Ferrera et al., 2000). This is generating fresh thinking across the EU about:

- What policies and strategies can help in reconciling such tensions?

- What kinds of education, training, employment, and guidance interventions could benefit unemployed young people?

- How can young adults not be made casualties in a globalizing world economy?

- What particular kinds of strategies may help reduce inequalities and positively mediate processes of social and economic empowerment?

The European commitment to 'reconciling' such objectives – something we applaud – is made central to this book (Ferrera et al., 2000). However, what remains little understood is how these more progressive policy directions are being enacted, experienced, and indeed exacted at local levels, and with what intended and unintended consequences?

This book provides insights into what we learned about these questions. In particular, we focus on paradoxes, tensions, and contradictions that we found to be recurring across Europe at the policy–practice interface. We show how these can be exacerbated by processes of policy funding, implementation, regulation, accountability and performance management practices, and evaluation. We consider how current processes may be impacting directly (and unnecessarily) on the lives of young people and the practitioners who work with them. Further, we will illustrate how pressures at every level of the system for greater effectiveness and efficiency in public and private services are giving rise to levels of manufactured risk that may be unsustainable – either at the level of individual lives, or in the European economy as a whole (Weil, 1998; Brine, 2001).

Rather than being a cross-country 'comparative' study, our intention here is to offer 'systemic' insights into patterns that we found to be recurring with disturbing regularity across national boundaries. Further, we explore alternatives that may engage diverse practitioners, professionals, policy makers, researchers in different forms of dialogue and systemic inquiry that might better serve 'learning for inclusion' at all levels of the system – and involve and empower young adults in non-tokenistic ways.

It is with the voices of these young adults – whom policy and practice related to unemployment and social exclusion is meant to serve – that we now offer some untold tales of social and economic disempowerment and empowerment across Europe.

Young People Surviving and Thriving in Europe: Opening up a Conversation

In order to set the scene initially, we bring in the voices of two very different young adults. Firstly, we hear from Jimmy. Jimmy would be labeled 'socially excluded' in current policy discourses and, at the time of our research, was participating in a national scheme for long-term unemployed.

> *It was their attitude... I mean, I'd just been made homeless and they expected me to continue doing Environmental Task Force. Put me under a lot of stress, nearly had a nervous breakdown... cuz I had to go on this option [to get my money] rather than sort out my own life... I've been through this so many times it does my head in. It's not easy to live... hard work... worst thing is just waiting for a job. I want to work. But this ETF [Environmental Task Force] – I don't want to do it. But I've no choice. It's not what I want to do. It's nothing to do with what I want to do. They say to me, 'It'll give you experience and it'll give you skills'. But it doesn't matter because that experience ain't going to be nothing to do with what my life's about (Jimmy, project participant, New Deal, UK).*

The other person's voice comes from a student-produced newspaper at the University of Leuven. The writer is in his final years at university. We suggest that many concerned with 'activating young unemployed adults' would perceive him as having no difficulties with 'economic and social participation' – the terms in which the challenge was framed by the EU when we began our research:

> *Mobility and change, instability and lost roots are striking features of our so-called modern times. Fifty years ago it was pretty self-evident that your grave would not be dug too far away from the place where your cradle stood. It's different nowadays. You are born one place, where you are also possibly raised, then you run off to university in another city, go abroad for Erasmus, perhaps you return, work a little, and may do a postgraduate degree in yet another place. All this before you take over an assignment with a multi-national enterprise, which basically takes you everywhere. Along with these personal displacements come intervals of cultural innovation, which just get shorter and shorter over time... We all came here with friends and a social life*

established back home. However, here we discovered how enriching it can be to meet new people, hear new ideas, engage in fruitful exchanges, and establish all these wonderful things in their 'institutionalized' form – in the relationship of a friendship (Stefan, university student, Belgium).

Many young people across Europe are struggling to survive – and thrive – in conditions of growing complexity and uncertainty. Jimmy speaks from the 'margins' and sees himself positioned thus. Stefan perceives himself to be firmly within 'the mainstream'. What choices for social and economic participation are open to Jimmy, who lives in England? At the time of this writing, he would be offered the 'choice' of *New Deal*, the government-funded 'flagship welfare to work' scheme for unemployed young people (Behrens and Evans, 2002; Percy-Smith and Weil, 2003a, 2003b). Jimmy is faced with 'choosing' to be 'activated' – a problematic term, to say the least, in the context of his story. And not on his own terms, as he protests, but on terms defined by others who have influence and power in his life.

Activation in *New Deal* takes the form of advice and guidance through the *Gateway* – the introductory program to the scheme. This provides Jimmy with four options: full time education or training; participation in a subsidized job; work in the voluntary sector; or Environmental Task Force (ETF) (Behrens and Evans, 2002).

In the excerpt above, Jimmy makes it quite clear that he does not want the ETF option he has been given. This may have been dreamed up as a 'sexy alternative' by the policy formulators. But young people participating in this unemployment project have learned that this is the option to which the 'no hopers' get sent. Despite Jimmy saying this is not what he wants, he is being coerced to choose it. Given what he knows about who gets placed on ETF, he cannot see how this is going to help him get a job. He does not understand why this pressure is meant to keep him motivated to stay in *New Deal*.

The use of the word 'choice' in the rhetoric of *New Deal* can be even more confusing to the young adults involved. Jimmy is caught in a cleft stick, and knows it, as illustrated by his words. On the one hand, if Jimmy and his mates choose *not* to be 'activated' on the terms offered by his advisor, they lose access to any form of benefit. On the other hand, if Jimmy decides to follow his personal advisor's choice, he will receive some income support, and conveniently for others, will not be a statistic on the unemployment register.

Stefan sees the notion of choice quite differently. He is eager to benefit from these changing economic and social circumstances of the 21st century and feels certain that he and his colleagues will surely do so. For this university student, speaking here as a journalist for the student paper, fragmented life trajectories and globalization promise fulfillment, excitement, challenge, and travel. Jimmy is unlikely to move out of his 'socially excluded' position over the next few years, if ever. Stefan, in contrast, sees the world that awaits him as full of choice and opportunity. He is speaking as a privileged university student for whom unemployment does not even loom. Yet what Stefan does not know at this point in his life, as he navigates a cusp that he finds exciting, is that as for Jimmy, there are no guarantees of full employment ahead. Middle class, educated, and skilled people are increasingly required to make many job changes. They are likely to face redundancy at more than one point in their career, given the unpredictability of corporate behavior in the globalizing economy. They can be made unemployed in ways that seemed impossible to contemplate a decade ago (Chomsky, 1996; Sennett, 1998).

Jimmy is probably already familiar with first, second, even third generation unemployment, as a result of experience in his family and that of the community where he lives. Such unsettling yet strongly emergent possibilities do not seem to have impinged on Stefan's lifeworld as yet.

Jimmy and Stefan are two young adults living in the same Europe. For one, an encounter with the labor market via a scheme for unemployed youth has given rise to a narrative of entrapment; and despair. Although he voices his desire to break out of this situation and make something of his life, he is experiencing no sense of choice. He conveys a keen sense of knowing that this option is not right for him, yet he cannot risk turning down this so-called choice. Jimmy gives us an initial glimpse of how hard it can be to maintain some sense of labor identity or empowerment as he, and others in the same situation, struggles to make his way through changing social and economic circumstances, mediated by such project encounters.

In what follows, the assumptions and impact of projects for others like Jimmy across Europe will be shown to hide a far more complex and worrying picture than is often revealed by statistics and performance indicators (Percy-Smith and Weil, 2003).

Stefan's story stands in stark contrast. It is one of eager hopefulness. He is keen to exhort his student colleagues to embrace the possibilities offered by the smorgasbord world that awaits them beyond the walls of academe. He uses the first person plural without any self-consciousness. He confidently assumes that equal opportunities await himself and his friends. They believe that they can and will construct their own biographical and social narratives of choice as they leave university and will encounter numerous chances to give these meaning through work.

Stefan's prospective employers will be pleased. They seek young workers who can flexibly adapt to changing conditions, who will be willing to transfer from one job to another without complaint, who will work long hours and accept non-permanence as a permanent condition.

But if we stand back from these glimpses of two young people embarking on different journeys in the same world, it is possible to consider how their seemingly polarized positions are themselves collapsing under changing conditions of global capitalism. Beck (1992), in his *Risk Society,* argues that 'just as modernization dissolved the structure of feudal society, modernization today is dissolving industrial society and another modernity is coming into being' (p. 7). In such a context, we see the 'emergence of a new perception of uncertainty on the one hand and, on the other, new means of dealing with risk' (Nowotny et al., 2001, p. 45). Individuals and institutions are having to become more reflexive (see for example Beck, 1992; Chomsky, 1996; Sennett, 1999; Edwards and Usher, 2000; Beck and

Beck-Gernsheim, 2001; Nowotny et al., 2001). By this we mean, they are having to invent themselves again and again in order to survive – with no guarantees attached:

> who we are becomes something that we experience as a question to be answered rather than the answers resting in a pre-given order of things .. The 'we' [too] is problematic if constructed as a universal (Edwards and Usher, 2000, p. 101).

Labor force decisions being made by individuals are becoming ambiguous and insecure. In the context of a rapidly shifting globalizing marketplace that creates recurring experiences of dislocation, people are being compelled to write and re-write themselves into ever changing (auto)biographies – vocationally, individually, socially. Reflexivity – in other words, the capacity to construct and re-construct our identities and new narratives of self in relation to constantly changing notions of the labor market – becomes an essential skill for survival. We might therefore expect support for the development of such capacity to be made integral to notions of 'activation'.

This 'Activation' Trend: What's it all About?

Over the course of our research project and the writing of this book, we noted with interest significant shifts in social policy discourses. The naming and framing of programs for unemployed young people as 'activation initiatives' became more and more apparent. In the not so distant past, the term vocational Education, Training and Guidance (ETG) would have been widely used as relevant terms for projects aimed at unemployed young people. Why is this no longer a 'taken for granted' form of discourse? Of course, many initiatives are still referenced thus, but the rhetoric has changed. What is being signified by these shifts and new absences?

We first encountered the term 'activation' in the Danish context where there was high national employment. Young people who were deemed 'unemployable' or who were choosing to opt out of the labor market, despite being well equipped to enter it – by virtue of education and family background – were seen as in need of 'activating'. This discourse has spread slowly and persistently across continental Europe to become firmly entrenched in Brussels.

We have noticed with similar interest how 'activation' as an official term remains little used in the UK. However, no country in Europe is a stranger to the underlying concept of 'activation'. During the previous decade, an emphasis on active citizens, active jobseekers, active senior citizens, active communities, and the active welfare state has been prominent in social policy discourse across Europe. A parallel tendency is present in policies characterized by lifelong learning and policy rhetoric related to the 'learning society'. In any of these domains, the message is the same. Individuals are meant to assume active responsibility for their own learning, employment, and community welfare.

These shifts in discourse parallel radical challenges and changes to notions of the Welfare State: notions that are now transformed ways across European nation states. Such language shifts – when they enter a field – are often welcomed as an indication of progressive innovation. However, increasingly, the coercive and controlling dimensions of the new discourses are being registered (Jansen and Wildemeersch, 1996; Edwards, 1997; Coffield, 2000a, 2000b; Edwards and Usher, 2000). The policy rhetoric that celebrates the transformative powers of lifelong learning becomes suspect. These authors ask whether such terms are disguising a conflict of interests between employers and employees, and spell out new gaps between the socially included and excluded.

This book scratches well under the surface of the rhetoric about 'activating' unemployed Europeans, aged 18-25. Our research raises powerful questions about activation for whom, for what, and with what unintended consequences?

Throughout, we try to stay in a collaborative yet critically reflexive dialogue with readers, as we work with and beyond the substance and springboard of our research. We attempt to open up spaces through which 'glimpses of globalizing processes can be discerned' and activation approaches can be re-considered. We believe that our insights that follow, derived from our learning alongside young adults and professionals from within the 'swamp' of actual everyday practice (Schön, 1983) warrant new forms of attention and inquiry at all levels of the system – and especially at this time of European expansion and diversification.

Chapter 2

The Research Wellspring for this Book

An Innovative Research Approach

The distinctions and descriptions of our research approach that follow here may seem irrelevant to readers who see themselves as mainly practitioners. However, our experience with this project has shown us how easy it is to underestimate – even discount – the extent to which EU policy and practice is driven by traditional forms of research and evaluation, rooted in a view of society – and science – that is limited in its reach and impact. In Part III, we shall explore this tension further, suggesting that the failure to explore this connection and its influence on EU policy and practice has significant consequences for both young people and professionals. But first, we wish to introduce ourselves, and the work we undertook together over three years.

The research project on which this book is based involved practitioners, professionals, youth, policy makers, and European researchers from across six countries. We were funded – unusually in the EU at that time – for an innovative co-inquiry oriented and qualitative approach, based on principles of emergent design (Lincoln and Guba, 1985; Denzin and Lincoln, 1994; Reason and Bradbury, 2001). In other words, we were not overly tied into fixed research decisions, questions and outcomes, determined well in advance of our engagement with the field of our inquiry, Instead, we built into our design, opportunities for ongoing joint learning after each cycle of research within each of the participating countries. In this way, regular critically reflexive cross-country inquiry, into our collective findings, underpinned and guided re-formulations and re-framings of research questions and approaches as we went along.

The full team met regularly over two years. Our work was enlivened and enriched by differences in culture, nationality, age, academic discipline, and professional/practice background. For example, our research approach was shaped by different team members' experiences of reflexive ethnography, narrative-based research, post-positivist qualitative research, as well as action research and systemic action inquiry. Group members had experiences of youth work, adult education, experiential learning, social change, and community development. We were all accustomed to drawing on a wide range of literatures and disciplines.

Our intention throughout was not 'to prove', but to stimulate new forms of critical and creative inquiry amongst ourselves and for others working in the fields of unemployment and social exclusion. Our shared commitment was to undertaking research *with* people, and not on them.

The project interwove cycles of within-country and cross-country data collection, analysis, and co-inquiry. The project began with a cross-country meeting where we shared and documented our starting assumptions, questions, experiences, and orientations to issues of unemployment, education, training, and guidance, social exclusion and other related issues, as detailed below. Each country then engaged in an analysis of policy trends and patterns of provision for unemployed young people, aged 18-25 within each country. This was followed by parallel strands of focus group and co-inquiry activity. The first strand entailed discussions with a diverse range of practitioners, professionals, policy makers, program funders, and project designers. The second strand involved young unemployed people who were, or had been, on projects that set out to get them (back) into work. In the case of most participating countries, these networks of co-inquirers, although often fluid in their membership, took on the status of critical reference groups. They provided a sounding board for testing out, elaborating, and exploring in more depth insights, findings, questions, contradictions, and paradoxes arising from both within-country and cross-country inquiry. The final two cycles involved in-depth case study work: at least two were undertaken in each cycle and in each of the six participating countries. These entailed detailed explorations of specific activation projects. The case studies were further supported by documentation, national policy analysis, interviews, co-inquiry sessions, and iterative dialogues with those involved, including the focus group/networks.

Our design enabled the full team to meet at the end of each cycle of within-country data collection and analysis. Researchers would prepare a paper, raising issues that drew on the full range of participant voices and research activity. Prior to each meeting, these national papers would be reviewed by one country in preparation for our subsequent meeting. A seventh cross-country paper would result, outlining key contours, contradictions, and questions arising across the six within-country data sets.

The richness of this data far exceeds what could be portrayed in this book. For readers who are interested, papers and reports generated throughout our research are available on the EU TSER 4th framework website.[1] These will be of particular value to those readers who seek a more in-depth analysis of each country's research activity and the cross-country issues raised throughout the project, beyond that which has been able to be detailed here.

In keeping with our principles of emergent design, the full range of country-based papers produced for each cycle would underpin the three-day co-inquiry sessions that involved the entire team. These meetings entailed intense dialogue and continual challenge. They kept us alert to emerging patterns and possible significations arising from the 'whole' of that which we were encountering on the ground. We could take account of new and surprising insights and questions.

So, on the one hand, we engaged directly with local practices and diverse young people and practitioners' narratives about their expectations and everyday experiences of activation at local levels in each of the participating countries. We derived grounded insights into what it meant for young people and practitioners to engage in education, training, employment and guidance projects aimed at improving 'social and economic participation'.

At the same time, our research design enabled us to subject our findings to an ongoing systemic analysis. We could explore differences and commonalities suggested across the six countries' experiences. We could question the implications of these, and the mutually interacting influences that might be giving rise to recurring patterns. New and challenging questions could be posed, and carried back into country-specific research activity. At the same time, differences could be valued and explored in more depth, since we were not compelled to produce typologies that might have squeezed out the complexity of what we were discovering.

We never aspired to produce a detailed cross-country comparative analysis. Instead, our approach was intended to be more illuminative. We set out to look afresh at this field of activity, from alternative research perspectives. Our combined approach of subjecting local and cross-country data collection and analysis to co-inquiry continually provoked new forms of critical reflection and unanticipated interpretations of findings.

Each meeting cycle also enabled us to review and achieve consensus on subsequent research design choices and methodological practices. We would seek a balance between competing tensions in the group. On the one hand, there would be pulls towards wishing to order and de-limit data collection, or to seek data that would uphold academic models, theories, and assumptions brought a priori to this research. On the other hand, there was the desire to follow new questions that had not been anticipated and that challenged taken for granted thinking and practices that were being opened up by our transdisciplinary and cross-cultural discussions. Insights emerged from our three-day meetings that often surprised us, or challenged us to re-think our taken for granted theories of practice and assumptions about unemployment, young adults, education and training, social exclusion, governance and project/policy funding effectiveness and efficiency. Emergent findings continually gave rise to new imperatives: to look more widely or closely at issues that seemed to have systemic importance in terms of EU, national, and local strategies, and the unintended consequences of certain discourses and trends influencing 'activation' policy, performance management, and practice.

As we progressed, 'fractal patterns' began to suggest themselves. In other words, we became more and more alert to how specific projects across Europe were manifesting tensions, dilemmas, and contradictions that 'echoed' wider system dynamics that, in turn, were acting back on the projects, and either constricting or enhancing their capacity to reconcile social and economic objectives.

Co-generating Socially Robust Knowledge

Our concern throughout was to learn from local practice and to support learning from this research in the 'real time' of the project. At the same time, we expected that a sustained cross-European perspective on our local findings over the entire project would reveal substantive issues and areas for further critical attention and inquiry – on the part of practitioners, policy makers, and academics.

We were committed to producing socially robust research (see for example Nowotny et al., 2001). In other words, we tried to engage in research practices and presentations of findings that would be considered valid by those whom the research was meant to serve, rather than merely in a narrow scientific sense. We also kept diverse 'practice-knowledges' (of both practitioners and young people) and 'academic-knowledges' in active dialogue throughout this project. We saw these mutually influencing forms of expertise and processes as key to enabling this research not to become divorced from the social contexts in which we were jointly located.

We worked with notions of 'grounded theory' (Glaser and Strauss, 1967) – learning from the voices and experiences we were studying – and what Derek Layder (1998) refers to as 'adaptive theory', that:

> attempts to combine an emphasis on prior theoretical ideas and models which feed into and guide research while at the same time attending to the generation of theory from the ongoing analysis of data (p. 93).

Essentially, our approach was participative and processual rather than prescriptive and pre-determined. We were committed to multiple viewpoints being incorporated, both from an academic post-disciplinary perspective and in terms of what Behrens and Evans (2002) call the 'official, unofficial, institutional, group, individual' (p.18; see also Smith, 2002). Behrens and Evans' work itself helped to break through traditional conceptual barriers in youth-related research relating to agency and structure, and to compare and elucidate differing opportunity structures and pathways open to younger adults. Our concern was to focus more on local and systemic dynamics and complex responsive processes (Stacey, 2001) in a context of globalization. We were also strongly influenced by pioneering developments in the UK in the use of systemic inquiry and large-scale action research. This work was post-disciplinary, multi-methodological, and brought multiple stakeholders into new forms of dialogue as integral to the research itself. It focused particularly on tensions emerging from the implementation of policy in specific contexts of practice, and on possibilities from timely learning in the present, rather than merely retrospective learning (Weil, 1998; Midgley, 2000). Some of this work was actively involving young adults as co-researchers in ways that challenged existing norms of participation (Percy-Smith and Weil, 2002, 2003).

Related to these influences, we were concerned to present our findings in ways that were recognizable to our research participants. It was important that their experiences of 'being activated' and how this impacted on their lifeworlds did not feel distorted or diminished by how we interpreted or wrote about these. We did not wish the contradictory realities, multiple perspectives, difficulties and possibilities embedded in their everyday experience of 'activation for real' to be subjected to the reductionist or 'sanitizing' tendencies that characterizes a great deal of academic research and evaluation reporting.

We also regarded new and powerful questions, rather than answers, as important research outcomes. We believed in the value of research that does not seek to prove something, but rather that focuses new forms of attention on competing choices, tensions, and possibilities in public policy and practice intervention. Our intention throughout was to generate knowledge that could stimulate new forms of choice, awareness, and empowerment amongst practitioners and policy makers, and therefore also stimulate more socially robust public decision-making:

> under contemporary conditions the more strongly contextualized a scientific field or research domain is, the more socially robust is the knowledge it is likely to produce...social robustness, in an important sense, is prospective; it is capable of dealing with unknown and unforeseeable contexts... [It] is produced when research has been infiltrated and improved by social knowledge. [It] has a strongly empirical dimension: it is subject to frequent testing, feedback and improvement because it is open-ended...this is a reversal of the traditional pattern of scientific working, which has been to restrict as far as possible the range of external factors, or contexts, which must be taken into account. Most of the most powerful scientific techniques – reductionism, normalization, sampling methods, control groups – are based on this presumption of containment or insulation (Nowotny et al., 2002, p. 167).

Throughout, we remained critically reflexive with each other as a team about how we were realizing such intentions in our actual research practice. We were challenged throughout by different assumptions within the research team about what constituted 'high quality' research, appropriate boundaries between 'science and society', who and what to include and exclude from presentations of findings, and how to use different forms of expertise and authority in the practice of research that had the intention of being participative. We return to these issues in Part III, when we consider possibilities for future research.

Involving Young Adults in Research

Perhaps most importantly, as far as was possible, we were committed to involving young people as a critical reference group in which they functioned as co-inquirers and not merely as respondent inquirers:

> Participatory and socially robust research is not just about improved research methods. It is also about achieving democratic participation and social justice for...young people. By influencing what is researched and how their lives are represented, they participate in institutional decision making processes (Kirby, 1999, p. 1).

To get even close to realizing these intentions, we had to be creative in how we approached and involved young adults. The following ideas for organizing and managing the focus groups were generated at our second seminar:

We would need a variety of methods in order to avoid less verbal youth having more problems with participating.

We could try to get in touch with organized youth in order to select young adults and to organize the focus group for young adults. We could develop a joint venture with youth groups that were working on the theme of employment.

We may need to use some incentives like free meals, drinks.

Meetings could be organized in a youth club.

Young people who are key actors in youth groups could be very interesting because they tend to make their attitude explicit in their youth culture and lifestyle. That kind of young person could be invited to the focus groups of the professionals. We agreed that in the focus group for young adults we would involve ordinary young adults and ordinary users of practices under study.

If the members of the focus group were interested, we could bring together the two focus groups.

In other words, in our cross-group meeting, we challenged each other about non-institutionalized approaches as to where and how we might meet, and how we listened to young people. We had to work through assumptions about formal interviews and fixed spaces that were unlikely to be workable in attracting diverse youth. We spoke about relational practices, thereby demanding that we go out to them and slowly build trust. Some of us used more creative ways of engaging them, such as through photos and drawings.

'Success' in attracting and sustaining young peoples' involvement in our work varied considerably across the countries, as illustrated below:

From our point of view, the co-inquiry practice, in order to really involve all actors at play, should be oriented in a meaningful way for both parties That is, the researchers' agenda must make sense and have a place on [potential] participants' agenda. If people we want to get involved in co-inquiry work are simply not interested in the issues we want to study and reflect about, the methodology falls into an empty space In the same sense, how we, as researchers, sometimes plan to put this into practice is not the way that matches participants' 'inner logic' In fact the starting point is obviously different; hence it influences the whole process.

From what we have experienced during this year and a half, we may state that there is a big difference between the professionals' and the youngsters' focus groups. The professionals we have been in contact with showed a truly [genuine] concern about the development of global competences and we really found most of them very interpretative and deeply open to critically discuss, reflect and question their own professional practices. The youngsters' focus groups were much more frustrating and we believe the methodological issues identified above had consequences for their functioning That was probably why most of them didn't show up in the last meeting and we could notice that the ones who appeared were strongly pushed by the institution to do so. Another factor that could have had an influence on the failure of that meeting was the place where it ended up. We chose our center to have the meeting because it was a 'neutral space', but perhaps the face of being a university in the [center of the city] may have had an inhibitory effect on these youngsters that, in almost all cases, are deeply marked by unsuccessful stories at school This situation made us wonder that maybe the best way to succeed with co-inquiry work with a non-professional group is just to take advantage of the situations and conversations that, casually or not, occur at moments during case studies, in their own environment. Even with certain youngsters in the second case study, we more easily got an idea of their feelings and opinions in an informal talk than in an arranged interview We cannot forget that we are dealing with people.. with diverse cultural roots, so we were trying to get in touch with youngsters with different conceptual, emotional and ethical frameworks which don't attribute to facts the same meanings as we do . The common constraints of deadlines and of the short duration of the projects also do not favor the deepening of the questioning and the attempt of other ways to get closer to people

This is but one example of the learning that was going on 'live' in the team and in Part III we summarize key considerations for engaging young people in research in non-tokenistic ways.   But such efforts, although variable in their success, enabled us to bring young peoples' voices into this book, in different ways.   On several occasions, when the full team met, we had the opportunity to visit participating local projects and meet with the young people and professionals involved.   Sometimes this involved young people sharing poems and insights that had been generated as part of their involvement in the case studies. They often spoke with us informally about their situation as unemployed young people, since they were aware that we might be able to influence their situation at a higher level through this research.   Throughout, however, we had to ensure that we did not objectify them, but stayed in conversation in ways that meant we too were fully present, as human beings and not merely researchers.

Despite the limitations we confronted in trying to live our research ideals and values in practice, we were well supported by the flexibility of our overall research design. This was structured yet open enough to allow us to learn as we went along. More importantly, it enabled us to pursue the extraordinary in the ordinary, the strange in the familiar, and the raw realities of policy rhetorics as systemic patterns began to emerge across particulars.

What has resulted, as presented in the website cited above and in this book, may have been far more limited in its scope and impact, had we not received funding for what, at the time of our initial proposal to the EU, was perceived as an exceptionally innovative design.   More traditional framings of issues and pre-specified methodologies can lead to important insights but they can also give rise to the possibility of more messy realities being 'edited' out of final texts. Instead, we felt we could find space for studying and voicing the emerging contradictions, paradoxes and systemic questions with which our research continually confronted us.

What seems important, however, is the extent to which the learning and agency built into our research approach contrasted with the constraints often built into the projects we studied.   Increasingly, projects are now having to meet accountability requirements and demonstrate how they have adhered to pre-determined success criteria and practices, such as, for example, the regular preparation and documentation of 'action plans'. But when a young person is homeless, struggling with a host of pressures and disadvantages, what is lost – and put at risk – when adherence to these practices is prescribed 'from above'?

The same applies to research. When there is pressure to adhere to fixed and standardized designs, we may compromise possibilities for generating socially robust knowledge in dialogue with diverse others. The irony of such contradictions – and their wider systemic implications – will remain a strong theme in this book.

National Contexts and Regional Choices for this Research

The variety of education, training, employment and guidance schemes available in Europe is huge. As discussed earlier, we did not, in our research project, set out to make a comparative study of these systems. Such a comparison has to reconcile such diversity across a range of varied social, cultural, and economic histories. Moreover, statistics are differentially gathered and interpreted in each country, and are soon out of date. For example, young adults as a group may be defined as, for example, 16-25 in one country, and in another as 18-25. Schemes and their relationship to the national post-school education, training, employment and guidance structure also vary considerably across countries.

What we wish to do here, is to offer some insight into the contexts within which this research was carried out in each country, and to indicate factors that influenced our choice of case studies within, and across the countries. This material is drawn from extensive within-country work, based on studies of national statistics, policy documents and analysis of trends.

Belgium

We encountered a Belgian economy that was shifting from an industrial economy towards a service economy, where the work force was growing. This in itself creates a paradoxical problem. There are growing numbers of vacancies that cannot be filled and a bulk of unemployed people that are very difficult to integrate into that labor market. As a result, a group of long-term unemployed and lowly qualified people was developing. The situation for young people – in comparison to other groups – also worsened during the 1990s. A hardcore group of long-term unemployed posed particular challenges.

At the time of this project, unemployment policy tended to be dominated by the idea of trajectory guidance, with a strong labor market orientation, with many different providers of education, training, employment and guidance, and increased competition for limited funding.

The region chosen by the Belgian research team was Leuven, in Flanders. This region is strongly characterized by a service economy, and, as a consequence, education, training, employment and guidance programs are strongly oriented towards the service sector. The Belgian team concentrated its research on a group of lowly qualified, long-term unemployed and underprivileged young adults who were squeezed by the paradox that the jobs they were qualified for (in other words unskilled enough for) were fast disappearing.

Denmark

In Denmark the unemployment problem from the 1970s and 1980s had diminished, creating a new and quite specific problem. From the middle of the 1990s, all young people under 25 had been the focus of some kind of 'activation' program, and it is in Denmark that this term originated. In this country, participation in some kind of education or project was mandatory. Programs focusing on more social or creative possibilities for participation were gradually closing down, as a strong labor market and goal-directed influence crept in. These new trends also affected funding criteria. This posed the Danish labor market with a growing problem concerning youth.

On one hand, the demand from the labor market for young people was increasing, and in certain sectors there was a desperate need for young people to get an adequate education, but such qualified youth were not coming through the system. On the other, there was a group of young people who had been unemployed for longer or shorter periods, but who simply did not want the jobs available to them. This was a group who were unwilling to fulfill the demands of the labor market, no matter what was being tried. They insisted on their right to creative and personally fulfilling jobs – but they were not qualified for these – and yet they were unwilling to accept the routine jobs that were left. Employers were faced with apprentices who were extremely unreliable in their commitment to work, and who preferred unemployment to a job they did not like. Traditional incitements that used to work simply did not any longer in the Danish post-industrial society. The authorities' more recent attempts to make programs more goal-oriented were proving no more effective.

So, although on the surface, as a result of enforced activation and the removal of young adults from unemployment statistics, unemployment among young people was perceived to be 'gone', there were deeper problems concerning the integration of the young generation into the existing labor market. One heterogeneous group of 'weak' youngsters was perceived as unable to hold the jobs available, while another group of 'strong' young people refused to accept unsatisfying jobs.

The dominant policy–practice trend at the time of our research was to focus on flexible individual plans of action, on the assumption that this may solve the problem for some of the stronger group and at least, keep the others 'active'.

The region chosen by the Danish team was Copenhagen where problems concerning young people's refusal of the ordinary labor market on many levels was most prominent. Both the 'weak' youngsters who could not hold a job and the 'strong' who rejected jobs were seen to be incompatible with the labor market.

Germany

The breakdown of communism in the former GDR set in motion a process of fundamental economic and social transition. The manufacturing industry, for example, faced pressures of competition that were leading to bankruptcy. De-industrialization has taken place without a service sector growing up to replace traditional industry. Moreover, many of the social services that used to be provided by employers, had not been adequately replaced. The consequences of these changes have been enormous for young adults. For example, some apprentices of firms that went bankrupt were unable to complete their education. Such young people, without a diploma in vocational training, have been highly vulnerable to unemployment. Moreover, people with good qualifications have often been employed below their skill levels, because of general high unemployment. This has led to low skilled workers and women in general being pushed out of the labor market.

Although in recent years, employment amongst young adults has decreased, unemployment rates have not risen. Short-term employment and educational projects have been used to reduce unemployment figures. Offers can be constructed as 'for now' measures, while 'waiting for improvements' in the labor market. So the surface impression of a flourishing labor market in fact covers up extensive long-term unemployment and unstable employment.

The German team chose Berlin as their region and focused on projects located in East Berlin. After de-industrialization, future hopes were attached to the development of the service sector, but at the time of this study, this was not yet prospering. There has been a strong voluntary sector in Germany, and many service and voluntary associations have been encouraged by the state to provide projects. Berlin has many youth projects, ranging from employment to lifeworld projects. These private organizations have been trying to bridge the gap between the traditional institutions and education, training, employment and guidance approaches, and to re-conceptualize learning for employment in new forms (for example differentiating target groups, experimenting with different time frames, combined tasks, and so on).

The Netherlands

The Dutch economy has moved past a point of being dominated by industrial production, with the result that from the mid-1970s, growing automation and international competition fundamentally changed the organization of labor in the country. New jobs arose in alternative areas for economic development, such as information and communication services. Job qualifications increasingly emphasized not only job-related skills, but more general competencies as well. Although work has been seen as important for social participation, the modernization process has also been leading to new forms of marginalization and social exclusion.

Although the Netherlands has a low unemployment rate among young adults, migrant youth and those from lower social class backgrounds are over-represented in official statistics. The main concern of the labor market policy has been to 'activate' the unemployed, rather than to create employment. Unemployed young adults no longer had any claim to social security benefit, but to a minimum job. Such jobs were created in the public sector. Many projects aimed to get the young to obtain minimum starting qualifications and to prevent early school leaving.

The Dutch team focused on early school leavers, and those who had left school without minimum starting qualifications. They also attended to processes of social exclusion. The region chosen was Amsterdam where such problems were most marked.

Portugal

At the time of our research, Portugal was facing the challenges of a growing population of young adults with low levels of education, where the majority still lived in small towns that fostered a complex mixture of rural and urban identities. There were also significant numbers of people of African and Afro-Portuguese descent living in cities. Portuguese youth have nine years of compulsory schooling, with a significant number (mainly boys) leaving after 4-6 years, perceiving school as not preparing them for 'real life'. The government has seen youth employment as a major issue. In addition to a focus on the lowly educated, those with university level education, especially young unemployed women, have been the focus of government initiative. At the time of this study, priority was being given to the newly registered, who were not yet in a serious situation of prolonged unemployment. Dominant trends included focuses on individual plans, and on vocational guidance that could lead to deeper self-knowledge. After this, training programs were available, and then projects that got young people placed in the labor market.

Portugal has many youth programs, but their failure to link offers to the interests of the young is perceived as an ever growing challenge. Success from projects is seen as smaller than anticipated. The region chosen by the Portuguese team was Lisbon: the most industrialized and urban region in Portugal. This is also the area that has the greatest ethnic diversity, and is considered to have the best and worst of what is on offer to unemployed young adults.

United Kingdom

The transition of youth from school to work in the UK has become increasingly fragmented by changes in local labor market conditions and a general collapse of the youth labor market. Young people are increasingly finding themselves competing for jobs with displaced adults, and all have become victims of economic and occupational restructuring, due to the decline in manufacturing. This has had a particularly serious impact on working class young males, who have traditionally followed family patterns of employment. This is even more serious in the case of those of Afro-Caribbean descent who also experience additional discrimination. Demand for higher qualifications in the labor market is expected to increase, and the demand for people with low-level qualifications to decrease. As in other countries, actual levels of unemployment are almost impossible to determine, given the numbers registered on training schemes.

At the time of this study, there had been significant investment in youth training schemes. Government preoccupations were social exclusion, the limitations of market forces in creating employment, 'joined up thinking' across agencies working with young adults, and 'client led' provision. The *New Deal* scheme was launched in the same year as this project began (1998) as a compulsory scheme for anyone claiming unemployment allowance for more than six months.

Northampton was chosen as the British research region: situated in a largely rural county with small numbers of urban centers, where problems of poverty, crime, and unemployment are concentrated.

Perspectives across the Countries and Regions

Our initial analysis of the unemployment, labor market, policy situation, and trends in each country made apparent the common existence of a hardcore of long-term unemployed, often lowly qualified, young adults, who were finding access to an increasingly knowledge-intensive labor market more and more difficult. But although the problem can be generalized, it took on a different character in each of the countries. Moreover, it made a big difference whether or not there were jobs available at all. For example, in Belgium, there were jobs, in the former GDR, not so many. With respect to the latter, what can be done with the new labor force in a society with no available work, but still with a strong ideology that labor is fundamental in life? With respect to the former, there seemed to be a growing group of young people qualified for jobs that were disappearing.

A related problem was appearing across all the countries: namely, that a hardcore was unwilling to accept the lowly qualified jobs that were available. In Denmark, this tendency was very marked, since there was full employment. In the UK, this problem is also well known. Similarly, the tendency of well-educated young people to reject work that does not live up to their expectations was also seen to be turning up especially in the post-industrial countries.

All the countries were dealing with these problems, but their concrete contents and forms could be seen to be different. And yet, looking more systemically, we were struck by the clear trend towards individualized rather than community-focused interventions. Individualization as a significant feature of late modern market-oriented societies is a familiar theme (see for example Beck and Beck-Gernsheim, 2002). But at what cost? And particularly, with respect to European concerns to find ways of meeting economic challenges in ways that do not enhance social exclusion.

Initial Research Preoccupations and Concerns

Our initial analyses of our respective national situations, and the regions within which we wished to concentrate our research, and particularly our case study work, helped us to shape the following research preoccupations and concerns:

> *Unemployed young adults' own situations, and their own processes of learning, meaning making, and identity construction with respect to activation for labor market participation*

In other words, we wanted to learn more from, and alongside, young adults about their 'own inner logics' in terms of how they perceived and reflexively engaged with these education, training, employment and guidance 'opportunities' and a changing labor market in the context of their own auto/biographies. We wanted to learn particularly from the experiences of the so-called 'marginalized' and the 'socially excluded' – and to consider terms such as exclusion, inclusion and participation from a wider range of perspectives than those that seemed to inform policy and practice at the outset of this project.

Program interventions and practice choices

We wanted to explore the diverse logics and assumptions that underpinned intervention and practice choices relating to education, training, employment and guidance being offered to young unemployed people and especially those who were now being perceived as 'socially excluded'. How did local practices diverge or converge with 'official' versions of what was on offer? Was there space to diverge from 'official' procedures? In particular, we used the notion of instrumental, biographical, and social competence to frame our initial concerns. For example, we assumed that an emphasis on instrumental competence (such as getting a job) would dominate in mainstream programs at the expense of the social and the biographical. (We return to these distinctions later in Part I.) Also, we wanted to explore tensions and possibilities around different 'activation' strategies in relation to varying labor market conditions. For example, when we began, there was low unemployment in Denmark and high unemployment in Germany after unification. What scope did professionals feel that they had to influence upwards? What scope did they have to generate insights into the limitations and possibilities of current policy thinking and development at local, regional, national, and European levels? To what extent were they feeling empowered or disempowered by changing 'rules of engagement' (such as the increased emphasis on performance indicators determined away from the ground of their pedagogical encounters with highly diverse and often disaffected young adults)? How were professionals themselves navigating and negotiating shifting education, training, employment and guidance 'encounter spaces', both within their actual work with young people and in their attempts to realize policy aims for 'social inclusion' with 'economic activation'?

The socio-political context and rapidly changing labor market conditions which influence the values, concerns, and assumptions – and practices – of policy and program development and funding (locally, regionally, nationally, and internationally)?

For example, what patterns and trends, if any, distinguished diverse education, training, employment and guidance programs? How were changing labor market conditions and globalization impacting on policy and practice? What different constructions of 'effective action/activation' were signified by policy directions? What kinds of strategies were seen to 'count' as valid and what kinds were being discounted, either implicitly or explicitly? What kinds of narratives were being influenced by the projects and the wider context? What was the impact of changing social and economic circumstances on how labor market identities and narratives of hope and empowerment (or their absence) were being constructed? What could the 'empowerment' of unemployed young adults in a changing labor market mean – especially in a context where professionals were increasingly expected to 'discipline' young adults' participation in activation projects?

No Easy Answers

We thus began with an exploration into micro-processes of education, training, employment and guidance. However, throughout, we paid attention to concrete ways in which locally situated interactions were being influenced by processes of social and economic policy making on a wider scale: the scale of the region, the country, the EU and the globalizing world.

Our dynamic systemic approach enabled us to formulate questions and hypotheses about the complex interaction of different forms of sense making, action and choice at different levels of the 'activation system'; about the intended and unintended consequences of particular assumptions and 'employment logics'. For example:

- How might current approaches and trends (such as more systematic audit and performance management of social policy 'delivery' vehicles) be compounding the very difficulties that European social and economic policy is seeking to address – such as reducing unemployment *and* social exclusion?

As will become apparent in what follows, we neither sought nor found easy answers. We did find unsustainable contradictions, such as between what was claimed and what was being experienced on the ground. We also found a host of paradoxes that were easily dismissed or misunderstood as such, that could be discounted as anecdotes, or framed as inevitable polarities. We acknowledge that many of these may be unavoidable in today's world. All the same, in opening them up to new forms of view, we hope to stimulate some fresh thinking and critical reflection on existing assumptions and choices for activation. As the

Chinese proverb goes, a fish does not understand the concept water when it has spent its whole life in it. In what follows, we invite you to consider a bigger story that deserves our attention and new forms of action, on behalf of young Europeans.

---

[1] http://WWW.improving-ser.sti.jrc.it/default/search.gx?_app.prePolicy=searchE.

Chapter 3

Three Starting Stories: Young Europeans being 'Activated' for Employment

As will have been evident in the previous chapter, as researchers, we wished to de-stabilize aspects of the subject–object, researcher–researched distinction that characterizes much academic research and especially that with young people. At the same time, we wanted to be sensitive to the dynamics of power that obtain in any such research. We tried to develop relational ways of knowing (Reason and Bradbury, 2001) on the assumption that the falsely distanced gathering of so-called 'objective data' can itself impede the quality of what might be learned through an inquiry like this.

But a further problematic arises when we come to write about such research. A great deal of traditional academic writing can fragment and distort the lives of those in whose name such research has been carried out. Instead, we want to bring you as readers into a deeper sense of encounter with what it may mean to live one's life as an unemployed young person in Europe, subjected to a host of different strategies for being 'activated'.

We therefore shift our emphasis at this point. We move away from clarifying our own intentions and approaches as researchers and now begin to open up stories that offer insights into key issues arising from our research from different perspectives. We wish to convey an overall sense of the complexity of what we discovered about paradoxes arising from trends in unemployment policy, performance management, evaluation, and project practice across Europe.

We have chosen to focus initially, as part of our scene setting for the book as a whole, on three countries. We have distilled a vast amount of data collection and analysis into three, multi-voiced narratives. Through this form, we present a multi-layered analysis that bring into closer view recurring aspects of the situation of young Europeans who are unemployed in Denmark, Belgium, and Portugal. These texts incorporate not only empirical material derived from in-depth case studies within these countries, but from the full range of within-country research undertaken as described in the previous chapter. For those who wish to study pen portraits of the full range of case studies, from which the following have been selected, these can be found in the Appendix.

It is our hope that these particular starting glimpses will generate a stronger sense of a dynamic, shifting, and contradictory terrain. The three narratives that we have chosen to present initially here in Part I unfold the full continuum of insights arising from this study: namely, into how the particulars of specific education, training, employment, and guidance projects, although seeking to 'act

25

back' positively upon the situations of young unemployed adults, were simultaneously being 'acted upon', by the wider context in quite complex ways. Our choice for initially presenting our data may, for some, violate 'some of our received and more or less unquestioned notions of just how and what...texts (and theories) are convincing' (Van Maanen, 1992, p. 135). We make no apology for this. We are inspired by authors such as Van Maanen (1990, 1992), Marshall (1995) and Richardson (1997) to experiment with writing that moves,

> against our customary aggressive certitude toward reality, a certitude that lies at the core of the foundational, scientific purpose that infects so much...theory... Novel writing strokes offer a promising way of doing theory, a way more in tune with current intellectual trends in many of the scholarly worlds that surround us and perhaps [that are] more in tune with the *culturally blended worlds in which we live* (Van Maanen, 1992, p. 139, emphasis added)

Real lives, actual projects, the politics and possibility of everyday action and choice, are full of contradictions and paradoxes. They are culturally blended. We therefore invite you to enter into these worlds for a moment. We encourage you to consider what might be the impact of such experiences on yourself and on your own 'motivation' to 'become socially and economically activated', as the jargon often goes. What explored here might cause you to actively opt out?

We are asking you to identify with young Europeans whose social, cultural, biographical, educational, and economic trajectories in life may be radically different from your own. Our intention is to offer a portal that supports imaginings into something about what it may be like to be experiencing the world from a different position. We ourselves were charged to do this through the undertaking of this research, when our taken for granted assumptions were dislodged by our own confrontation with difference that we had not previously imagined. Moreover, traditional academic writing that remains detached may itself impede the emergence of the very human connections and dialogic possibilities that may generate different forms of policy, practice, and research in this field.

Returning to van Maanen:

> The language we use to theorize about organizations is not a symptom of the problems the field faces but is a cause of such problems... Our theories of the world are not mere reflectors of the world but makers of this world, and this is why the words we use are so terribly important... Theorists are lost because they are blind to what words in context can teach them (1995, p. 139).

Each encounter with the worlds of unemployed youth, initially in Denmark, Belgium, and Portugal, can be approached as a kind of passageway into a wider view. In other words, each narrative offers us a 'point of departure' whereby we can begin to unfold a different view of the 'everyday'. We use specifics as springboards to call into play systemic influences that may seem a long way away from everyday living realities. Although such influences may seem to be acting upon them in ways that may seem 'neutral' and 'invisible', after our first few cycles of research, questions gradually came into focus that helped us to see that this is anything but the case. For example:

- What is the impact on young people, professionals, and the projects themselves of social and economic policy discourses that construct unemployment as something for which individuals are responsible, or in which unemployed and socially excluded young people are described as having 'deficits' that can be rectified through some form of educational, training, employment or guidance related intervention?

- In what ways is the 'audit culture' sweeping across Europe itself generating new paradoxes, pressures, and unintended consequences for professionals and young adults alike?

- How is a globalizing world market, with its demands for a ready supply of casualized, flexible labor, itself giving rise to entirely different project and program trends?

Each narrative is followed by such critical inquiry questions that kept coming up for us, as we progressively learned more about that with which we were engaging. These questions are meant to beckon you further into a more holistic view of politics, policy, projects, and practices in Europe, and to stimulate your own inquiry about whether, and the extent to which, they may be successful or not in opening up alternatives for young adults' social and economic participation. We invite you into assuming a more critical perspective on the unintended consequences of different kinds of influences across Europe, and a more reflexive orientation about what is and is not possible.

Put another way, each narrative may at first appear merely anecdotal, as just a dot in a random connection of dots, each unrelated to the next. But we hope that the way in which we unfold our research and our theorizing through the book will reveal narratives such as these as indicative of 'fractal patterns' that speak wider 'truths' with which young people, professionals, and policy makers need to grapple. We shall continue to nuance and explore what we open up here in different ways in subsequent sections of this book, through a variety of narrative voices and styles.

So, in this 'just for a moment' experiment, from within this 'artificial' role reversal, we encourage you to 'feel' your way into what seems promised by these projects and what seems not to be. Perhaps recall the voices of those with whom we began this book: Jimmy, who is on the *New Deal* scheme in the UK, and Stefan, who is at university in Flanders. What might be some of the difficult choices, dilemmas, and paradoxes you might have to wrestle with, were it you who were categorized as 'long-term unemployed' or 'unemployable' and also, perhaps, 'socially excluded'? If you were a practitioner in such projects?

For example, do you have any idea what it may be like to be living in Denmark, compelled to attend an activation project all day, all week, because you are deemed unemployable and, if you don't attend, you lose any access to state funds.

Encounter in Denmark

Imagine you are there. Imagine this *you* is really 'you':

> *It is Denmark, Copenhagen, a grim city suburb. You are unemployed and have been so for some time More than that, by virtue of being referred to this House of Projects, you have now been officially deemed 'unfit for the labor market' This is because you and your unemployed friends who participate in this 'activation scheme' are regarded as having a lot more to contend with than unemployment alone. most of you have family problems, criminal records and drug and alcohol abuse histories (past and present). Some girls amongst your group have experienced sexual abuse. Some of you were not born in Denmark Some of you are descendents of first generation immigrants. As a group, you come from a wide range of cultural and ethnic backgrounds*
>
> *Many of your parents have the same problem as you· struggling to find and keep work or to survive through whatever they can do on the back streets, behind closed doors, away from the official gaze. They, like you, have tried out several different jobs and gone on various courses, but they have run out of ideas since nothing seems to shift things for the better.*
>
> *You hear the professionals saying that you lack 'work experience'. Or when they write reports about you (which they have to do all the time), they explain that you have had 'interrupted training, work, or education trajectories'. But you think that's true for most people you know and not just those in your age group. What confuses and amuses you and your friends – and sometimes make you really angry – is that on the TV you hear people speak about 'full youth employment' in Denmark Yet you are not employed. Nor are your parents. So what is going on here?*
>
> *The building where you go each day is set amidst a raft of official places, where not just young people come Unemployed people of all ages arrive here daily to get counseling, guidance, and training You, however, have been given the 'opportunity' of a special 'clarification project', aimed just at young adults, aged 18-25 This is meant to help*
>
>> *the largest possible number of participants to gain the confidence and ability needed in order to enter the labor market or educational system For those young adults unable to reach such goals, the aim is to support them in finding a more permanent solution to their situation, by offering them rehabilitation, flex-jobs, pension, abuse treatments, etc. The primary aim of the course is to 'clarify the situation' of the participants rather than actually solve their problems and to help improve their 'biographical and social competences' as the lack of these is the main obstacle, rather than a lack of 'instrumental competences' (Project documentation, House of Projects, emphasis added)*
>
> *In this project, they seem to have given up on you ever getting a job You have heard people say, this project is for people who are 'unemployable' It sounds so final, as if there is nothing out there for you But unless you come here, you cannot afford to live So, it is necessary to pretend that coming to this project is like coming*

to a job. A lot of you even put on work clothes each morning yet wouldn't think of wearing these clothes to go out at night

There is no time limit as to how long you can remain here, nor any regular admittance to courses. It is all arranged in a flexible manner to meet you and other participants 'wherever they are' as you heard one professional describe it. There are, however, a few specific daily routines they expect you to keep, although they are not sure how to enforce them.

At 9 am breakfast is prepared in the kitchen, although only a handful turn up for this half hour slot There is lots of 'healthy food' because the staff sees nutrition as a big problem. You and your mates don't often eat anything regularly and don't care so much about the food they make for you. You and your vocational teachers are then expected to choose your workshop for the day, or follow the counselors to their offices.

Four workshops are on offer each day, where you can stay until finishing time, as most of you tend to do. You don't ever have to do the same thing in a row. Yet, it is easier to 'stay put' than to have to keep making decisions about what to do all day. Every 45 minutes or so there is a huge burst of energy as a bell rings: smoking break time! You and your friends all charge out from your different workshops towards your special smoking room, laughing, talking, and passing your cigarettes around the group. But no matter what, time passes incredibly slowly. It seems different here, strange.

> *...during the 'active periods' the level of activity is very low. It makes me feel restless. There is no goal and nothing seems to be more important than anything else. I feel empty and the atmosphere is dull Breaks are taken randomly. The dullness vanishes the minute they come Everybody suddenly becomes active and leaves the workshop within seconds (Researcher, House of Projects, field diary, Denmark).*

Some workshops are more intense than others, but then you can never predict what is going to happen on any particular day. If it is too hot, too cold, or raining, there are always people who do not come in. This influences what happens. Sometimes you do the same thing for the whole day, or for longer:

> *Like we were meant to be doing a project on drugs and violence for a week (Project participant, House of Projects, Denmark).*

> *Or you just surf the net or play animation games. Or you can learn word processing. Sometimes you feel like you are doing nothing really (Project participant, House of Projects, Denmark).*

> *Just killing time (Project participant, House of Projects, Denmark).*

If you have a problem, you are meant to see the counselors down the hall 'who are there to listen to you', as your teachers say. In some ways, this program is not much different from the House of Keys project you and some of your friends were on before This was held at the local job center, before you were formally declared 'unfit for the labor market' and sent to this House of Projects. But the professionals call both projects 'clarifying activation projects' You are never quite sure what these

words mean, except that they don't seem to be about getting a real job. But at least at
the previous project, you and the teachers spent a lot of time talking about getting a
job As one of your friends said about it.

> You have to try out everything until you find the right job – and that may well
> take forty years. After all there is a lot of working possibilities nowadays. You
> can become everything Carpenter, cabinet maker, bricklayer, and you can just
> keep on going on and on. Illustrator Fuck! (Jannick, 23 years, project
> participant, House of Projects, Denmark).

There was almost too much choice Jeanne, who you met there, said what many
of you felt:

> I don't know what I want to do – it is difficult, there are so many different things
> (Jeanne, project participant, House of Projects, Denmark)

It was like people were complaining at the House of Keys that there were too
many choices, but at least there was a lot of emphasis on helping you find out what
you wanted to do The classrooms had lots of new paint, in bright colors. There were
two computer rooms and a smoking room. There were some posters and a few plants,
but it still looked like a Job Center You had to do math, Danish, English, computers,
psychology It was also a lot like school, because the teachers and others decided
what courses were important and you couldn't skip any of them. At that project, they
kept going on about you getting motivated or getting skilled for a job or about doing
training to get specific jobs.

Not like here. At this project, they don't pressure you at all. They talk about
communication and social skills a lot more. You also know you are here because they
see you as having problems that are more than just being unemployed. But that
doesn't mean that it wasn't boring in the project before Just like it still is now, here
at the House of Projects One conversation went as follows

> Martin·   Well, the first week it was ok, fun, but afterwards [makes a
>   snoring sound] .. Sleeping! Do not bother!
> Researcher: What did you think about when you woke up this morning?
> Martin   That I did not bother [laughs]

And another conversation

> Rashid·   No, I don't [feel lonely] because I have my PlayStation
> Researcher· Yes, okay. Is that your friend?
> Rashid   Yes, it's my friend. Because it's just like automatically
>   relaxing You don't think about it. I mean, you don't think
>   about... you just think about playing and when you have played
>   then .. when I did so many games I go down to rent a video or
>   something, hang out in a café. Fuck, sometimes I've been to a
>   pub all alone and I had a beer – no more – and just chilled out

At the previous project, you had 'trainee service periods' where you could try on
different jobs The teachers there were ok. It was not like at school They at least
treated you like adults And they didn't put you down But there were not as many

counselors in that project as in this one – nor half as much pressure to talk about your problems.

In a research group, we heard from someone who had been on various projects like the House of Keys and the House of Projects. She told us,

Elisa:	*They* [the practitioners on activation schemes] *are nice people, most of them, but it* [the project] *has had nothing to do with dreams or anything like that. I have been attending, 'find your self' courses I do not understand why they spent so much money on something that is worth nothing Incredibly expensive Personal development in education courses, which we just get thrown into ad hoc*
Researcher:	*Was it not good then?*
Elisa:	*If I had a purpose. If I had something I could use it for, then it would have been all right. But I have not. I have not asked to join this Not that I would like to sit at home and do nothing, but I want to do something where I can have some self-esteem and where I can be used for something. Instead of just being placed somewhere.*

Lots of people you meet on these schemes have lots of other problems though; there are more drugs around than in the other projects and it's getting tougher to keep your benefit The staff are really friendly, but still they have this power over you. They can tell the authorities to stop your money , if you don't show up or if you mess up. Since most of you and your friends are already considered school failures, it's sometimes hard to understand how what they are doing now is going to make any difference.

I left school in the sixth grade. I'm 24 years old and no schools want me... It's many years since I've left school, so why should I sit with my pencil and put my hand up to a teacher? I wouldn't be able to stand it. I would explode... Never. Because I couldn't stand it. I would explode if a teacher said to me 'It's not your turn'. I would go crazy because I'm not used to it. I'm not used to people snarling at me. Do you know what I mean? It makes me angry. But really what do you want me to do? It's too late for me. I don't care about education Do you know what I mean? I just want my own business and earn a lot of money (Jannick, project participant, House of Projects, Denmark).

Yes, you would like some steady money. It's expensive to keep up with fashion these days. You need money – and want a bit of security. That's the way you see it. The researchers have their own way of seeing things·

Generally the way in which the young were talking about such projects signaled an ironic distance and stultification. Such courses seemed almost unworthy per se and linked to a 60 or 70's discourse of emotional pawing. Maybe such trajectories even worsen the subjective perception of being invaded or colonized by the system as they involve the entire system, not just the more instrumental projects. Maybe ('find yourself') courses like these are increasingly being instrumentalized and accordingly putting their participants off? Maybe it is a question of how such courses are being promoted or thematized? Maybe the participants would rather focus on instrumental competences? And how do we understand the relationship between projects aiming at social and biographical competences and alternative projects? Are we beginning to experience some distance between these two concepts?

There are quite a few projects and training schemes that have instrumental competences as their formal objectives, although in practice these are meant to develop both biographical and social competences. At present we have not had the possibility to investigate these schemes further In terms of raising questions for further investigation, we need (of course) to dig deeper into such social, biographical, and instrumental elements in relation to experiences of positive and negative activation (when young adults participate in one pointless training scheme after the other just in order to be 'in activation') (Researcher, House of Projects, *field diary, Denmark)*

There are teachers who feel strongly that even though you are on this project, you must not stand still.

That's just storage The goal is to get them going, heading for the best possible place And its okay if it takes time finding the right place. No more quick solutions where you just send them off to yet another place We have been tossing people around long enough. Some of them have been in 8-10 projects Now is the time to analyze (Teacher, House of Projects, *Denmark)*

You can hear the way people who are between projects talk about their next one

So right now I am just waiting to be summoned to a meeting at the employment office and then they will probably send me into something enormously exciting once again! And no matter what you say in terms of, 'I would like to . ' if it does not correspond with what they have on their lists of areas of the labor market that's lacking workforce, you can forget all about it (Tomas, ex-project participant, Denmark).

And you wonder what they will get, or more to the point – not get – when they get assigned to their next project.

They sometimes forget that we are unemployed and that we want to get further in life. WE WANT TO GET A KICK IN THE BUM That is why we are here!!!! (Project participants, excerpt from letter to teachers, House of Keys, *Denmark)*

We have lots of jokes about being unemployed Some are funny; some jokes are not so funny (Jannick, project participant, House of Projects, *Denmark).*

Being Kept Busy Doing Nothing: Raising Questions

These young people were officially 'deemed unsuitable for employment'. The Danish activation projects, like others we studied, increasingly promise individualized personal support, counseling, and development opportunities. Policy and program documents also reveal a trend that became more and more apparent to us: the extent to which considerable emphasis was also being placed on the development of 'communication skills' and 'social skills' that were meant to 'equip participants for life and work'. However, the initiative was focused almost entirely on redressing 'deficits' in young peoples' social learning and in their repertoire of skills. We found little indication of value being attached to the skills they had generated through surviving, often difficult backgrounds in their trajectories thus far. In other words, the standardized rhetoric about 'social competences' was the starting point, rather than the raw material of their life.

The 'emotional pawing' dimension referred to above by the researchers also became familiar and indicative of the extent to which humanistic discourses about human potential (an individualized discourse) had entered into the unemployment field. As the project progressed, and we spoke about our findings and insights from within our countries, we became aware of how this shift in emphasis seemed to be used to disguise and dress up a much harsher reality.

Tensions within the project or hardships faced outside by individuals, however, were seldom seen as material from which to learn social and communication skills. Instead, these tensions were often wrestled with in silence or away from the group, such as in the counselor's office. The young people sometimes reflected on paradoxes and contradictions that characterized their existence, noting them cynically, in their smoking area, away from 'official hearing'. They could recognize that professionals were doing their best, to understand and help them; yet young people were also alert to some of the professionals' powerlessness. At the same time, the professionals were increasingly legitimized as the gatekeepers for the state. If project members did not participate 'appropriately' in these schemes, they lost their income support. Individual professionals became the arbiters of the personal, social, and political norms by which 'appropriateness' might be judged, leaving the door open for a host of inequalities to be sustained. We increasingly became aware of how such approaches could promote further disconnection and disaffection, rather than 'enhance participation'.

What became increasingly evident was how projects such as this one in Denmark seemed to create a 'life of their own'. The choice was clear (or was it?): either lose your benefit or participate in this 'world', no matter how disconnected it may be from the labor market or your communities. The complexity of this choice for young adults seems to be denied by these activation schemes. What became apparent across Europe, however, was how official statistics on youth employment changed to include as employed young people on schemes such as this. The reference by the teacher to young people in the *House of Projects* often having been on 8-10 unemployment projects takes on a different cast. We began to see how young adults were being placed in projects that were meant to reduce social exclusion and increase employment, but instead too often we found young people could be further dislocated by the projects that were meant to serve them.

We also found that professionals and young adults could feel equally imprisoned by these discursive practices, as we shall explore in depth in Chapter 9. They faced growing pressures to be accountable for the money spent on these projects and to provide evidence of 'successful activation'. Action plans, examples of competence development, portfolios, and other generic protocols were becoming co-opted as technologies by which the state scrutinized and standardized what was going on. Yet their instrumental application seemed to undermine possibilities for learning, rather than serve these; to undermine choice on the part of professionals and young people, rather than to extend it. When professionals are increasingly pressured to participate in practices that seem wholly disconnected from young peoples' lifeworlds and the world of work, it is inevitable that various forms of creative subversion of the 'accountability bureaucracy' will become essential, professional survival skills. But this became increasingly apparent to us as wasteful of energy, skill, and potential: that of professionals and the young adults. The space required to mediate complex social and economic tensions and possibilities instead becomes reduced to: How can we fulfill external demands to show successful competence development for these young people while simultaneously keeping them meaningfully engaged in this project, on terms that matter to them?

Consider the following scenario, today, in the *House of Projects*. Imagine that a new directive from the Department of Unemployment now requires young people and their teachers to complete 'portfolios'. These are meant to track their competence development, against criteria that have been determined outside that community of practice. These will be subject to external 'independent' scrutiny, such as by audit teams or evaluators.

So, imagine a cake-making workshop as a basis for finding something that can comply with such a directive. How do the professionals and young adults fit this experience into the boxes that they have been given, in order to track evidence of, for example:

- ✓ 'decision making skills' (deciding what kind of cake?)
- ✓ 'negotiating skills' (getting others to agree on this?)
- ✓ 'communicating skills' (reading the ingredients and seeing what is in the cupboard?)
- ✓ 'successfully transforming' and adapting to unsatisfactory conditions for learning and working situations (turning familiar ingredients like sugar and flour into a cake?)
- ✓ 'teamwork skills' (cake cut, eaten and enjoyed by all?).

In such ways, we saw concerns with pedagogy becoming increasingly marginalized in the service of technocratic rationality. The treadmill of ticking boxes and feeding some distant bureaucratic machinery with such data was becoming more and more self-perpetuating. And what if yet another Directive, written out of concern about so many people staying on one project after another, requires action plans to prove further that time and money are not being wasted? Plan: to go apple picking with a group of unemployed people with learning disabilities and make pies and cakes out of what we find. Might a further set of boxes relating to 'active citizenship', 'environmental consciousness' and 'sensitivity to diversity' be made 'tickable' thus?

When any such pattern was encountered in an individual project, some narrative about its potential value could be written. They often are: by policy makers, young people, and professionals. But to encounter this pattern repeatedly, as the pressures of the 'audit' culture seemed to spread from the UK across Northern Europe, was profoundly disturbing. In our three-day co-inquiry sessions as a full European team, we began to become more reflexive about the unintended effects of such seemingly 'innovative' practices.

In one sense, participation in what instead become artificial practices may create a false sense of solidarity between professionals and young adults, as they jointly try to subvert a meaningless system and manage their shared sense of disempowerment. In engaging with the irony of such everyday rituals, professionals and young people can assure themselves they are not entrapped by these frameworks. They can 'buck the system' together. But are they empowered...? On whose terms? For what? And where is the space for improvisation and working with the raw realities of what is already present, in the local and specific practice of that project and the lives and communities of those involved? These are the kinds of questions that kept recurring for us.

Looking longer term, and encountering directly young people who had gone from project to project, we gained a powerful, grounded sense of the cumulative despair around what it must be like to do this again and again.

Being kept busy while going nowhere. The situation becomes increasingly Kafkaesque. We began to wonder at what the tyranny of repeating such procedures again and again does to the spirit (and indeed motivation) of young people and professionals. Moreover, we saw how such engagements can feel controlling, coercive – and demeaning – for young people and professionals alike.

We also began to see across our research into lived realities of such practices how quickly 'the world out there' can fade out of the view of all who participate. Competence boxes can feel miles away from anything that young people who are already multiply disadvantaged experience when they go out back into that world at night. The artificiality can further de-value the grounded and contextualized competences young people have had to develop to survive on the borderlands and boundaries of society's different social landscapes.

But this same picture, from a managerial or policy maker's perspective, can seem quite different. Such approaches can provide assurance of greater 'efficiency and effectiveness' in the delivery of public services. Protests about compliance can be all too easily dismissed with some narrative about professionals being resistant to being accountable, and to 'modernization', as it is put in the UK. For politicians, targets need to 'be seen' to be met and clear action plans formulated. Ministers can be reassured that 'competence development' is taking place and that these programs are activating difficult youth, including those deemed unfit for employment. The investment is justified and the unemployment statistics remain untainted. Policy makers are further re-assured that standardized yardsticks can be devised since the fulfillment of these accountability criteria 'proves' that even in such tricky social policy arenas, success can be measured.

Further evaluation studies can be commissioned to formulate new criteria to make sure that such projects can be statistically compared across the country and Europe. All variation and complexity can be neatly reduced. All illusions of being in control are maintained. The messy and painful realities of this for those having to perform such bizarre rituals are kept safely at a distance.

Of course, we are deliberately using irony here to bring these systemic tensions more clearly into the foreground, before looking at these in more depth in Part II. Yet how does 'the system' gain insight into, indeed learn from the overwhelming sense of emptiness and despair we witnessed amongst counselors, teachers, and the young adults and that indeed we experienced ourselves? Moreover, our research showed how these particular Danish projects are being profiled nationally as 'innovative' and highly responsive to the long-term needs of marginalized and multiply disadvantaged youth. But the actual participation of the young adults cannot be used as a yardstick of success, since across Europe welfare benefits are becoming linked to mandatory participation in such schemes.

Paradoxically, although we are highlighting here the extent to which lived meanings of empowerment or activation can feel illusory, disconnected, ungrounded, and inappropriate, from another perspective, young adults exert their own labor identity and agency in this drama of endless preparation for illusory labor market choices. Rather than settling for lowly paid jobs that no one else wants, these young adults begin to feel legitimated in sitting it out, waiting for the 'best choice' to come along. They assure the professionals that they are waiting for the 'right job', the 'right thing for me'; in other words, something, anything – however unrealistic – which nonetheless has some meaning or signifying power in their own lives. The professionals too, as indicated, speak about finding the 'right thing' for each person. The unemployed youth begin to feel that they have this right. This is what they have learned. They are actively participating in the discourse of market choice. But is this the only choice?

Encounter in Belgium

Imagine:

> You are unemployed in Flanders. Until recently, there were very few special schemes for people in your age group, even though there are more and more unemployed young people like yourself. Before, when they put you on a project, you had to mix with people of all ages and backgrounds. You keep hearing yourself called 'hardcore unemployed,' 'lowly qualified'. You hear in the news that this is a 'socially undesirable situation' since you get into other problems and cannot get out of poverty. As if it were all your fault. As if you were a scrounger.
> You have never been employed. You have always been lumped into a group of others 'like you' and no one really seemed to care much about whether you got on or not. But recently, it is like they have started caring too much. You now have to meet

*regularly with someone at The Public Counseling and Training Service (VDAB - The
Flemish Labor Guidance Office) They write to you all the time, track you down and
give you appointments to talk with a local 'trajectory guidance officer'. They think it
is their job to keep pressuring you to make some efforts to do something. As if you
weren't doing that all the time.*

*They keep offering 'orientation programs' where you can learn what is
available. You get to choose a training of 1000 hours in a vocational training
program preparing for jobs, like restaurant and catering or cleaning – all lowly paid.
You and your friends often think that the money you get for this hardly makes it worth
it:*

> *I was working with meat. All day meat in front of you. Hup, hup!! It is nice but
> crazy. If somebody talks to me after 6 hours of work, I have the feeling of being
> without head, without voice, closed ears. It is awkward. I come home and do
> not hear my television. I do not want to hear any sound. I have a headache. It
> disturbs me. Production work is different. To pack, not to stand and look
> straight all the time and work constantly (Project participant, FlexiJob,
> Belgium).*

*You can also take an 'application training program' of only 40 hours, like for
bricklaying, house painting, and working with children or elderly. Most of your
friends, like you, don't have any qualifications But these programs don't give you
real qualifications. At least, not any that seems to count with employers. The person
you meet with at the VDAB is supposed to make sure you stay busy and report on how
you are doing at the end. If you mess up, they can decide you are not trying hard
enough and can take your benefit away. The fact is – not that many employers want to
take people like you But you and your friends often get blamed for not being
'motivated enough' or for being 'irresponsible'.*

*The counselors talk a lot about helping you 'adapt' to the new job situation.
They really get on your case and don't let go. They want to pry into your personal life
in all sorts of ways You and your friends know they're just doing their job, but more
and more it feels like what the professionals call 'help' means constant pressure,
constant meddling, telling you how to get things right in your life. If it were that easy,
you would have done that long ago. It isn't like you don't want a job. As long as it is
an interesting one You and your friends know the mantras too well:*

> *...boring jobs...*
> *..meaningless work...*
> *.. rotten work conditions...*
> *...constant pressure...*
> *...doing more and more for less and less...*
> *...Jobs that other people don't want either. .*
> *(Quotes from young unemployed people in Flanders, Belgium).*

*I cannot imagine that you can know something like work pleasure if you have to
work at an assembly line for many years. How would you be yourself? It is not
inferior, but the idea is that if you do not want this, you have to make sure you
do not end up there (Danny, project participant, FlexiJob, Belgium)*

*The last project you were on was meant to train you for 'sales and distribution'.
It had people of all ages, all women, ages 24-55. You had to be unemployed for two*

years just to get in and then you were going to get one year's work experience It sounded good. You were going to sell things made in your area like wine, jam, honey. Going to local markets and other places, and also helping to manage a shop at the training center and at the mobile farm. You would be helping farms in the region too. It was pretty good. You liked that 'they didn't talk at you'. You 'learned by doing things'. They also wanted to give women, and especially those with children, some choices that were different – not just cleaning or cooking. But although they said that, they did not offer you much real choice. The trainers would just give you tasks without asking what you wanted or if it suited you. They decided what products to sell You couldn't really criticize or ask questions. When you and the others had ideas about how to improve things, how it could be better for you, the trainers did not want to know. They thought you were hassling them So it just felt like 'filling time' in some ways, but not in others. At least it lasted a year. And you got used to it But the program could have been for anyone. It was nothing special for the people you know. It was just about doing the job At least, that's how it felt when it was over and you were still unemployed

But now you are on a brand new project that lots of people seem quite excited about it. They say that this is better. it has been designed for people just like you, all under 30. It's called 'FlexiJob'. You even heard the politicians on the news talking about it This felt a bit strange, although you thought that maybe you and your friends were going to get famous!

What you like about this new project is that it is connected to a youth organization that you and your friends think is ok. The youth workers get out on the streets and really talk to people. Lots of you don't know what you want to do and don't feel you have many chances to realize your dreams. But what you do know is that you don't want to get stuck in

> boring lowly paid jobs. Where people treat you like you are nothing But on the street, if you make it there, selling drugs and such, you can become a hero real fast. Sometimes you wonder if it's worth it, going to all these schemes (Christian, project participant, FlexiJob, Flanders, Belgium)

And you aren't going to let those people make you let go off your dream jobs either·

> Like being a footballer or a pop star – or even a policeman, even if there is not much pay in that (Piet, project participant, FlexiJob, Flanders, Belgium)

Lots of the people who come into FlexiJob, like you, have been through the 'normal' temporary employment agencies or various training schemes that did not work. As for you and many other young people you know, these didn't change anything for them But as long as you are on this project, but you are not officially unemployed and you get some extra money – a bit more than you get from the State But the deal is that you only do short time jobs:

> 1 to 30 days MAX (Project promotional material, FlexiJob, Belgium).

It's not like a lifetime commitment. You can get a bit of extra money without getting in trouble – or selling your life away. If you get bored, you are guaranteed to move on. And you can have a holiday whenever you want. When you saw the poster '30 Days MAX' you and your friends said:

That's ok. No commitment. Won't be stuck (Claudine, project participant, FlexiJob, Flanders, Belgium).

And going to FlexiJob means you don't need to go near the unemployment office. It is based near where you live. And you don't have to spend your life in dingy gray horrible buildings. The youth organization and this FlexiJob agency seem to work together somehow. You're not sure how they do this. What you do know is that the youth counselor doesn't just sit in his office. He gets out:

Doesn't wear a suit or anything (Project participant, FlexiJob, Flanders, Belgium).

Whereas before they were trying to force you into the labor market, here they want you to be 'flexible'. It helps get you money in an emergency without getting into trouble:

...Gives you some experience...
...Gives you some time...
...It's cool...
...It's quality of life that matters...
...You don't want to kill yourself working all the time...

Everyone knows about work stress, from watching television. But before, when you tried to explain that to the workers, they'd lecture you. Now they say it all the time to encourage you to do '30 Days Max': you can have a rest or a holiday when you get stressed or bored. It's strange they say that now but didn't say things like that before. Why is that? And with FlexiJob, the jobs aren't all boring like the ones the Employment office wants you to go into:

Some people even get to help organize concerts (Project participant, *FlexiJob*, Flanders, Belgium).

But what the workers still don't understand is that you still just get minimum wage and that you can't really live on this.

I find the people here very friendly. In other temporary employment agencies you have to speak Flemish. Here is it ok (Klaus, project participant, FlexiJob, Flanders, Belgium).

Although you like the '30 Days Max', you secretly hope that FlexiJob hasn't given up on getting you a real job. Maybe they will find something that is interesting and lasts more than 30 days in real sales and distribution. So you don't have to turn to crime. And won't be so poor.

I have to earn money because I have a wife and two kids (Project participant, FlexiJob, Flanders, Belgium).

I want a job because I would like to give my kids a good home, not to spoil them, but I would not like to have to tell them that I do not have money to buy them something (Lotte, project participant, FlexiJob, Flanders, Belgium).

You are getting used to FlexiJob and it suits you in some ways. But recently, you have noticed that something is changing. Ever since the project was featured on the TV and everyone was going on about how well they are doing with people like you, the workers don't talk to you so much about helping you get long-term chances or a good training. They have also stopped prodding you about your personal problems. That's a relief. You just can go in, get your job assignment and get out of there fast without any hassle.

But also, it's almost like they want you to keep coming and going and filling these job gaps. With no commitment from any one – employers, them, or you even. So it can feel pretty confusing still.

I would like to care for people in a hospital and you need training for that. To study again, to invest time, you cannot earn money at that moment. I want to marry, to buy a house and a car. This is normal, no? I was wild before and I accept that I did not study. I was hanging around in the streets. Smoked shit and so on. I feel sorry for that and that is why I am here (Project participant, FlexiJob, Flanders, Belgium).

Sometimes employers call with complaints·

When the youngsters came to the temporary employment agency, the youth-worker would call the employer and switch on the loudspeaker in the telephone. She did not ask the young person for an explanation, but let the employers draw their own conclusions (Researchers, FlexiJob, field diary, Flanders, Belgium).

Jobs Just for a Moment?

Here we continue the line of questioning and inquiry that became integral to our thinking together as a full team, as we considered the reports from our within-country research. As before, we are opening up trends and patterns that, in their particularity, can be treated as 'neutral', indeed as inevitable. For example, how can we *not* be concerned about how public money is spent? Isn't some experience of a job, however slight, worth something? Yet, the ways in which these experiences impact upon the lives, choices, and 'motivation' of young adults and professionals is anything but neutral.

So, for example, in the *House of Keys* project in Denmark, the professionals and the young adults seem to be corralled in a multiplicity of ways. However, the professionals were still trying to engage with some notion of meaningful pedagogy in that context. Notions of relationship, encounter, activity workshops, dialogue and attention to individual and collective identities still seemed to have some currency, however episodic, however cocooned from the wider world.

But in *FlexiJob*, steps have been taken to eradicate any notion of pedagogy. Getting a young person into any low-paid job, even if only for a few days is all that matters. In other words, low-paid work experience becomes silently re-positioned as educative in and of itself, separated from any opportunities to construct narratives or to learn from this experience.

During the period of our research, the *FlexiJob* project was hailed by the Minister of Employment as representing an important breakthrough in activating unemployed youth. It was argued that through this innovative approach, a prospect of a job can now be virtually guaranteed. So too can access to regular income, diverse job opportunities, and neighborhood support to make sure young people participate. A so called 'fit' between the dilemma of unemployment, changing labor identities, and young adults' changing lifestyles is said to have been found.

We can understand the enthusiasm. As in Denmark, we encountered in Belgium much cynicism amongst professionals who had long been involved in education, training, employment, and guidance initiatives for unemployed youth. This 'radical solution' can seem to offer a promising alternative. We can imagine how '30 Days Max' might make professionals feel as if they are engaged with a more meaningful and realistic 'activation' strategy – one that is more attuned to young adults' fragmented lives. The partnership between the private agency and the youth workers can also seem progressive. Rather than resist or deny the fragmentation or bemoan the lack of genuine work opportunities for lowly qualified and multiply disadvantaged or 'socially excluded' youth, why not make work 'work' in young adults' favor – or so the narrative might read.

But again, when viewing this situation from numerous perspectives over the course of our project, we questioned, on whose terms. Is it the 'needs and wants' of young unemployed that is driving the enthusiasm for such projects, or corporate demands for casualized flexible labor?

At one level, what is presented is the chance to 'try on' jobs as if they were new clothes. No pressure for real pay. But these are not designer labels. Instead, they are short term, poorly paid, low status 'jobettes'. They serve an increasingly de-regulated and 'competitive' global market economy. The rules of engagement are clear: '30 Days *Max*', not '30 Days Minimum'.

From another perspective, might we not see *FlexiJob* as stifling the aspirations of young adults? Is it in the economy's interests to encourage them to indulge fantasies of 'choosing the perfect job'? This question emerged from the Danish research and we develop it further in Part II with respect to the theme of labor identity.

Lay people, including the professionals involved, are all too aware of the severe shortages of skilled craftspeople and people in the building trades, for example. But rather than equipping these young adults for self-employment in highly paid areas of skills shortage or for entrepreneurship, instead the emphasis is only on a smorgasbord of endless job nibbling. *FlexiJob* at first seemed an extreme example of a trend. Yet by the time of this writing, it is fast becoming normative across Europe.

As Richard Sennett (1999) puts it, youth are enjoined to enjoy 'life lived as a series of episodes'. But as he comments, such enticements are 'woven into the everyday practices of a rigorous capitalism. Instability is meant to be normal'. Moreover, Sennett's analysis of the changing American job market reveals the extent to which private companies (such as the one which is involved in the pioneering partnership with *FlexiJob* in Belgium) take on contracts with companies that include them persuading young adults to keep taking on work placements in

FlexiJob (a kind of 30 day max recidivism target). Increasingly, private sector recruitment agencies are winning state and European funding, as more and more work is contracted out. These agencies are some of the fastest growing companies in the economy (ibid). Some even wake up, feed, collect, and deliver these 'temporary' crews, to ensure that employers' contract specifications for temporary labor are fulfilled.

Is this how Europe is to reduce social exclusion and decrease unemployment? Where is the space to consider questions such as, for example, for what, for whom and at what cost are schemes such as *FlexiJob* hailed by Ministers and professionals as great success stories? Are we to be surprised and delighted that employers are now so keen to participate in *FlexiJob*; to 'help' these unemployed youth with a minimum wage; to give them a 'chance to try out' different forms of work? And as the discourse and the performance record of *FlexiJob* is compared to schemes such as the Danish ones, what will become the new norm for intervention? We are reminded of Vietnam. Robert MacNamara introduced the 'reform' of greater corporacy and targets into the US military establishment. However, he was reputed to have said, just before America pulled out: 'By all *quantitative measures*, we are winning this war'.

And what if projects such as *FlexiJob* outperform other 'activation projects', against performance indicators based on getting jobs (although not keeping them)? Will time and space continue to be funded for schemes that support alternative forms of identity and labor work, and the integration of social, instrumental, and biographical competence – in non standardized ways?

It is with such questions in mind that we now turn to Portugal. Here we find strong contrasts with the trends introduced above, as found in Denmark and Belgium, as well as in UK mainstream projects. Here we found people working with similarly challenged young adults, but with greater freedom and autonomy to work with the raw material of the young people's socio-cultural and biographical histories, and to be more improvisational with respect to interpreting labor market possibilities. Project accountability was not yet constrained by generic, standardized frameworks and narrowly defined targets.

Alternatives such as the one now explored below helped to give rise to our conceptualization of 'paradoxes of restricting and reflexive activation' and to theorize alternative forms of European policy–practice dialogue, project governance and research, as explored in Part III.

This third case study and the final set of questions we pose will complete our introduction to the major systemic questions that were raised by this study, and which we continue to unfold in this book.

Encounter in Portugal

Imagine you are in Portugal:

> It is a typically bright sunny day in a very poor area at the edge of Lisbon. You know that many people call the place where you live a 'slum' or a 'ghetto'. As you

make your way to the local Community Association, located close to where you live, you see many people you know along the way. As usual, they are talking, working, cleaning their windows, selling things. You and many others who live in this area feel good about this Community Association. It was founded in 1987, and it gets a great deal of money from the EU. It attracts many visitors, from across Europe. It is always starting new projects that come from ideas that involve the community. For a number of years now, your friends, and family; people of all ages have been coming to the Center for lots of different activities. They feel, like you, that the Center has become an important part of their lives in the community and has had a positive impact on quality of life in the barrio. The Center's work has also helped people to feel less powerless and to discovery ways of doing things for themselves.

The sound of Portuguese you hear on the street and as you pass through the markets has a different music and rhythm from what you hear at the center of Lisbon. Almost everyone you meet on the way has come from, or has parents who have come from, different parts of the former Portuguese empire in Africa, mostly Cape Verde. You know they came here, like your own parents, because they wanted to make a better life for their children than they could find at home, often because of war and poverty. People in your community share stories all the time – about the hopes and courage that brought them here and about what they have experienced since arriving.

You and your friends like the course you are doing at the Association. This has been developed for young unemployed people in the community. You are being trained as 'cultural mediators'. This is a relatively new job. The first program was run in 1997. It is still not yet officially recognized, but you feel good about it. It's special and it is about helping people like you. You know that if you are successful in getting a job, you will help to sort out problems between teachers and students, parents and children, and between the school and people in your community.

People are accepted for this program because they are seen to be suitable, even though half of you have not even completed your 9 years of compulsory schooling. All of you feel proud to have been chosen for this course. Your ages range from 17 to 28 and out of thirteen of you four are young men and nine, young women. Only two in the group come from outside the community, the only White participants. One is Portuguese and is 19 and another is a young French woman, with a university background. They tell you that they are here because they feel fed up with formal education and want to do something that is meaningful:

> *It is them [the local people] that build each training session, because there is lots of participation They belong to the lived reality of this area and I don't. It is not what I have studied at university that will give me that (Participant from outside community, Cultural Mediators, Portugal).*

The program is like school, but it is also not like school. You are being trained for something your experience has taught you is needed. That makes it different. Also, the eight-month course provides not just classroom training, but also practice placements in the community. Sometimes you feel ashamed of how poor it is where you live, but also, you want to make things better for people in your community (Mieneke, local participant, Cultural Mediators, Portugal)

What you hear all the time, in the project and outside, is 'Here, immigrants without work are nothing'.

The program is broken up into 'modules' that introduce you to different kinds of subjects and skills. One cluster teaches you about social services, psychology, the labor market and mediation   You never had subjects like these at school   Other courses get you to think about other things you never talked about at school, such as present world, cultural diversity, prevention of school failure, parent education   You also have time just for 'personal development' and to discuss 'exploitation' and 'social justice' and learn skills in a course called 'instrumental enrichment'.   The teachers talk about you learning lots of personal, social, and political 'strategies' for dealing with the many worlds you will have to understand in your role   You like that word, 'strategy' even though you are not always sure just what it means

Even though the modules always finish too fast, just when you are really getting into things, what you like is the time you have to discuss and practice what you are learning, in real situations   The practice time increases as you go along, moving up to four days per week over the eight months you get to be on this program.   You often hear group members saying things such as·

> *We learn things that are with us (Izelda, participant, Cultural Mediators, Portugal)*

> *I feel that I learn much more in this school than in others (Salonge, project participant, Cultural Mediators, Portugal)*

> *Many in the group also see a big difference between their school experience and this vocational training.. that question is very important, because teachers have a content to teach and that may mean one, two, or five books.   And they do everything to teach it, without paying attention to whether students are learning or not, at least they are teaching   If the student is looking outside, he [the school teacher] doesn't care and keeps on teaching   But I think that is not the case here.   Here it is very important because trainers try [to ensure] that every mediator is trained, or that they have done their best to learn   Because many times they pay attention to if we are attentive or not, which is very important for not letting [us] escape anything that may be useful in the future (Ines, project participant, Cultural Mediators, Portugal)*

You also meet regularly each month with a coordinator, to talk about how you are doing and evaluate together your ups and downs with the program   They ask how you feel about what you are learning, the trainers, and anything else of importance to you in your life that may affect your getting the most from the program

> *We are making part of the training session and they are making part of us (Izelda, project participant, Cultural Mediators, Portugal).*

You and your friends think that the teachers are quite nice and you know they want to do the best they can for you   They are here because they have chosen to be   Most of them are White, very experienced with young people who have had problems.   They come from very different backgrounds   education, law, psychology, special education and rehabilitation   So, not just vocational training   They are committed and they work hard   There are 17 people involved all together, with eight people responsible for the core modules   They often speak about 'empowerment' and they feel strongly about the value of this program being located where you live, rather than outside your community   They meet regularly as a group to talk about what you say to them and to discuss how to improve the program and your overall experience of it in relation to your lives and possibilities in the Labor Market.

When you learn things you never feel you are doing it alone. Unlike school, you can talk to each other, laugh, and share things that matter to you. You knew many of the people in the group before you started. But you have become better friends here and often see each other outside the program now.

> *I use to say that the cultural mediators are like a family and that is very important (Raziz, project participant, Cultural Mediators, Portugal)*

> *The teachers let us speak. We don't feel intimidated to ask something. Doubts just come out. Besides, we both are part of and contribute to the training session (Zaz, project participant, Cultural Mediators, Portugal).*

You like how the teachers involve you and your friends in decision making about what to learn, how, when and where – and how to make things better. They want you to make links between things: your discussions, experiences of your own life and your family, friends, and neighbors, and what you are learning about in your placements and in terms of different subjects. Unlike when you were at school, what you are learning here has meaning in your own life. You like how the teachers want you to ask questions and to think about things. You like how it helps you see things differently from before

The professionals also seem to like working with you and coming into your community to help you learn in ways that might make a difference. It also makes a change from thinking that you can only get lowly paid jobs no one else wants. Although you and your friends still dream about being world famous footballers or musicians, this is also something you can do that is useful. It gives you hope, especially when you look at others in your community.

> *Sometimes I used to feel anger when I heard about something and then what I would feel like saying was, 'Hire a bunch of boys and beat them up'. But not now... We have to live life calmly. We have to know how to understand people and why the person does that, as Raziz says. And this I think I'm learning very much, that is not with violence we can change things.. (Mota project participant, Cultural Mediators, Portugal).*

> *In that first contact we can discover the individual, how he is working, then understand where does he come from, that moment is also interesting...what culture do they bring...that encounter for me is essential (Teacher, Cultural Mediators, Portugal).*

> *The only job we know is cleaning work, because we don't have opportunities for other kind of work... That's why I say slavery for me has not finished yet Discrimination still goes on (Midjin, project participant, Cultural Mediators, Portugal).*

> *They are very much in the here and now. This raises a big concern about how they will manage to give a satisfactory performance as mediators, since it is work with people who have problems who will not change behaviors so easily. Deeply rooted in their rationalities is that everyone is against them. Can they be strong enough to open themselves to the external world...? (Teacher Cultural Mediators, Portugal)*

One other thing, on which the professionals agree is to empower these young adults for autonomous responsibility, because in their future professional intervention they will be fundamentally alone, left by themselves and in need of supporting others   However, they doubt if the eight training months will be sufficient to consolidate that (Researchers, Cultural Mediators, Portugal).

At the same time, it can feel quite scary to think about being an actual mediator 'in the real world' without the professionals' support – especially outside the community where you feel less confident and with people you don't know   Sometimes you hear the professionals talking about this as if you are not mature enough, or ready:

> *on the one hand, I try to transmit confidence   As I'm here, I can support them, but I won't give them all .   More and more I will let them assume their responsibilities, having me behind, and slowly I will leave them by themselves   but I need to warrant that I'm here (Teacher, Cultural Mediators, Portugal).*

There is a certain immaturity on their part and a perception of the world characterized by a 'victim perspective', resulting from past experience.   They seem in need to strengthen 'winner' strategies to prevent them using 'survival strategies', and solutions related to their prior state as 'victims' (Researchers, Cultural Mediators, Portugal)

They are keen to imagine themselves going to support others coming from the same background as they themselves do.   They perceive this as a major contribution to their own personal and professional development.   These young adults are mostly fighting against the lifestyle usually offered to African immigrants in Portugal.   They are aiming for a profession other than the lowly qualified jobs commonly available to ethnic minorities in Portugal.   But, when the analysis involves a questioning of their own behaviors and attitudes, they still don't demonstrate enough openness to go ahead with it   Nonetheless, it is recognized that while they are feeling more empowered and more self-confident, they are becoming more and more able to integrate learning and to be aware of the surrounding reality   This is, anyway, a long path they will have to go through (Researchers, Cultural Mediators, Portugal).

Sometimes you and your friends talk about how these teachers interpret what you live with everyday.   They come to the project and then they go home every night   When they leave here and go straight into places where people aren't so poor, and aren't so Black, they do not get people shouting abuse at them   They don't need to feel scared that people will beat them up just because they are children of immigrants and different from people out there   All the same, you know they pay attention to future prospects for you working as a cultural mediator   Even though the schools support this project, saying it is important, it is not yet a real job.   But as long as you can make some money and do something that doesn't feel useless or like slave labor, that's what matters to you   You know that the first group all have jobs in schools, but only because they are making a positive contribution   There are no guarantees, though, that they will continue   The Association is making a lobby now to pressurize policy makers to recognize mediation as a career, either on its own, or with others *doing professional training. You like to hear about that. It makes you feel important. Like things can change.*

> *If they are needed, I think sooner or later it will be possible to recognize them as professionals (Teacher, Cultural Mediators, Portugal).*

> *what concerns the professionals the most is that trainers are really willing for a place [for the participants on this program] to work as mediator. They are in training with the precise aim of opening a door in their lives and not meeting this level of expectation can be a serious and frustrating experience for them (Researchers, Cultural Mediators, Portugal).*

> *They are doing a remarkable job (Project participant)*

> *Eight months might not be enough to prepare them for such a complex professional activity in view of their pasts (Teacher, Cultural Mediators, Portugal).*

Learning From and Through Contradictions?

This case study confronts us with an alternative lived notion of activation in practice. The majority of the young adults involved here would be perceived by many professionals to be similar to young adults in the previous encounters: 'socially excluded' and 'difficult to employ'. Their problems would tend to be seen as compounded by being labeled by the larger society as 'ethnic minorities' and being scapegoated as 'alienated' from 'society'. But what is different about this scenario in Portugal, in terms of working with multiply disadvantaged young adults, of largely Afro-Portuguese descent, in a severely marginalized community?

Firstly, the program was being experienced as directly transformative by young people and professionals alike. We encountered virtually no dispute over this: dialogue about how to do it better, yes, but nothing about it being meaningless, or of little use. Moreover, this was recognized not only, by those participating, but also by others in the neighborhood, by virtue of the project's association with a highly and long respected Community Association that was trusted by the community, based on its previous track record.

Professionals and unemployed young adults seemed to be learning alongside each other how to create narratives of hope. This was rooted in working with, rather than denying the complexity, contradictions, and paradoxes both groups were navigating at various ethnic, cultural, and economic borderlands.

We also saw this project as not yet under 'surveillance' in the ways that were so evident in others in this research. Teachers were more protected from the barrage of demands for 'accountable and evidence based practice'. On the one hand, any such tensions would be mediated by the main Community Association who had raised the funding from European and other sources for this project. On the other, at the time of our study, the tenacious hold of the 'audit culture' (Strathern, 2000) that was so evident in Northern Europe was not an issue in Southern Europe – an issue that itself deserves further research, particularly with respect to its unintended effects on the quality and meaningfulness of work that can be undertaken with socially excluded and unemployed young Europeans.

Our co-inquiry based research orientation was not difficult to establish with this project. Unlike others, where we could often be perceived initially as a threat, contact with the young adults was neither as controlled nor as strongly mediated by the professionals. Opportunities for learning from our participation were seen as compatible with the overall ethos of the project.

Pressures to achieve time–space compressions, so characteristic of a globalizing economy, were thus not impacting upon the project as forcefully, as with, for example, *FlexiJob*. In the Portuguese case, the funding and governance dimensions of the project allowed for a different time–space dynamic to be jointly constructed and enacted. The lack of external demands for compliance with quantitative and standardized performance indicators, seemed to open up space for continuity, struggle, and learning, and for working through difficult questions more so than in other projects.

At the same time, an eight-month, overall time-frame for this training was imposed by funding. This exerted significant constraints and pressures. The professionals spoke in different ways about the difficulties posed by having this short amount of time to prepare the young adults with histories of past failure, for a complex professional activity. The teachers and the young adults would convey differently how they experienced the 'difficult cusp' after eight months. The young people seemed unable to retreat to previous aspirations and earlier internalized assumptions about what they might 'legitimately' achieve in this world. Yet simultaneously, they were unable to move fully into expressing the alternative aspirations and futures that had been 'activated' by this training for cultural mediation. The teachers felt similarly that something was just opening up, that would serve these young adults well in many ways, with respect to both their economic and social participation, irrespective of their placement as cultural mediators. But the time scales that were a condition of their funding were too short to realize the full potential of what they were unfolding and supporting in the young adults and the community, through the Center.

This 'premature end' of the project, could be seen (in this particular case) as somewhat counter balanced by the sustained European funding supporting the community association as a whole. In other words, discontinuity at the end of the specific 'activation project' had the opportunity to be counter balanced by other interventions. This has become a key issue in research on social exclusion and more and more challenges are being posed to policy makers who expect that projects can redress major disadvantages, such as poverty. But how many projects have such culturally embedded associations working hand-in-hand with them?

Many of those who were participating in the *Cultural Mediators* project also had strong levels of social and personal identification with this Association: its aims, its values as they lived them and its activities. For example, it was this Association that had identified the need and possibility for training as cultural mediators, in the first place. It had worked hard to gain the necessary funds for setting up this innovative project. The idea for training in cultural mediation had been neither imported into nor imposed upon the Community. It was culturally and locally contextualized, and derived from collective social learning supported in part by the Association.

Recognition of this difference seems critical in the context of another European trend that we first noticed in the UK. This was the idea that it is possible to identify 'best practice' ideas, irrespective of the histories, contingencies, and power relations that have had to be navigated in order for a project to be perceived locally as 'successful'. Such policy and practice operates on an assumption that socially contextualized knowledge can be extracted and exported elsewhere, as if such knowledge and practice has a life that can be dissected from the relationships and dialogues in which they are embedded. These will have been negotiated, navigated, and co-constructed over time. They cannot be 'packaged' as instant solutions to be formulaically implemented elsewhere. There needs to be time and space to 'grow' new meanings, values, and histories for an idea that has not emerged out of local relationships and knowledges. New practices cannot be commanded into being. They need to be nourished through dialogue and relationships, and given expression in forms that find their own life and meaning in a particular community in order to be sustainable.

Here, there was evidence of a strong commitment to making this project a 'genuine activation': a meaningful one, for the individuals and the wider community, even though the role of cultural mediator was not yet officially recognized. It had meaning in terms of the young people's experiences, at the interfaces of school, street, and home. This disjunction itself would be worked with as raw material for the project's social and instrumental learning.

There were questions that this project also raised for us, that have wider import. For example, why is it that some external observers of this project tended to de-value and discount as 'untransferable' the capabilities that *were* being developed in this project? What other social processes are at work, such as institutionalized racism, that discount the validity and potential value and importance of this learning on the part of largely Afro-Portuguese young adults? What if alternative performance criteria became the yardstick of value, such as evidence of how participants are being helped to deal with the unknown and the unexpected and to learn from contradictions they meet in their lives and the labor market? This project would fare far better against such criteria than *Flexijob* or *House of Keys* or *Projects*. How might alternative expectations of what counts as competence shift the space for what is possible in projects such as this?

This project also raises questions about whether and how participants in this project may be implicitly or explicitly encouraged to assimilate to the dominant White middle-class culture in order to succeed in school and in life. Or alternatively, to prop up a school system that itself has not yet come to grips with what it may mean to mediate cross-cultural meanings, expectations, and interpretations of school experience, or to empower, educationally, youth who are both perceived to be on the margins and are simultaneously pushed onto these? The tensions around professionals 'working with' or 'working for' the young adults in these projects manifested in some form across all the case studies. In this scenario, however, 'working and learning with' was the dominant mode in evidence – in the founding, the funding, the implementation, sustainability, and improvement efforts of this project.

What was evident here is the extent to which tensions arising from such complex interactions could be jointly negotiated and learned from, through dialogue and everyday forms of reflexive co-inquiry. Everyday lived practices within the project engaged with notions of meaningfulness in many different ways. In the external world, this included lobbying the government and other professional bodies for recognition of cultural mediation as a valid and valued professional activity. Within the project, it meant engaging young people in dialogue that gave them different ways of understanding and navigating their own situations. The rhetoric of empowerment was not disconnected from pedagogy. Young people were being helped to claim and name their actual situations in various ways, to stay reflexive about difficulties they and their community were facing (such as school drop out) and to devise personal and collective strengths, skills, and strategies for navigating them differently.

But how quickly might current policy and governance trends unintentionally undermine projects such as these? What if this project were to lose some of the autonomy it currently has? What if 'more efficient time scales' and pre-specified performance targets and pedagogical outputs were prescribed, at the pre-funding stage? In terms of the complexities being worked with, who decides '8 months max'? On the basis of what criteria?

At present, the longer-term European funding for the wider Association, which gave birth to this project, provides a certain amount of ballast to stimulate and support such innovations in a Portuguese barrio. Moreover, all participants from the first project were, and remain, employed – an output that many in Brussels would welcome. But will they in future be able to continue? But what of other projects, that grow out of local efforts, imagination, and improvisational pedagogy in the face of complex social and economic realities to generate new forms of social and economic empowerment for young adults? We think not, given the power of the more restricting trends we have signaled in the other two narratives, and that threaten a newly expanded and more diverse Europe.

These lines of inquiry lead us to wonder how discontinuities and inequalities may be perpetuated not only through power relations influenced by class, gender, and race, but also unintentionally by activation policy, funding, and accountability frameworks. We were confronted with the contradiction that the metaphors and models that currently guide activation policy and practice may be highly influential in strengthening inequalities and further socially excluding those who are already on the boundaries. We shall return to this sobering insight in Part III and suggest ways in which such possibilities might be given new forms of attention, by policy makers, practitioners, program designers, and researchers.

Chapter 4

Youth Transition Research:
Changing Metaphors and Languages
in a Globalizing World

Beyond Agency-structure Dualisms

The ways in which we are unfolding the research findings and questions that have been stimulated by this project suggest how our research project has 'pirouetted' on what sociology has framed the 'agency–structure' boundary. In the UK, until fairly recently, this has tended to be approached academically as an either/or duality. This has been manifest in two very different traditions of youth research namely, the cultural studies approach to youth (Nava, 1992; Griffin, 1993, 1997; McLaughlin and Heath, 1993; McRobbie, 1994; Cohen, 1997; Skelton and Valentine, 1998), and the sociological approach. The latter has been preoccupied with investigating structural pre-determinants of young adults' lives such as social class (Bynner, 1987; Banks et al., 1992; Bates and Riseborough, 1993; Roberts, 1995; Dolton et al., 1999; ESRC 16-19 Initiative). The former has been characterized by a 'quasi-anthropological concern with exotic instances of youthful deviance and difference' (Cohen and Ainley, 2000, p. 89).

Youth researchers have, however, increasingly acknowledged the interplay of both dimensions in youth transition research (Gayle, 1998; Rudd and Evans, 1998; Percy-Smith, 1999). Cohen and Ainley (2000) argue for the need to create a third space between these two traditions for example by focusing on how young people learn to 'culturally labor' (Lave and Wenger, 1991; Ainley and Rainbird, 1999). Karen Evans' work has also been pivotal in this respect. Her own research on youth unemployment reveals youth transitions in terms of a process of 'structured individualization' as young people reflexively negotiate the realization of their own biographies with respect to the 'risk society' (Cieslik and Pollock, 2002). Her 1998 analysis of trends in youth research shifted the metaphors for such studies to the language of niches, pathways, trajectories and navigations (Evans and Furlong, 1997):

- Pathways and filling niches, which emphasize 'age-related normative tasks, and identity and certainty if tasks [are] completed successfully'.

- Trajectories, which emphasize 'reactions of alienation [and the] social and cultural reproduction of roles' with an emphasis on 'social structures and power relations'.
- Navigations with an emphasis on 'negotiation of 'structures of opportunity and risk', giving sources of stability or instability in the life course' (Evans and Furlong, p. 74).

Our case study material will continue to show ways in which the navigations, pathways, and trajectories of young unemployed and socially excluded Europeans might be located and dislocated by attempts to 'activate' them. Karen Evans (2002), in her more recent work, speaks about 'bounded agency'. Our project revealed an array of contradictions and paradoxes arising at the interfaces of policy intentions, intervention practices, and the lived realities of young adults and professionals. In retrospect, our decision to pirouette at the interface of agency and structure in this project (at a time when the binary tradition in youth research still prevailed) was proven sound. Our empirical data helped to untether us from implicit moorings of linear, developmental, and progressive concepts of youth transition. We were enabled to bring a multiplicity of lenses to a field where considerable systemic complexity is being enacted and experienced within the particulars of 'encounter spaces' on a daily basis. Postmodernist notions of multiple identities, reflexive autobiography, and (dis)location were meaningfully contextualized through this project, as will be further revealed in Part II.

Balancing Competences: A Socially Robust Line of Inquiry?

This study made apparent the extent to which participating EU member states were all experiencing difficulties in their efforts to reconcile both economic and social objectives of educational provision. There has been a steady growth of initiatives relating to social exclusion and unemployed youth (Brine, 2001; Hammer, 2002). Apropos these trends, our original research proposal documented our intent to examine what we called, 'mainstream' and 'alternative' cases of education, training, employment, and guidance interventions with unemployed youth. However, we found this conceptualization difficult, nigh impossible, to operationalize. This dilemma itself raised questions that warranted further co-inquiry.

For example, we had anticipated that we would find radical differences in the pedagogy of various providers such as state, private, and voluntary. We assumed that approaches to activation across Europe would be strongly influenced by different national, structural, socio-political, and historical factors. This is not to deny the great variety in concrete practices we researched, nor their diversity in terms of meanings and implications as enacted in specific national and local contexts. However, it became more and more apparent that patterns of provision were becoming more and more standardized in their format and their objectives, and ever more regulated by the same evaluation and funding criteria, despite the diversity of circumstances or participants. Green puts this finding into perspective:

Education and training policy can increasingly be seen as a global commodity. Armies of international think tank experts and consultants analyse, develop, adapt and package policies to order for governments, corporations and other interested parties; international organisations – notably the OECD, the World Bank and the European Commission – evaluate national policies and seek to persuade national governments to adopt their favoured measures, with more or less potent forms of persuasion, and national education ministers keep a watchful eye on developments in other countries which they may adapt or borrow... Where education policy was once a largely national affair, now – thanks to improved communications and cross-national data, and because of the global pressures of competition and *transnational* politics – it is a fully internationalised, and at times internationally – traded, commodity (Green, 2002, p. 611).

At the beginning of this project, we also hypothesized that 'mainstream' projects would attend primarily to the development of 'instrumental competences'. In other words, as we suggested in our original EU proposal, such projects would seek to (re)introduce unemployed youth to the labor market through their capacity to influence interactions with the help of material and symbolic resources, in such a way that the actor(s) involved would realize their goals.

We also hypothesized that 'alternative programs' would have a less restrictive and more radical pedagogical focus. More specifically, we anticipated that programs operating outside mainstream funding regimes would give as much emphasis to social and biographical competence development, as to instrumental competence and indeed to their interrelationships. In our original proposal, we clarified these other dimensions as follows:

- *Biographical competences:* the capacity to create consistent narratives of one's (inter)actions and experiences, guided by frames of reference (images and discourses) that are meaningful and valuable to the actor(s) in interpreting themselves and the world.

- *Social competences:* the capacity to participate in various social networks which directly or indirectly creates possibilities of participation in the labor market.

We set out with the assumption that attempts to understand the 'content' or meanings of such competences would be explored in relation to the meanings and differing socio-cultural and biographical circumstances that influenced individual lives and choices, as well as specific national trends with respect to projects that were responsive to changing economic conditions. We set out to learn more about how different contexts of practice might shift the focus from one kind of competence to another. But the overall assumption that we made explicit in our original project proposal was that all three kinds of competences were important if young adults were to 'realize their potential for economic and social participation'.[1] We even subtitled our research proposal, 'balancing competences'. We believed that local practices would mirror the systemic dilemma faced by

Europe of seeking to balance economic competitiveness with attention to social exclusion.

In other words, we regarded our research project as an opportunity to inquire into whether and how Educational Training and Guidance (ETG) programs and practices were attempting to work with tensions and possibilities of giving these potentially conflicting policy objectives meaning in concrete practice.

What we discovered, however, was that not just some, but *all* of the programs we studied paid attention to social and biographical competence in some way. This was often supported by a discourse about progressive activation practice. This was a surprise. We began to ferret under the surface of such practice. As illustrated through our case study narratives in Chapter 3, we found ourselves confronting the dilemma posed by Chambers (1994): namely, how globalization is giving rise to the re-invention and cooption of terms, in ways that cease to be self-evident, in terms of our taken for granted sense-making.

We came to the conclusion that in spite of regional variations, few aspects of European educational policy and provision for the unemployed could escape tensions of instrumentalization and commodification. This inexorable pull was always there, even if disguised by the rhetoric of 'choice', familiar features of corporate globalization eventually surfaced. Further, we became aware of the extent to which these forces were becoming institutionalized and therefore constricting the spaces for 'alternative' forms of experimenting with (and learning from) attempts to reconcile social and economic tensions. So, although policy makers might be reassured by the resulting evidence of greater 'efficiency and effectiveness' in education, training, employment, and guidance initiatives, this view may be distorted, in its distance from research that generates more grounded understandings of how these 'regulatory controls' may be undermining the very innovative local practices Europe needs at this moment. As Jackie Brine argues:

> The concept of globalization may seem far removed from the practices of the classroom... It may also seem somewhat distanced from nation state education policy makers and policy itself...however, the economic, cultural and political reality of globalization is the context within which supranational and national education policy is made, and furthermore, it is the context within which the practice of education takes place (Brine, 2001, p. 120).

The Discourse of Activation: Further Questions

As discussed earlier, our study paralleled clear shifts in policy discourse: namely, from an emphasis on education, training, employment, and guidance, towards this emphasis on social and economic participation, and principles of 'activation'. Its initial use in Denmark was in the context of high employment. Many programs there were targeting unemployed youth who were seen as socially excluded and unemployable. The use of the term 'activation', although still little used in the UK with regard to unemployed youth, is now acutely manifest in a range of present day EU social policy and discourse (Kazepov, 2002).

It was midway through our research that we began to discern how existing patterns of exclusion and inequality could be reinforced and indeed exacerbated by this 'activation rhetoric', and by its governance. As complex and mutually interacting processes became apparent through our initial case studies, we chose – as our second case studies – projects that were targeted largely at multiply disadvantaged unemployed young people. In other words, principles of emergent design enabled us to learn from the research thus far, and to shift emphasis. This further deepened the quality of our questions about whether and how dominant discourses and ideologies may be squeezing down possibilities for pedagogical and social innovation with respect to 'successfully activating' young people who were labeled not just unemployed, but also socially excluded. They can be condemned to a perpetual doomed existence, in what Rob MacDonald (1997), on the strength of his own research with marginalized and unemployed youth in the northeast of England, has called 'schemelands':

> the vast number of government schemes [jobless youth] had encountered. Few knew anybody who held down 'proper jobs'. For them, their friends, their brothers and sisters, working life now consisted of a series of marginal activities: short run community or cooperative ventures, unpaid volunteering, self exploitative small business, low-paid and part-time jobs, risky fiddly jobs, and time on government make-work of 'training schemes' interspersed with periods of idle unemployment (MacDonald, 1997, p. 170).

In Part I, we introduced different kinds of 'schemelands' that were being navigated by young adults deemed unemployable and often also 'socially excluded' in Europe. This 'scene setting', for the book as whole, raises challenging questions such as:

- Can such projects be assessed as successful if unemployed young adults are merely kept 'schemelined' in order to be kept off welfare, off the streets, out of trouble and out of the official statistics on unemployment?

- How long and how many times can young adults be 'corralled in the holding pen' (as one worker at New Deal put it), lest they face further social and economic hardship?

- Is success being measured on the basis of criteria that may only support those who are most likely to succeed?

- Is there sufficient 'space' at local and policy levels to allow for, and learn for, a diversity of practices, in attempting to reduce social exclusion and unemployment?

We believe that EU ambitions to influence reductions in youth unemployment and social exclusion are of considerable importance. We contend that this is especially so, at this historical moment of major expansion of member states. This continuum of trends we have begun to unfold in Part I, and their intended and unintended impacts, suggest some of the complex systemic dynamics and trends we have surfaced through our research. Many paradoxes are having to be managed at current policy, practice, and governance interfaces across the EU. Some of these may be irresolvable, or unmanageable. But others may be ameliorated and shifted through alternative forms of policy–practice dialogue, research and governance. But, firstly we wish now to widen the lens on this landscape, in a different way, and introduce readers to the full range of projects we have studied across the six participating countries. We shall then focus in particular on questions and paradoxes arising from our data in relation to the themes of working identities, agency, and empowerment, and shifting pedagogies and relationships between professionals and young adults.

---

[1] Our use of the term competence at this time was influenced by the work of Anthony Giddens as well as by ideas on social learning theorists coming from mainland Europe. Our understandings of competence could be understood more in terms of contextualized 'capability building' or 'capability' and were related to our interest in concepts of education, training, employment, and guidance that engaged the notion of an alternative social contract within Europe.

PART II
LENSES ON THE SHIFTING
LANDSCAPE OF 'ACTIVATION'

Chapter 5

Activation Practices:
An Emerging Topography

In Part II we consider how concepts of education, training, employment, and guidance are being transformed through the emerging emphasis on 'activation', and with what intended and unintended consequences. We now open up the full landscape of the projects we studied in depth. We reveal subtle yet powerful ways in which taken for granted assumptions, perceptions, and possibilities relating to what might constitute 'effective' education, training, employment, and guidance interventions with young unemployed people are being de-stabilized. We suggest how traditional notions of time, space, and the nature of work are being de-stabilized, not only in the labor markets in a globalizing economy, but also in these activation projects.

As we draw on our empirical data in different ways, we invite readers to continue to reflect alongside us on current policy obsessions with 'active' and 'activation', for example:

- Where does this discourse come from?

- What tensions or contradictions is it trying to resolve?

- How are activation discourses being realized through concrete everyday practices and procedures of activation?

- How are paradoxes and contradictions on the interfaces between policy 'rhetoric' and the lived realities of young people and professionals being sustained by larger systemic forces and with what unintended consequences (Weil, 1998; Percy-Smith and Weil, 2002, 2003)?

- In what ways might we value, the activation tendency in policy discourse and practice?

- What alternatives for 'activation' remain under-explored or are being constrained, in their discovery by communities, their funding, and their support?

Discernible Trends: Four Cultures of Learning

We shall now depict four 'cultures of learning' that were suggested to us by our research into the cases studies, supported by interviews, focus group work, and policy document analysis. Throughout this section, we draw upon case study material, as prepared by each participating country throughout the project. For more in-depth pen portraits of each project, readers can turn to Appendix 1.

This particular view of the educational landscape will offer a further lens onto ambiguities and dilemmas that we encountered in local interpretations of EU influenced education, training, employment, and guidance policies and trends. Concerns to maintain economic competitiveness that influence European economic policy are not easily reconciled with equally legitimate concerns for social equality and participation. This structural contradiction gives rise to a host of paradoxes and tensions, when there are attempts to 'activate' young unemployed adults.

We have chosen the phrase 'culture of learning' to refer to different clusters of practices, perceptions, beliefs, norms, and rules. These express and give direction to the arrangements and daily expression of activation-in-action. Each in their own way reflects a particular interpretation of social and economic policy imperatives for 'activation'.

A culture of learning can therefore be understood as a particular kind of 'discursive practice', aimed at reconciling labor market and social participation objectives. Weinberg (1999) has used the term to refer to educational and training strategies being adopted to support the development of competences within and outside the formal education system. We discovered that the culture of learning that prevailed in a particular activation initiative had a significant influence on:

- a project's communication processes,

- its explicit goals,

- what counts and is discounted as valid contents and processes for learning,

- the kinds of expertise required of participating professionals,

- the expression of power relations between the professionals and the young people,

- relations between the project and the wider social and economic environment,

- the kind of experiences that are emphasized and encouraged or vice versa.

Four Orientations

The four cultures of learning we identify below are not particular to specific countries. Instead, they capture indicative patterns in the approach of different projects as reflected across the six countries. What will become evident is how discourses and concepts of 'activation' mutate within each of these approaches to influence the trajectories of unemployed young adults. Although we believe that some key distinctions can be made, at the same time processes of standardization are all strongly in evidence within and across the first three cultures. We will see that these cultures of learning are engaged in an intricate dance with the wider environment and forces of globalization, and discourses of neo-liberal economics.

We 'name' the four cultures of learning we discerned and how we relate them to the 'activation' projects[1] we studied as follows:

1. Getting them working no matter what or where
   - Belgium: *FlexiJob* and *The Farmhouse Shop*
   - Netherlands: *Right Match*
   - Germany: *JobXchange*

2. Targeted and tailored training
   - Netherlands: *Community College* and *Vocational College*
   - Germany: *Female Electricians*
   - Portugal: *Vocational Training School (VTS)*

3. Informing and helping
   - Denmark: *The House of Keys*, *The House of Projects*
   - Belgium: *First Advise*
   - UK: *New Deal/Gateway*

4. Situated social learning
   - England: *Bridging the Gap*
   - Portugal: *Cultural Mediators*

By foregrounding one culture of learning for a specific project, we do not imply that the same project does not exhibit characteristics of other cultures of learning. Nor would elements of one culture be completely absent in other cases. But the cases referred to for each culture of learning demonstrated most strongly the dominant named strategy.

After introducing the dominant orientations, we consider limitations and possibilities in each culture of learning with respect to claimed intentions to mediate tensions between the forces exerted by changing labor markets and forces that give rise to social exclusion. The data presented here represents a distillation of data from the full range of within- and cross-country papers produced throughout the project.

This exposition enables readers to re-visit key questions and paradoxes introduced through the narratives in Part I. This kaleidoscopic unfolding of data will continue to be used as a deliberate strategy in this book. We consider this 'style as theory' orientation (Van Maanem, 1995) appropriate to a research approach that sets out to explore tensions and possibilities in the field. Overall, our intention is to stimulate new forms of dialogue and co-inquiry about taken for granted actions and choices in different domains of the system and the unintended consequences of these for young Europeans.

Getting them Working no Matter What or Where

I have to earn money because I have a wife and two kids (Project participant, FlexiJob, Belgium).

I want a job because I would like to give my kids a good home, not to spoil them, but I would not like to have to tell them that I do not have money to buy them something (Lotte, project participant, FlexiJob, Belgium)

Sometimes people without children live on unemployment benefit They could work if they wanted, but they don't. I have problems with that. I do not show it, but I find it difficult that they come here and tell me several times they want to work When I give them a job, they don't go Towards the society I feel responsible to report them to the employment office and tell that they have to stop the unemployment benefit On the other hand, I find it difficult to do that, because it will bring those people severe problems for a period of six months (Private sector consultant to FlexiJob, Belgium)

In this culture of learning the emphasis is predominantly on learning through work itself. The emphasis is placed on work attitudes that will accustom young people to discipline. These may or may not be seen (by young people and professionals alike) to connect to the actual labor market.

Projects that we would associate with this orientation vary in the way they provide this kind of work experience. *FlexiJob*, introduced in Part I, and the German *JobXchange* project offered participants actual short-term jobs in low paid segments of the labor market. Others, like *The Farmhouse Shop* in Belgium, combined work-based training with actual work experience in the retail shop that was established as part of the project. Others again, such as the Dutch *Right Match* project, provided work placements outside the project in combination with training in practical and social skills within the project itself. Common to all of them, however, is the predominance of work placements and real work experience over training and counseling.

The German **JobXchange** *and the Belgian* **FlexiJob** *projects both offer short-term jobs (and thus also, 'fast money') to young adults. The jobs are located in the lower segments of the labor market (working on a construction site, cleaning, renovating or transport). There was no training offered by these projects, but there were voluntary options to get some counseling and advice, with the professionals mediating between the employers and the* *young adults. The professionals regarded their work as outreach work, since they were trying to make contact with young people who had not been able or willing to do any training or full-time employment.*

The Farmhouse Shop *project in Belgium gave women a one-year work-based training in sales and distribution, although the emphasis was more on learning by doing rather than the actual content of such training. The women practiced their skills in the project's shop although there was often little to do. Participants were, however, pushed to make specific decisions and were expected to find their own way in the project.*

The Dutch Right Match project provided training at EU level 1 for low skilled and unskilled labor. The courses alternated between practical training, social skills training and a work placement. The clear goal was to find a job through work placements and to sustain that job.

Young adults applied and were selected for participation in these projects; they were not open to all unemployed. The notion of getting them working, no matter what or where was assumed to be the most promising road to labor market integration. Getting them working was also a key driver for the professionals. Indeed, most projects could point to a relatively high percentage of employment for ex-participants. However, processes of selection and exclusion may have helped to play a role in assuring such 'clear outputs', in terms of 'activation success'. Also, such as in the case of *FlexiJob*, presented in Part I, we need to question whether we are merely measuring episodic work experience in the labor market. Further, what labor identities are being co-constructed through experience of such projects?

The focus on workplace experience and the development of work attitudes adopted in these projects was a direct response to a specific client group of young adults. This group was perceived as either not willing or not able to make a commitment to long-term training or full-time employment, but was assumed to be inherently capable of doing so, with the support of this particular culture of learning. It seemed that increasingly, professionals, practitioners, and policy makers were making distinctions about 'activation schemes' for those who were likely to remain long-term unemployed and 'activation projects' for those who would not. What became apparent was how such discrimination was itself being influenced by funding criteria and governance practices.

The same power relations that maintain existing processes of social exclusion could thus still be seen to be at work. Those who were seen to have severe social and/or personal problems (such as drug addiction, homelessness, psychiatric disorders, family breakdown) were on the whole excluded from participation in this form of provision. Yet, paradoxically, many of the young adults who were admitted to workplace schemes showed a personal record of early school leaving, an aversion to regular education and a lack of a clear perspective on how to move on.

Professionals working in the Dutch **Right** Match *said that for many of the participating young adults, this was the last educational resort, since all previous attempts to establish a regular school career failed.*

In some projects, such as the German JobXchange, *the participants represent a mix of young adults who were lost in the challenges with which regular education and employment confronted them. Participants that had a more or less clear perspective on how to move on, used the project to solve urgent financial problems.*

In the Belgian FlexiJob, *the participants consisted mainly of young adults who were said to have deliberately chosen a lifestyle in which periods of work and leisure alternated, and to whom full-time and lifelong employment was not an ultimate aim at all. This assumption tended to reinforce the proliferation of programs that denied the possibility of making any kind of difference in terms of young adults' trajectories and lives.*

In The Farmhouse Shop *project, the young women on exit had very high employment records, indicating both the impact of selection strategies and/or flexibility and transferability of the learned skills.*

Funding requirements and instrumentally focused project objectives can also make it difficult, in practice, to pay much meaningful attention to biographical learning in these projects. This was especially the case for those projects that focused almost exclusively on merely 'brokering' short-term opportunities for work like the *FlexiJob* project. However, in a number of projects we found professionals trying to hold onto the possibility of stimulating reflexive, biographical learning, despite the 'getting to work' orientation. The main problem professionals faced was how to help the young adults bridge the gap between short and long-term time perspectives on work. Yet, paradoxically, as explored in Part I, projects were working with ever-shorter notions of time and space, and in a field that itself is becoming more episodic, both in terms of job placement, work experience, and training. The field of education, training, employment, and guidance, therefore, offers a parallel view of many aspects of a globalized changing labor market, where time–space compression and flexibility without long-term security figure strongly.

Some projects we associated with this learning culture were also often trying to maintain some kind of group pedagogic space, structure, and a sense of coming together at specific times. When this was possible, the professionals tried to create an open and tolerant atmosphere and to show respect for the views and biographies of the participants. In such projects where this was achieved, there was often a strong emphasis on group work and on group discussions. In group meetings participants were often challenged to exchange and respect different views and outlooks, and to reflect upon their meaning. They were encouraged to perform tasks collectively, while at the same time learning to take individual responsibility for a successful outcome.

Professionals in these projects realized that the school records of the majority of the young adults they worked with were marked by negative experiences. Therefore they were often concerned to enact the projects as an 'open space' with the intention of enabling an 'authentic' encounter, between themselves and participants, which kept imposed obligations, formal rules and strict regulations to the minimum.

Most participants welcomed the relaxed atmosphere. Some could recognize that they were learning to function better in a group situation as well as developing skills of negotiating to meet their own personal needs and desires. At the same time their feeling of being taken seriously sometimes could help them in opening up to the options that were offered to them, including 'instant' possibilities in the world of labor. This in turn might support them in framing clearer goals and orientations for their near future.

By contrast, in *FlexiJob*, the activation project hailed by the Minister of Employment as representing a significant and innovative breakthrough in work with unemployed young people, there was no fixed time and space. Individual members that could fill short-term needs for a flexible labor force were met on the streets, in places where they hung out. Transactions between workers and the young adults were limited to brokering the possibility of a job 'just for a moment'. Or they were encouraged to 'drop in' at the center that would place them.

However, the alertness of the young people to the double messages was most apparent:

> *Although you like the 30 days max, you secretly hope that FlexiJob hasn't given up on getting you a real job. Maybe they will find something that is interesting and lasts more than 30 days in real sales and distribution. So you don't have to turn to crime. And not be so poor.*

Both in the case of the German *JobXchange* and in the Belgian *FlexiJob*, our data clearly indicated that these projects tended to confirm existing views and needs of the young adults involved, rather than presenting incentives for young adults to challenge their perspectives on life. The projects fitted well with the short-term perspectives of the participants and the needs of organizations for flexible and cheap labor. The young unemployed are merely temporarily stabilized and provided with a means to an end: in other words, they can improve their financial situation by gaining temporary access to the world of labor. Projects are not much help when it comes to the question of how to rise above the level of low-skilled, short-term employment. Some of the participants were aware of this dead-end perspective, but without support, they had no clue as to how to find a way out.

However, to a certain extent these projects that emphasize 'getting them working, no matter what or where' can be seen as having some potential for a transformative impact on the biographies of the participants. This impact seems to be reinforced by the opportunity to obtain paid work within a relatively short time. At the same time, if projects such as *FlexiJob* become the norm, with no opportunities for reflexive dialogue, social exclusion might become less episodic and more sustained. The social dimension is missing altogether, since this culture works in individualized ways. Nor is much attention given, within the instant job projects, to the development of instrumental competences that might otherwise empower the young adults to build some kind of career identity or to explore options that realize their capacities and aspirations (Thijssen and Lankhuijzen, 2000). Such projects may suit employers who want a large labor pool to be readily on tap to meet their needs. But to what extent do they contribute to the economic and social participation of young adults or communities? How many times can a long-term unemployed person tolerate nothing but episodic periods of non-specific work experience with no extra support to encourage social, biographical, and instrumental reflexivity about that which is being encountered?

It may be politically expedient to depress youth unemployment statistics through requiring placement in such schemes. However, we pose the following question:

- In what ways might these understandings of activation sustain or even exacerbate the problems that socially excluded and unemployed young adults experience anyway?

Targeted and Tailored Training

The specific character of the projects that we associate with this culture does not so much originate from their content, but from the special provisions and pedagogical principles developed to help these young adults to engage with the content of work. In other words, these 'tailored training programs' are attuned to the specific needs and situations of the target group of unemployed young adults. Projects for this culture include the German *Female Electricians*, the Portuguese *Vocational Training School (VTS)*, and the Dutch *Community College* and *Vocational College* projects.

Contrary to the other cultures of learning, the focus here is almost entirely on the acquisition of instrumental competences. The participants are trained for vocations and professions that are also the subjects of regular vocational education. Innovation was the norm in these case studies, with the intention of widening opportunities for unemployed adults to benefit from vocational training.

> **The German project of Female Electricians** *was exclusively directed towards young women, who were being trained to become electro-technicians during a three-and-a-half year course that fitted in the general framework of the German 'dual system'.*

> **The Portuguese case of the Vocational Training School (VTS)** *offered three-year courses in the field of ICT and in the field of communication and marketing, accredited by the Ministry of Education. But the learning was not only focused on instrumental competences. Rather a more holistic perspective was adopted. Learning for citizenship, empowerment, and self-development were integrated into the program.*

The Dutch cases of the **Community College** *and* **Vocational College** *offered one- or two-year learning trajectories within the regular vocational training programs of e.g. business administration, child-care, and electro-technology.*

In general, there was a powerful assumption being enacted across these very diverse projects: namely, that only the emotionally most stable and motivated young adults would perform well in this culture of targeted training. Demands on trainees were high. This was because these projects were meant to offer admission to established professions in the labor market through this specially designed door.

In most cases there was a relatively strict selection of applicants for participation in these projects. Participants who were perceived to lack a certain degree of social and personal stability were often assumed by the professionals involved to be unfit to cope with the challenges they would meet. We often encountered the rationale that this exclusion was in the young peoples 'best interests'. In other words, it was considered that further failures would not only discourage the young adults themselves, but also put at risk the innovative impact of the project as a whole.

The German project **Female Electricians** *only admitted young women with a rather stable social background and a rather well developed sense of actorship of their own lives.*

The Dutch researchers in the case of the **Community College** *project concluded that the students were able to relate what they learned to their wider life perspective that they identified with the content and aims of the course and they showed a high intrinsic motivation.*

What struck us about these projects was that although the focus was on instrumental competences, we observed efforts to integrate social and biographical competences as well. However, such professional skills, knowledge, and attitudes were directly related to the labor market jobs for which they were being prepared. Sometimes this was due to explicit objectives of a project. For example:

The German **Female Electricians** *aimed to integrate more women into a male dominated profession.*

The Portuguese **Vocational Training School (VTS)** *demonstrated a holistic perspective on work. Vocational training was perceived as located in the wider social context where empowerment and active citizenship were desirable outcomes and where the professionals needed to serve as role models for the learning of democratic and human values – as well as being experts in the vocational subject area.*

Further, there was often explicit attention being paid to how pedagogical concepts and practices could support the integration of different kinds of competences. Attempts to combine theoretical, experiential, and practical learning through group work and self-directed learning were often apparent. Of course there was huge variety in the ways the different projects did this. Some, such as the Dutch *Community College* and *Vocational College* cases were quite curriculum-oriented and adopted a school-like learning environment. Others challenged participants to take initiatives, to deploy self-reliance and to trust their own ability to make decisions and find out. Group work was also often common. Professionals perceived this as relevant to increasing the young people's sense of social responsibility and the quality of their involvement and interaction with others.

Each of the targeted and tailored training projects that we studied also offered some form of counseling and guidance, but not in the all-pervasive ways depicted in Part I in relation to the Danish cases. Rather, within this culture, participants were encouraged to access specialist help with the social or biographical problems that were preventing participants from concentrating on their training, or in order to mediate problems between participants on the one hand and teachers or employers on the other. Once again, problems were almost always conceptualized as individualistic, rather than as symptoms of wider pressures and barriers.

In spite of their differences, each and every project providing tailored training made ample room for practical training, using work simulations, trainee service placements or real-life work experiences. Furthermore, all the programs showed a shift from an initial emphasis on instruction towards more self-directed (individual and group) learning activities over the course of the project. The time orientation was often more long-term than other types of projects, supported by funding. We did, however, discern a trend of greater pressure being exerted to achieve long-term outcomes in shorter time frameworks.

Looking at provision related to this culture of learning, and the kinds of young adults who were allowed to participate, it is perhaps not surprising that we found high levels of satisfaction, amongst learners and professionals. In general, we encountered feelings of relief and contentment. For young people, these were often associated with having an experience of learning that they perceived as positive and meaningfully related to the labor market, irrespective of this landing them a job. This seemed especially significant, since most young adults in this culture had a previous record of school failure or at least of school frustration. Many of them were experiencing education for the first time as contributing to the enrichment and stabilization of their lives. It could be argued that they might draw positively on this experience, in defining their own social and economic participation. The value of such projects and longer time-scales can enable young adults to realize alternative possibilities for re-authoring their lives.

As for the professionals, they seemed to find satisfaction through the fact that they were not just teachers but could also function as stimulating and committed agents whose impact really did 'make a difference' to the lives of the learners. What struck us about projects in this frame was the confidence in the competences of the participants that was shown. In other words, the participants were not being met as 'deficient individuals' but rather as whole people who came with a variety of backgrounds. However, this does not imply that this culture of learning is without problems. Each project demonstrated its own tensions and dilemmas:

In the German project **Female Electricians** *the professionals often found themselves lacking the know-how to support young female learners confronted with stigmatizing prejudices and discrimination in the male dominated world of electro-technicians. Experiences like that made the participants question their outlook on future professional success and the amount of satisfaction they might anticipate in the labor market they were being trained for.*

In the Portuguese **Vocational Training School (VTS)** *participants tended to perceive a large gap between, on the one hand, the competences they were being trained for and the positive atmosphere they experienced in the school and, on the other hand, the harsher realities of the actual labor market on the other. As a consequence, some of them developed action strategies to postpone their entry into the labor market, thereby delaying their anticipated confrontation with a hostile environment.*

The Dutch **Community College** *and* **Vocational College** *projects from the point of view of labor satisfaction and career perspectives seemed the most promising example of targeted and tailored training. But these projects only attracted and met the needs of a relatively 'privileged' category of young unemployed adults: those with a stable background and high intrinsic motivation. The ones who lacked these characteristics were almost never allowed to enter this project, since they were perceived as having little chance of coping with the challenges they would meet and a threat to overall success rates.*

At this juncture in our book we invite readers to consider this question:

- How might this approach to activation, including its selection processes, be confirming and reinforcing inequalities of opportunity for economic and social participation (Hake, 2000)?

Informing and Helping

This culture of learning places at its center a strong emphasis on counseling guidance and 'personal development'. This was clearly evident in both of the Danish case studies *The House of Keys* and the *House of Projects*, the Belgian *Advise First*, and in *New Deal* in the UK. These activation schemes were targeted predominantly at young adults who were multiply disadvantaged, seen to be living at the fringes of society and perceived as 'hard core' unemployed. The projects exemplifying this culture were firstly oriented towards introducing participants to the prerequisites, possibilities, and demands of labor market participation. Secondly, they were geared towards helping young people with their many problems, including schooling, rather than actually preparing them for specific employment trajectories or jobs.

This culture of learning was thus focused almost entirely at stabilizing and (re)orienting these young adults. They were provided with knowledge, information, and experiences that were deemed by the professionals significant for supporting their integration 'back' into society and/or the educational and economic system. In addition, the projects required adherence to rules and prescriptions that were constructed by the project. These were treated by the professionals as analogous to rules that participants were likely to encounter as members of a low-skilled labor force. However, this was not necessarily the way they were perceived by the young adults. The unintended consequences of such orientations will become more evident as this book unfolds.

A key feature of such schemes was the provision of specific guidance about options for further schooling and jobs. Experts and time for individualized specialized support with personal, social, and emotional problems also figured strongly. An exception to this was *New Deal* in the UK, where young people's advisors were performing this full range of roles, often in ways that they themselves found superficial and inadequate *New Deal* also offered 'remedial' education and training as an option, whereas in other projects, if it was provided in some form, this was often compulsory. The way in which this mix was organized varied within each project:

In the Danish project **The House of Keys** *participants were required to attend a six-month labor office run program. This entailed a combination of classes in typical school subjects (math, computing, and Danish). They were given opportunities to learn about various domains of labor, including through 'taster' experiences. Counseling here was offered on a voluntary and individual basis, and was intended to help participants clarify the possible significance of the options on offer, in relation to their lives as a whole.*

In the Danish **House of Projects** *workshops in textiles, woodwork, metalwork, and ceramics were seen as instruments for improving the social competences and self-confidence of the participants. 'Learning through doing' and producing products were meant to provide experiences of success and improve participants' self-confidence. Unusually, there was no specific time frame for participation in this project.*

New Deal/Gateway *in the UK provided a four-month initial period of individual support and assistance before young people were obliged to choose one of four further options. These comprised full-time education or training, subsidized employment, work in the voluntary sector and work in the Environmental Task Force. The initial period entailed the provision of information and/or support in gaining access to these four different options, while the options were 'delivered' by a range of providers, including Further Education colleges, employers and voluntary or private sector organizations.*

In New Deal, *those who choose an educational option joined in classes at their local colleges with others, despite often having early histories of problems with mainstream schooling. Moreover, they and the participating professionals were compelled to comply with an additionally demanding regime of paperwork that differentiated them from their peers. Funding was at risk for both the agency and the young person if administrative tracking procedures were not strictly adhered to. Failure on the part of the young person to participate could result in loss of their benefit.*

Advise First *in Belgium provided a trajectory guidance program. Individualized counseling was required to support the choice between a vocational training program (1000 hours) and an application program (40 hours). Coercion to participate, lest benefit be withdrawn was a key feature of the 'counseling' provided by the Labor office.*

The various social and instrumental skills and knowledge emphasized by a project are often perceived by the professionals as helping the young people to gain self-confidence and to experience 'being successful' on terms that conform to professionals' perceptions of success. As will be explored in the next chapter, their own radically different experiences of career and the labor market have often shaped these perceptions. Paradoxically, attention to standardized or generic competence development often seemed only obliquely, if at all, related to the actual challenges of a changing labor market.

In all projects that we associated with this culture of learning, the emphasis was on enhancing participants' ability to take responsibility themselves for their decisions and actions, and on being 'responsible individuals'. Yet, how this was given life through specific forms of pedagogy, relationship, and activity varied considerably. The emphasis on individualized responsibility also often clashed with the distinctive trend towards professionals being required to engage in coercion and punishment. For example, on projects targeted at 'hard core unemployed', professionals were increasingly required to alert the relevant authority if the young adults failed to participate to a satisfactory standard. This would in turn set in motion various kinds of sanctions and threats, including potential withdrawal of income benefit. The norms determining 'appropriate participation' could vary considerably, from seeing an individual as failing to adhere to, for example, fixed time frames or prescribed organizational rules and procedures or to expected conforming behavior. Another paradox lay in how the professionals' espoused claims to be enhancing the young adults' responsibility seldom extended to inviting them to participate in socially reflexive learning processes that focused on mutually negotiating norms of participation and collectively agreeing forms of maintaining these.

The strength of this culture of learning can be seen in the recognition that was given to the comprehensive character of problems experienced by long-term unemployed youth. These young peoples' pasts have given rise to what were perceived as 'instabilities' in their lives. They were seen to have difficulties in setting clear goals and orientations for their (working) lives. They may have long had to cope with processes of social exclusion. The combination of guidance and counseling was assumed to be an effective approach in helping young people to overcome these impediments and to achieve successful integration into the late modern societies of Europe today. It is significant that the Danish activation strategies were being developed to help the hardcore of unemployed youth, even in a context of claimed full employment.

The weakness of this culture of learning lies in the neglect of the social, collective, and political dimension to many of these so called 'individualized' problems. Moreover, its promise to provide comprehensive individualized support clashes with pressures to fulfill agendas for surveillance and sanction. Behrens and Evans (2002) in their study of *New Deal* point out the differing intentions from previous Government funded interventions in its attempts to: 'tackle problems at different stages in the transitions of young people and [in its recognition] of the variability of situations and requirements within the extended age range of up to 25' (Behrens and Evans, 2002).

But when operationalized through guidance- and counseling-oriented strategies, the impact was often experienced by participants as too vague, inadequate, or irrelevant to generate any significant change in their biographical and social competence, much less their instrumental competence. Further, it often made little if any difference to young peoples' actual unemployment situation: something they soon learned as they encountered other young people coming in the same front door again and again.

In the Danish case **The House of Keys**, *a course was provided that had such a broad content and offered such a diversity of options, that it did little to bridge the gap between the unrealistic dreams of 'becoming whatever you want' and the realities of the labor market for largely unskilled and unsettled young people. Neither did it help the young people obtain specific qualifications for a particular vocation.*

In the Danish case of **The House of Projects** *participants experienced the setting of the workshops as too 'artificial'. Even though participants were supported in improving a general work attitude, as claimed by the professionals, this experience was not acknowledged as having any value within the 'real' world of labor outside. The workshops were detached from material, economic, and labor market conditions.*

In the Danish cases neither the participants nor the professionals experienced their joint activity as very worthwhile in helping participants feel socially or economically empowered.

In the UK's **New Deal**, *the patterns of enforcing relatively strict procedures and limited options often failed to support any meaningful engagement with young adults' individual problems. Many of the young adults on New Deal complained about feelings of disempowerment because they were not allowed much freedom beyond the advice and choice determined by the guidance* *counselors. The counseling dimension in this project suffered from a lack of flexibility with virtually no personalized options from which to choose. Conforming to one of four standardized trajectories became the only option. Young adults like Jimmy, with whom we opened this book, ended up having their prior experiences of exclusion and alienation reinforced. Many were forced to choose the Environmental Training Force despite having learned that this was the place for 'no hopers'. For those who were not able, nor prepared, to follow the trajectories set out for them, their participation in social and economic life became further compromised, through the imposition of sanctions and withdrawal of benefits – and ultimately, exclusion from the project. Those who chose normal further education college courses (despite often having a history of school failure) had three times more paper work to comply with than ordinary students.*

The Belgian case of Advise First *favored a high adherence to fixed procedures, options and guidelines, with little room for flexible and personal variations or alternatives.*

Such contradictions almost inevitably exacerbate the power differentials between professionals and participants, and can increase alienation and disaffection. We see a disjunction between the state's agenda of getting young people off the dole and into work, and young people's desire for rewarding work. As will be seen in the next chapter, work often needs to have some resonance with young peoples' identities and perceptions of meaningful economic participation. It could be argued that these are shaped more by the media and other influences in young people's lives than professionals on the projects or direct encounters with work. As a result, young adults are learning to become new kinds of 'unemployed consumers' of economic possibilities, and to see choice as their right; not necessarily their responsibility. For all the political and educational rhetoric about the latter, this too can be seen as a paradox and to have unintended consequences. We shall develop this paradox in more depth in the chapters that follow.

The general picture in this culture of learning is that both groups of actors enter into these projects with sufficient enthusiasm and determination to turn their 'enterprise' into a success. The disappointments they jointly experience, however, in many cases ultimately give rise to resistance, apathy or even dropping out – on both sides. The agency of both professionals and of the young adults involved becomes highly restricted. The double binds become significant in terms of the possibility of sustaining the motivation to participate in the project at all. Professionals are made responsible for maintaining prescribed standards and procedures, which in pedagogic terms, are increasingly externally determined. They are also meant to function as experts on knowledge and information. Moreover, they are meant to provide surveillance for the system as a whole, with respect to difficult unemployed youth who are not seen to be 'participating effectively'. Yet, at the same time, the course documents for these projects stress their uniqueness in that professionals can now provide individually tailored emotional support and stronger relations with hardcore unemployed youth. This can be portrayed as an innovative process, compared to projects that mixed young adults with others of all ages, and were seen as more standardized in their responses.

*In the Danish **House of Projects**, the young people seldom shared the professionals' goal orientation. They wore their work clothes to the workshops – and were proud to do so. But they never got the feeling that their production was recognized as something important by the world outside. So a good and open atmosphere did not necessarily stimulate a process of learning. A fluid structure and goals did not seem to give participants the orientation they claimed to seek.*

*In the Danish **The House of Keys** participants' learning became neither a means of finding an orientation nor a way of getting a qualification.*

*The UK's **New Deal/Gateway** expressed client-centeredness was found to be characterized by very asymmetric power relations between the advisors and the young people, despite the formers' attempt to be responsive to young people's individual trajectories. The language of options disguised the more mundane choices on offer. We could not help but wonder, for example, what low-paid job would ever involve young people in the kind of paperwork trail they were forced to comply with in New Deal. The compulsion to follow the advice given seemed to diminish their sense of agency and responsibility. Learning seemed to mean conforming to the fixed procedures of the scheme. The disciplining effects on the conformers may have further excluded the non-conformers.*

*In Belgium's **Advise First** learning meant conforming to the fixed procedures of the scheme and integrating oneself into the trajectories on offer. Pressure was on young people to conform to the expectations of the professional advisor.*

Predominant across all four projects that constitute this culture of learning was the feeling on the part of young adults that they had not been taken seriously enough in their desire to qualify for the labor market. We also found professionals often tempted then to label participants as 'non-motivated' when they resisted emotional investments, and then withdrawing the care they started to provide so abundantly. For instance, researchers observed some professionals making a distinction between youngsters, who in their view were capable and who were not. It seemed that this distinction was based largely on differences in the young peoples' positive responses to the professionals' efforts to 'come close'.

So the question that lingers for us with respect to this culture of learning is:

- Who and what is being activated here and how – both within and outside the projects – and according to whose agenda?

Situated Social Learning

The two projects which we associate with this culture of learning, are:

> *The* **Bridging the Gap** *project in the* **UK** *that worked with young unemployed adults who, amongst the many challenges they faced in their life, were coping with homelessness.*

> *The Portuguese* **Cultural Mediators** *project, introduced in Part I, that trained young Afro-Portuguese people in a deprived area to become cultural mediators, a profession for which accreditation was being sought at an official level.*

The first of these two projects might at first glance be perceived as an elaborated and situated system of informing and helping multiply disadvantaged young adults in transition. The second might easily be considered as an example of targeted, tailored training. But an in-depth look at how these projects worked compelled us to challenge these assumptions. On the strength of our within-country research and cross-country dialogue, we came to appreciate in more depth the distinctive alternative approaches to reconciling economic and social tensions that these projects were attempting to realize in practice.

What characterizes these two projects overall is the attempt on the part of the professionals to work 'for real' with the actual problems and contradictions faced by the young people in their own local and social situations and at the boundaries of the many worlds they were navigating:

> *In England's* **Bridging the Gap** *project, the target group of homeless young people was provided with accommodation, in-house programs, financial and relational support services and challenges to reflect on their actions and achievements in the situated learning context of a round the clock residential service. Individual empowerment and the enhancement of social skills and self-confidence, combined with practical support in providing a stable home base, were seen as indispensable conditions before integration into the labor market made any sense at all. Guidance, skills development, and learning for and from life were related directly to young peoples' actual experiences of the problems of coping and living in the world and the community of the project.*

> *In the Portuguese* **Cultural Mediators** *project, the professionals were alert to opportunities for personal and social development that arose from the complex and lived realities of the trainees in their daily life. These were also made integral to the vocational training process. The very nature of that which they were being trained for related directly to the need for new forms of cultural mediation and understanding between Black families' lives and the institutions that were meant to serve them (schools in particular). The role had been identified as necessary, based on actual narratives told and re-*

told within the participants' community. The idea for the project was not 'imported' into the community, but rather grew out of learning through work and relationships with the community by the local association. It was the association, which sought funding and in partnership with the community, helped to devise and continually revise the curriculum in relation to changing circumstances and needs. Therefore, any notion of instrumental competence development was permanently interwoven with (and included reflection on) the social context and power relations in which participants were situated. Further, dialogue about individual and collective biographies was made integral to project-based learning, in contrast to projects where personal and social skills development felt like an instrumental 'add on'.

What most struck us was the extent to which the social, biographical, and instrumental competences of the young adults were seen as strengths, not 'deficits'. We found that the 'entering competences' of the young adults – those with which they begin the program – were being re-valued as skills that did and could matter greatly in the context of the projects' and the young peoples' aspirations to improve their choices and competences for social and economic participation. There was active resistance in the cultural mediation training against de-contextualizing the development of biographical and social competence from the narratives of this particular community. At the same time, there was clear recognition of the need to re-contextualize narratives and strengths in relation to the role of cultural mediators. The aspiration overall was to enable these young adults to work effectively with members of their own community to prevent problems at school and between school and home, from escalating.

In these projects, we also encountered professionals engaging in continual relationally grounded improvisational work with these young adults, in ways that were characterized by a great deal of mutual respect. The emphasis was on learning alongside each other, in ways that worked actively with the particularity of the group's biographical and social situation and confusions. Professionals did not feel compelled to provide easy answers or clear directions, but instead, were prepared to get inside the skin of the young people with whom they were working and help them look differently at what they were encountering. They were unafraid to support learning that went beyond merely experientially grounded descriptions of their lives. Paradoxically, the capacity on the part of professionals to not fear a loss of control or not knowing 'everything' seemed to contribute to capacities on the part of young people to be less daunted by the uncertainties and complexities they were encountering in their lives. At the same time, the adults were not afraid to set limits, and set high expectations, based on respect. The young adults were encouraged to make choices and to reflect on these and their subsequent actions in ways we did not find in projects that were driven either by counseling and guidance preferences or more narrowly defined competence orientations.

Project practices were not drawn from some generalized set of formulas or competency protocols from on high: for example, 'effective communication' was not approached as if this could be understood as separate from actual social contexts where power operates in fluid ways. Nor was learning approached as a linear instrumental process. Instead, approaches emerged out of relationship and critically and creatively reflexive dialogue. The overriding commitments were to learning and co-inquiry alongside young people, rather than delivering standardized practices, such as action plans and portfolios.

Articulations of any 'formal' curriculum in both of these projects were of a very different character than other projects. In both cases, professionals were attempting to support more seamless learning. Learning and the curriculum were co-constructed out of specific challenges that the young people were facing and the contradictions and confusions that they themselves identified. These later became a point of departure for opening up assumptions, exploring choices, listening, and experimenting with alternative ways of perceiving and acting. To do this, however, required relationships of trust that were not fragmented by arbitrary movement from one activity to another, or by compulsions to comply with clearly evidenced outputs.

In England's **Bridging the Gap** *project, what came across was its striving for an 'organizational philosophy' and the creation of a culture of challenge based on the organizational motto, 'Success through empowerment'. This involved regular, critical reflection and conversation on the views and actions of all involved, both professionals and participants, in an open non-judgmental climate of equality and mutual trust. The project was intended to 'stay on the move' and to stand by the young adults as they negotiated their way through life at this particular juncture, but in ways that involved neither 'emotional pawing' nor a formulaic or coercive approach. They provided opportunities for skills development and experimentation with different versions of life and work, supported by ongoing discussion, inquiry and re-attunement to ever-changing circumstances.*

So, in each case, it was not perceived as merely a matter of using specific methods to deliver a well-organized curriculum. Instead, critically reflexive dialogue and learning and substantive content were all organized around issues that young people recognized as grounded in their lives and to the program (for example cultural mediation). Alternatively, the curriculum was structured around relationships that supported learning from problems related to specific social and psychological situations being experienced by the young people (such as in the case of the *Bridging the Gap*).

As with all the other cultures of learning, there were tensions operating here that could be experienced as both positive and negative by all involved:

The **Cultural Mediators** *project could be viewed as largely White professionals doing something 'for' young Black adults. Insights from critical race theory alert us to the explicit and implicit cultural deficit narratives that prevail in 'majoritarian stories' explaining educational inequality (Valencia, 1997; Solorzono and Yosso, 2002). As a result of this initiative becoming a case study in this research, however, dialogue on these* *issues was made less marginal and more central to critically reflexive co-inquiry of professionals in the project, the Community Association and the research team.   Such tensions were themselves seen as integral to the professionals learning as well as that of the young adults.   With the professionals being seen to be reflexively engaged as learners themselves, in ways that remained alert to contradictions in their own practice in the situated circumstances of their practice, the young adults were offered role models of a very different sort than those to which they were accustomed.*

The **Bridging the Gap** *project was 'picking up' clients that* New Deal *didn't know what to do with.   The cruel paradox here being that with certain young people – often perceived as the most excluded by virtue of their homeless status (Rosengard, 1995)* Bridging the Gap *was making a difference.   This is in spite of funding streams working in favor of the statutory agencies rather than voluntary organizations.   This paradoxical position of* Bridging the Gap *with respect to the mainstream was felt through the tension the workers faced in 're-engaging' young people.   As the then Principal officer stated 'We are concerned that in providing respite we are simultaneously breeding a culture of dependency'.   However, rather than choosing one side of the fence or the other, as researchers, we found that the holistic and critically reflexive culture in the organization allowed them to successfully hold the tension between providing a safe haven and challenging young people to move on.*

These projects also brought into sharper relief important questions concerning other cultures of learning, and how discontinuities and inequalities can be perpetuated through power relations influenced by class, gender, and race.   As activation projects overall become more individualized and more influenced by externally determined performance indicators, they may become less responsive to possibility and difference. In being so restricted, they may inadvertently contribute to the social exclusion of those who are already on the margins.

The **Portuguese group** *experienced tensions between the positive atmosphere of the project and the harsher realities and racism of the wider community. Despite conveying to funders how frequently the young adults felt 'stranded at the cusp' after only an eight-month course, unable to return to earlier versions of their world or to choices that they once might have made, there was no scope for re-negotiating the time frame, in light of this learning. Moreover, attempts to gain professional recognition of the role of cultural mediator were meeting resistance.*

The **Bridging the Gap** *project at the time of our research, decided to secure additional funding in competition with other statutory and voluntary sector providers. They believed they could play the game, in terms of meeting funding goals, pressures for specific target related outputs, and greater financial accountability.   Bridging the Gap felt confident that it could resist being constrained by these restrictions.   For these professionals, the work* *they were undertaking was what mattered and something they would do anyway. The proven quality of this work was used to barter, contest, and consequently negotiate project 'outputs' with new funders. However, soon, this became a 'merry dance up against the wall'. Paradoxically, what became evident throughout the period of our research was that as the* Bridging the Gap *was compelled to formalize their work and produce evidence of clear outputs. It became more and more locked into the instrumental rationality of mainstream funding streams, as action plans and activity portfolios were required to demonstrate evidence of competence development. The more this happened, the larger became the threat to the quality and impact of its work, and the nature of the relationships that had sustained them previously in generating forms of economic and social participation on the part of these homeless young people that were often deemed impossible.*

A critique of projects in this culture of learning may be that the young people were not being trained for 'real jobs'. Our questions would be:

- Who decides what is 'real'? Based on what constructs?

- What power do professionals and young people have to demonstrate how 'unreal' and undermining targets, strategies, and protocols for reporting evidence of 'real activation' work, can be?

- How do such projects become undermined when driven by policy discourses about the development of transparent 'transferable skills' that have become so dominant in recent years?

- How well do dominant practices enhance the capacity of young people to cope with uncertainty, complexity, and finding answers for themselves, and thereby make them feel more empowered?

We found in these two projects a particular kind of approach to working with the 'spaces' available. These spaces could not be pre-defined, nor neatly organized to produce pre-specified outputs. They were full of tension and possibility. But in each case, professionals had considerable autonomy to re-define what was possible within the constraints. They could develop relationships and a particular quality of dialogue with the young adults that did not exacerbate power differentials or generate a sense of disempowerment, alienation, and disaffection. In these projects, paradoxically, we see a reducing tension between the state's agenda of getting young people off the dole and into largely low paid work, and meeting young people's desires for more rewarding lives, in which paid work may be but a part.

What also connects these two projects is their socially organic nature. They both emerged out of specific historical and social circumstances, and the attempts of local participants to connect action to needs in a specific community. They sought funding to support needs and intentions that they themselves had identified as potentially relevant, in dialogue with local people. They tried to ensure that this funding was not tied to overly prescriptive requirements to comply with centrally specified performance indicators and targets, including for delivery of people into jobs or specific evidence of key skill areas. When strings were attached, they negotiated a re-interpretation, in ways that they believed would not undermine work that had previously been shown to be successful. In our view, however, young people and professionals alike were increasingly constricted by such partnerships and funding. More and more energies and time had to be invested in playing 're-defining games' or directly re-negotiating the terms of engagement with the external funding body and producing evidence to demonstrate the unintended effects of such constraints. Although, in comparison to other cultures of learning, they were less subjected to the highly regulated process of external scrutiny and audit that were fast becoming the norm for the other publicly funded activation projects we had researched. There was more scope for social and economic empowerment in the action space on terms that had meaning for these specific communities.

Both projects offer a glimpse of the potential meaning of 'activation as a situated social learning process', where ongoing contextualized learning and improvisation are made more central. Our questions, at this point, are therefore:

- What kinds of funding, support, and freedoms may be required for activation projects to work in such a locally responsive way?

- How can the EU support community based initiatives that - out of the very ground of their experience – evolve alternative ways of reconciling the complex tensions that abound at the interface between the objectives for reducing youth unemployment and social exclusion?

- What forms of external governance might be less constraining *and* support more examples of socially situated learning?

Emerging Issues: Standardized and Non-standardized Approaches to Activation

The questions at the core of this book are:

- How do, and how might various activation projects, work effectively at the interface between generating learning for the labor market and learning for social participation?

- How, from this perspective, should we address issues of instrumental, social, and biographical competence development?

On the ever shifting landscape of activation, we have brought into relief four cultures of learning: one that emphasizes getting young adults into work, whatever, wherever; one that emphasizes targeting and tailoring vocational training for young unemployed people; one that focuses on informing and helping; and one that emphasizes socially situated learning from the complexities that define and impact on young people's various social and individual biographies.

The differences between the first three cultures are strongly related to assumptions about young adults as destabilized in their personal and social life. They suggest the need, above all, for 'activation' and what we might call 'rectification'. This deficit orientation becomes a starting point for constructing and funding 'relevant' options for increasing labor market participation. Guidance and counseling obtains overall, with the intention of addressing the development of social and biographical competences. Yet professionals are expected to undertake 'surveillance' duties.

In the first three cultures of learning, the prevailing social construction of the young adults is that they are 'groups-at-risk'. In other words, specific young people are seen as lowly qualified, with blurred perspectives on the future and poor school records. For them a fast entry in the labor market is assumed to support and give structure to their lives, both socially and financially. Therefore they are perceived as in need of instrumental skills and social attitudes that will enable them to get a job as soon as possible. But, as we saw in the above, how these skills and attitudes are developed – and their relevance to the actual labor market facing these young people – is becoming more and more suspect. In the example of *FlexiJob*, such competence development seems to be expected to emerge through immersion in a 'job episode'. Such a culture emphasizes instrumental and social competences, but not necessarily their 'active' development.

They must 'be made to be included'!

Thirdly, a relatively small and 'privileged' group can be seen as capable of being stabilized and motivated enough to participate in a systematic training trajectory. This sets out to prepare them for regular and more demanding specific vocations and professions. This trajectory seeks to integrate the development of social and biographical competences for long-term unemployed people along with the instrumental competences that will help them qualify for specific jobs and vocations. Selection is carefully monitored, lest the innovative quality and success of the project (in terms of getting young people into jobs or further education) be put at risk.

The fourth culture of learning does not attempt to 'clean up' the complex, messy nature of the learning that is rooted in the actual circumstances of peoples lives nor to reduce or fragment what these young people must do and learn in order to be socially and economically empowered. As such, it raises important questions and contradictions about the previous cultures of learning. The young people at whom the Portuguese *Cultural Mediators* and the *Bridging the Gap* projects are targeted could just as well have been channeled into other projects. How easy to get away with categorizing, for example, young black people in Lisbon as socially excluded and as requiring more guidance and counseling, stabilization, or instant experience of the job market; to disregard cultural mediation as something that is 'unreal' and contrived and not relevant to the 'real' labor market. But at what cost?

So what have we been learning thus far about 'learning for inclusion'? Professionals increasingly have to work with more standardized and regulated protocols for 'activation work', with more externally predetermined cultures of learning that fit dominant trends as outlined above. Moreover, they must do so in shorter and shorter time frameworks. Irrespective of all the variation in projects and cultures of learning, this burdens nearly all of them in struggles with different forms of input–output rationalities. Such rationalities may fit well into the world of economics, but are not easily reconciled with pedagogical demands related to young adults at risk. Their problems are in many cases so comprehensive and their situations so turbulent that projects, of a few months supported by a few sessions of counseling, will have little impact on their biography and life chances. That is why, apart from the more specific problems highlighted earlier in the chapter, the majority of professionals and participants are experiencing a lack of flexibility and autonomy as the main flaw that prevents these projects from achieving more convincing successes.

Different young people have different needs. How can we address their situations in different ways, with different methods, different challenges, and different objectives? So, at what cost do we de-contextualized and 'de-situate' – and then formulize – such learning? The projects we researched do not only show clear differences in their focus on the development of more instrumental, more social or more biographical competences. They also show how the content of these three sets of what we might better refer to as capabilities, as understood and enacted, varies significantly across the different cultures of learning. The interpretation of these in action and in context is influenced further by often untested assumptions about the needs and backgrounds of the young adults involved.

The one characteristic that young adults share – being unemployed – falls a long way short of determining who they are. It can only partially reflect aspects of their multiple selves. Between, and even within, the different cultures of learning, participants often exhibit a considerable diversity in their narratives of who they are, where they come from, and where they want to go, in all the readings and contradictions such narratives reveal. Yet, they are first and foremost being addressed as unemployed.

In policy terms the success of the professionals who work in these projects is exclusively and increasingly judged by the number of participants who are transformed into active members of the labor market. The contradiction between an 'external' focus on an identity of 'being unemployed' on the one hand, and on the other, the 'internal' narratives of being unemployed along with the social narratives that are further constructing those involved, gives rise to a variety of dilemmas and tensions within each culture of learning. The professionals in these projects find themselves permanently navigating on edges between participant's emotional and social involvement with the struggle for a more decent life, and the charge to mould them into suiting the demands of the labor market.

What we see in response to this is a kind of dichotomization that is supported more and more by highly mechanistic understandings of success and of pedagogy itself. Some projects begin to direct their attention to biographical and social development and away from instrumental competences, as is the case in some projects in the culture of guidance and counseling. Alternatively, others focus on short-term instrumental and social skills that give instant access to the labor market, but that overlook the variety of biographical needs and wants that characterize these diverse (young) adults, as is the case in the culture oriented to getting them into work, whatever, however. It is significant, therefore, that the projects experienced as truly satisfactory by both professionals and participants, were those that both gave room for social and emotional commitment, acceptance and mutual respect, while simultaneously providing a challenge to develop knowledge, skills, and attitudes that could be recognized and valued in the 'world out there' in the here and now of the young peoples lives.

Looking from a distance at the picture of the landscape in motion that we have sketched here, it is clear that the overall tendency is to privilege economic rationality in activation policies. This, on the whole, tends to overrule social rationality. This does not deny that in the majority of the projects attention was also given to biographical and social competences, or that there was a true commitment of the professionals to remain responsive to the needs and desires of the participants. Neither do we underestimate the seriousness and commitments evident across the various cultures of learning for different target groups.

However, almost all projects suffered from an 'economization' of the learning trajectories they tried to develop. Activation is being tied ever more closer to the world of calculation and control. This is in direct contrast to the more open-ended and seemingly disordered processes of social interactions that we saw in the cases of the *Bridging the Gap* and the Portuguese *Cultural Mediators* project. But when we embed learning in actual contexts amidst lived contradictions, it is never a tidy business. The last culture offers an alternative perspective on the limitations of what is on offer at present and a glimpse of what may be possible in transforming perspectives, and fostering social and economic capability over time.

Anticipating what Follows: Different Lenses on the Same Landscape

We now wish to bring back into the foreground the voices of young people and professionals. We shall offer a more in-depth consideration of three issues, the importance of which has been signified through material presented thus far:

- Changing labor identities.

- Transforming competences and notions of agency.

- Shifting pedagogy.

Changing Labor Identities

Programs and projects for the unemployed are inevitably challenged by issues of changing labor identities. On the one hand, from the perspective of government policy, projects are supposed to transmit and reinforce the meanings, values, and norms that young adults require for labor market participation; in effect to socialize them into the 'logic' of the work ethic that is assumed to be implicit in effective labor market participation. On the other hand, the unemployed people who participate in such programs cherish their own narratives, dreams, aspirations, and experiences. Many bring these with them into the learning situation. These stories about their 'selves' and their hopes in many cases contradict the labor identities that govern labor market policies and activation projects. Young adults' stories are constructed and validated by particular experiences, values, and expectations. Therefore they cannot be ignored, nor simply stripped of any significance and value.

The flexibilization of production and organizational functions, the ever-increasing significance of the information sector and the impact of information and communication technology on social and communicative skills have become basic requirements for all kinds of professions and jobs – these are only the most striking changes that future workers have to deal with and give meaning to in their own careers. At the same time globalization is influencing youth cultures and lifestyles that also affect young adults' relationship with and attitudes to changing labor market opportunities and in turn education (Edwards and Usher, 2000; Miles, 2000; Cieslik and Pollock, 2002). Further, those who work with young unemployed bring constructions of career and labor market identity and practice orientations that are embedded in their experience. However, these constructions may no longer have validity, in the context of the young adults' lifeworlds and the system into which they are meant to be 'activated'.

In Chapter 6, we offer a lens onto the various inner and outer logics that we found young people and professionals to be attributing to the idea of 'labor-identities' in 'activation programs'. We were interested in the influences of globalization on the construction of such identities, and how these constructions varied. For example, professionals trying to help and/or employ young adults who have had a fairly stable career path and a fairly fixed sense of labor identity may be working with very different assumptions and aspirations for these young adults than those of employers and the unemployed themselves.

We explore how the young adults we met during our research coped with tensions between the internalized stories or biographies of their 'multiple selves' on the one hand, and the 'logics' of the labor market as (re)presented in the programs they took part in, on the other. Furthermore, we will show that their struggle to construct meaningful connections between their own biographies, and the images, assumptions, and expectations of work they met in activation projects constituted one of the major challenges to policy and educational practice. We take extant notions of 'career-identity' and 'labor market identity' to explore the idea of 'working-identities in (com)motion', and to show further how standardized norms and processes of activation can seem a nonsense.

Transforming Competences and Notions of Agency

A core concept in our original research project was that of competences.

- In what ways, and to what extent do the researched practices support unemployed young adults in the development of the competences they need to become agents of their own labor careers and lives?

Starting from the notion that competences nowadays can be restricted no longer to instrumental skills and capacities, we focused mainly on the question of whether, and how, instrumental, social, and biographical competences – and their interconnections – were constructed in the practices that we visited.

The more deeply we examined these interconnections, however, the more we became aware that our particular focus was itself fraught with tensions and ambiguities. The logic of management and measurement that pervades the labor market and in turn project funding and project evaluation, is giving rise to a 'standards' approach to the definition of competence (Weil and Frame, 1992). Competences are now often constructed as 'outputs' that can be pre-determined and understood as separate from specific communities and contexts of practice. This pattern is extending to all levels of education across Europe. The acquisition and possession of competences are increasingly attributed as an individual need (or deficit), and perceived as something that can be broken up and listed and in turn, 'packaged', 'delivered', and therefore learned. As skills, attitudes, and knowledge are increasingly pre-specified and treated as uniform and generic terms, they are assumed to be capable of development and testing, irrespective of the circumstances in which a person lives and acts. In other words, competences in this perspective are predominantly perceived as normative and necessary requirements, without which, young adults are assumed to be maladapted to the demands of the current labor market.

On the other hand, due to the unforeseen and ever changing circumstances of the 'risk society', competences can be seen differently – as more associated with capacities and the capability to learn from and cope with uncertainties, changes, and complex situations that require multiple forms of intelligence (ibid). Competences from this perspective are difficult to develop in isolation from concrete cultural contexts, and specific 'communities of practice' (Wenger, 1998). Learning for the unknown is more dependent on learning from the actual interplay between actors and their communities, as they respond to their changing environment through many different forms of knowing: for example, relational, social, technological, and imaginal. A contextualized perspective on competences does not lead to abstract lists of skills and knowledge. Instead, it directs attention to how young unemployed people learn to embed and organize themselves in a range of specific practices, to deploy and assimilate, in a meaningful way, the skills and knowledge they need for that practice, and to transcend and set limits within changing conditions. In other words, from this point of view, educational practices conceive of competences not only as adaptation, but also as the transformation of present conditions. They focus on opening up possibilities for influencing and acting upon and within concrete practices, placing an emphasis on social learning as itself a force for developing agency.

In Chapter 7, we explore tensions and contradictions generated by these different constructions of competences. We will show how this inherent ambiguity can so easily impede a developing sense of agency. At the same time, we suggest ways in which, if such ambiguities and contradictions are named and made integral to a situated and social learning approach, they can help to empower and skill young adults. Otherwise, professionals do little more than try to balance contradictions.

Shifting Pedagogies

The ambiguities and tensions that are embedded in issues of identity and agency for learners in late modernity are further reflected in the shifting pedagogical efforts of the professionals involved. The logic of the world of labor and of European policies to combat unemployment and social exclusion, exert a strong pressure on educational programs to produce calculable and short-term results. As with the post-Fordist economy itself, education becomes characterized by a compression of time and space in which professionals are directed towards an output-oriented, just-in-time delivery of the 'products' that they are responsible for. Strict time management, narrowly defined objectives and clearly delimited 'packages of knowledge' are among the major instruments used to cope with this pressure for fast and measurable results.

At the same time, we discovered in many practices how professionals struggle with the impairment of genuine pedagogic ambitions and ideals that might influence the time–space compression of their interventions. They experience the extent to which the deprived status of the young adults they work with is rooted in wider factors well beyond that of being unemployed and beyond the reach of educational interventions. Often they are captured in a complicated web of personal, social, emotional, and material pressures, of which unemployment is just one dimension. Despite the practical constraints they experience, many of the professionals sought alternative ways of taking this awareness into account, in order to try and widen the 'action space' for meaningfully bringing the life-world experiences of the learners and the educational programs into new forms of educational relationship.

In Chapter 8, we explore how professionals in the researched practices work with such contradictions between pressures for an 'output orientation' and their desires to enact genuine pedagogic intentions in their work with young adults. One of the key issues affecting young adults' experiences of interventions was the role of the education, training, employment, and guidance professional. This echoes research elsewhere (Kinder et al., 1996; Percy-Smith and Weil, 2002, 2003; Percy-Smith and Walsh, 2002) which also highlights the considerable impact that a perceived lack of respect from professionals can have on young people's experience of education and social policy interventions. In this chapter, we explore how professional relationships with young adults might be reconstructed as a process of interpretation, or negotiation, between the policy objectives implicit in interventions and young people's agenda.

Promising Cusps?

In Part I, we discussed how youth studies have traditionally been caught between research that leans either towards sociological explanations or more social-cultural or psychological explanations. This study, instead, was positioned at the interface. Each of the issues that we now bring into the foreground of our landscape signals possibilities at their cusp. We have done this through our formulation of them, deliberately calling upon the ambiguity of words such as 'changing', 'shifting', and 'transforming'. On the one hand, we can construct young adults and professionals as 'being subjected to' dominant discourses and structures that actively 'write or speak through' their actions and choices, and constrict how they perceive the politics and possibilities of their situations. In other words, our grammatical formulation can imply something that is being 'done to'. On the other hand, we can construct them as actors, who can exert their collective and individual agency through re-constructing what can be presented as normative and neutral 'givens'. In other words, changing implies agency and the notion of 'speaking back' to that which is experienced as constricting. In the context of unemployment and social exclusion, the former carries within it notions of being subjugated into merely adapting to the labor market as given. The latter signals possibilities for social learning that are themselves potentially transformational and act back and re-construct notions of economic participation that are not at the expense of social participation. The remainder of this book will deepen our exploration of the tensions and possibilities at such cusps.

---

[1] These project names represent a mix of pseudonyms and actual ones. See Appendix 1 for pen portraits of all project case studies.

Chapter 6

Working-identities in (Com)motion

Socially Excluded Young People in Relation to the Labor Market

A substantial number of young adults whom we met in this research were perceived as a hardcore of long-term unemployed, lowly qualified young people. Many of them not only shared the experience of being unemployed, but also a common background of serious social and personal problems such as unstable family relations, uncertain living conditions, poor school records, abuse, discrimination, and multiple addictions. The existence of such a category of young people – increasingly referred to as socially excluded – is a common phenomenon in late modernity, but has different structural and cultural implications in different countries.

What we found to be common to all of these young people was their need for additional provisions and support in finding their way through cultural ambivalences and social restrictions of various kinds. In certain ways, as we shall explore in this chapter, these can block their access to participating in the labor market in quite complex ways. Yet these young people cannot be seen as a homogeneous group. Work and employment have different meanings for them, depending on their biographical, social, and cultural contexts. Some choose unemployment as an optional step on the road towards the promise of more challenging work. They expect that subsequently they will discover work that will fulfill their personal interests and goals. Others were desperate to find a job – no matter which kind, as long as it could support them financially. Others again had already tried many different types of employment or educational options, so far without developing a clear picture of what they actually wanted to obtain and what might be realistic possibilities for them. Some were on the boundaries of opting out of trying altogether, regardless of the consequences.

Whatever their various stances in relation to the labor market, those who were participating in activation projects still showed some concern about finding a niche in the labor market. Their aspirations presented them with obstacles that had vocational as well as social and biographical implications. To gain access to the labor market, they needed access to more than mere opportunities to develop specific technical or generic skills and knowledge. They needed some means of mediating the gap between their own 'inner logics' about themselves in relation to the labor market, and the 'rationalities' that prevailed in changing local, regional, national, and global economies and within the 'activation projects' that were meant to 'help' them.

The gap they had to bridge also included the challenges of the constantly shifting roles and functions, the ever changing character of qualifications, the fast succession of projects and profiles, the pace of technological developments, and the concomitant need for sophisticated social and communicative skills.

However young adults define 'success' for themselves, the wider agenda at play requires them to be socialized into the social and psychological implications of what are perceived as emerging labor market 'rationalities'. Adaptation to these is often seen as a precondition to surviving in the knowledge and service economies of today. Yet, a key issue for the projects that we researched was how to support young unemployed adults in even identifying themselves as potential participants in the labor market, much less getting to the point of adapting to it.

The meanings and values associated with work and working-identities have always been susceptible to change over time and place. The image of the dutiful and committed craftsperson with pride in his or her skilled knowledge was as much a construction of the age of industrialization as the image of the volatile and multi-functional flex-worker is of the globalized economy today.

However, the individualization of possible options in all domains of social life that dominates late modern societies is mirrored in the de-standardization of working-identities. The reference points are less clear for young adults seeking to situate themselves in the world of labor. The notion of work, and its meanings for a person's social being and aspirations, gives rise in our current age to a variety of contingent mentalities, identifications, values, and attitudes. The world of labor does not provide many solid standards or blueprints for 'the good worker', except in abstract idealized terms. An example is the ubiquitous idea of the flexible, autonomous, self-motivated, customer-oriented, professional, knowledge worker (Myles, 1991; Harrison, 1994; Mingione, 1994; Hammer, 1996; MacDonald, 1998; Farrell, 2000; EGRIS, 2001).

From 'Career-identity' to 'Working-identity'

Various authors speak about a 'career-identity'. This is used to refer to sets of beliefs, values, orientations, knowledges, and the capabilities that are available to a person in their social setting moment by moment (Meijers and Wijers, 1998; Farrell, 2000). This notion of identity is perceived as being the outcome of an internal conversation. This internal work becomes a process of relating narratives of oneself as unemployed and oneself as who one wants to be, as internalized through interactions with others and the media, to the implications of labor market participation and various choices of workplace working-identities. These working-identities are being constantly (re)presented to them through their projects and work experiences, as well as through the media, and are continually being reconstructed in dialogue with the narratives of other adults and peers.

We agree with Farrell (2000) and Meijers and Wijers (1998) that the development of a career-identity does not just happen, such as through a job placement. It requires reflexive dialogue about previous experience, expectations and the different values they (might) attach to different choices of work. It requires a consideration of specific career pathways or jobs open to them with respect to their own biography and life course.

We found in this research the extent to which such processes of identity formation cannot be approached as merely an advice or information giving activity. They require active attention to what work means within the lifeworlds of these long-term unemployed young people.

- How does work even fit into the narratives they tell about and to themselves and others?

- How and to what extent may the demands and promises of work that they encounter be reconciled with the dreams and desires they harbor within?

We therefore might consider what kinds of professional relationships and learning experiences might be able to constructively support not only the reconstruction of working-identities, but also the deconstruction of existing ones. In other words, we became more and more alert to the kind of 'attunements' that seemed to influence the various attitudes and strategies these young people (might) adopt in navigating and negotiating their way through the landscape of educational and labor market imperatives and choices.

In the current chapter we will focus on these internal conversations and 'inner logics' of young adults and their wider implications. In particular, within the remit of this study:

- What perceptions and meanings of work do young people construct when they travel on the road to social and economic participation via an 'activation' project – recognizing that this is seldom a linear process?

- What action strategies do they deploy within the projects in which they participate?

- How do these give insight into their struggles to reconcile personal aspirations, desires, and capacities with the possibilities and limitations of the labor market demanding their participation?

We have chosen to adopt the notion of 'working-identity'. The alternative terms, 'career-identity', or indeed, 'labor-identity', suggest modernist conceptions of both career and the labor market that we resist as a result of this research. Both are more and more subjected to fragmentation and erosion, and are therefore fraught with commotion in a globalizing economy.

The term 'working-identity' suggests less fixed positions and provides room for reflexivity and re-invention. In other words, we signal something that is provisional: that 'works' for now. At the same time, for us, the term holds the possibility that a working-identity can change, in response to different forms of individual and social learning, and in response to changing social, cultural, political, and economic circumstances. It also allows for the inclusion of paid and non-paid work.

In particular, we consider four working-identities that signify young adults' various stances towards the labor market today. The notion of stance is drawn from Salmon (1989) in her discussion of experiential learning:

> Because personal stance refers to the positions which each of us takes up in life, this metaphor emphasizes aspects of experience which go deeper than the merely cognitive, and which reflect its essentially relational, social, and agentic character. In this, it offers a view of learning as a vehicle for social change (Salmon, 1989, p. 231).

The distinctions that follow may be useful in generating greater insight into the different ways in which unemployed, and often socially excluded young people, relate their inner logics and conversations to their specific perceptions of the outer logics of work. They offer another way of understanding how and why young adults react to different learning cultures in different ways. They offer insight into different meanings of fostering a sense of agency and empowerment in today's world.

The four working-identities are not intended to provide some easy typology into which young people can be categorized. They are only indicative of recurring patterns we noted in the various stances that young adults, in this study, assumed in relation to the labor market. Moreover, young people often exhibit characteristics that combine features of one kind of stance with those of another or employ different kinds of 'inner logic' as they confront unfamiliar situations. Yet, heuristically this differentiation may help to clarify how projects that 'meet' unemployed and multiply disadvantaged young adults well, might simultaneously fail to meet policy driven instrumental targets for economic 'activation' within ever shortening time scales. Moreover, the standardized competence lists and performance targets can ride roughshod when working with young people whose participation in a project is embedded in stances such as those that follow.

We will conclude this chapter by focusing on some of the tensions, dilemmas and contradictions that exist between the assumptions and intentions of the case study projects, the inner logics, and the perceived working-identities of the participants.

Four Working-identities

We summarize these four stances not as easy labels, but rather metaphorically, in order to invite reflexive contestation and action inquiry on the part of readers (Percy-Smith and Weil, 2002a, b):

- Tenacious duty.

- Instant satisfaction.

- Disorienting freedom.

- Self-expressive ambition.

Tenacious Duty

One has to have a job in order to get along.

In response to the question, 'What does work mean to you?' one participant in the German project *JobXchange,* responded:

> *Wow! Every time I'm very relieved· 'I got a job today '. You need something which occupies you and even if it is anything, but everybody has to be occupied. Your body is there and you have your skills Everybody can find his skills and work means a lot to him. To know I'm needed (Marc, participant on JobXchange, Germany).*

To this participant, work is a human need. Work itself is important – not so much because of the character of a specific job, but because of the social value he attaches to work. In his view, work warrants dignity to a person. To have a job signifies that one is needed, valued, and has a role in contributing to the benefit of society as a whole.

This stance towards work was expressed by a number of the young adults in this study. Their understandings and interpretations of work are closely linked to the mentality and attitude of the modern wage earner in traditional industrial society. In this context, the value of work can be understood as part of a broader configuration of arrangements and basic values, centering on a gender-based division of labor. This is characterized by breadwinning as distinct from household activities along with the assumption that full-time, life-long employment is possible, necessary, and that relatively standardized and stable stocks of qualifications will assure this. According to this perspective, work is associated with a fixed set of values and meanings, which can be internalized by subsequent generations.

The young adults in our research who assumed this working-identity stance tended to believe that the perceived security of (long-term) employment would outweigh whatever struggles were involved in qualifying for a particular kind of job. Moreover, to them, having any kind of a job was preferable to being unemployed. The majority of those who adhered to this working-identity were young males. They associated 'traditional' life aspirations, like getting a girlfriend, getting married and having children with their ability to earn a regular income by gaining access to the labor market. They perceived their participation in the projects as a necessary first step to their desired status of becoming a 'decent' and 'valued' worker, family man, and citizen.

As a consequence, some of the young adults in this group expressed a strong desire to perceive their training and activation the same as performing a job in the traditional sense of the word (Ainley and Rainbird, 1999). When they described their training, they often use expressions like 'going to work' and 'getting wages'.

Some even wore work clothes while they attended a project, even if there was no need for it.   One of the participants in the Danish *The House of Projects* mentioned:

> *Things are actually going okay. No problems. I'm okay, I do my job, go home and relax... Everyday I come here, then I get off work and go home, and dinner is on the table and everything (Participant, House of Projects, Denmark).*

Work and training in the view of these young adults are thus seen almost synonymously. They clearly distinguished them from, and prioritized them over leisure time. Only when the duties related to work and their training were done with, did they feel they had the right to relax and enjoy themselves. They spoke as if this were 'true' not only in the short-term but also in the long-term. Work was not sought after as a source of self-fulfillment or as a value in itself. It was an obligation that had to be done. Its output justified the enjoyment of a better life. This stance was seen as good for the present, because of the possibilities for stability and material security that went along with the earning of a regular income. It was perceived as even better in the long run, because of the possibilities of earning respect and establishing a family life that they saw implied in having a steady job.

According to this perspective it was understandable that the young adults who identified with this type of a working-identity showed a remarkable endurance. Even the young adults who had experienced a disturbing past expressed a working-identity that accepted hardships and imposed obligations as the inevitable conditions that preceded the realization of a meaningful and satisfying life; more often than not revolving around images of traditional lifestyles and traditional family lives.

Instant Satisfaction

> *I want a job. I just do not know how to keep it (Participant).*

The young adults who adopt this working-identity stance towards the labor market show a more fragmented and less robust commitment to the values of education and work. Those who adopt this stance show low endurance when challenged with the demands and obligations of effective performance or with jobs and educational trajectories that are not short-term. Many of them manage to stay in a particular context for only a limited period and some of them have started up to ten projects in education or work, without ever finishing one of them. One of the young adults in Denmark, who was 22 years old, described how, since he left school, he had worked for a couple of months in a kindergarten, as a carpenter's apprentice, a fitter, a painter, a home-help, a butcher's apprentice, a landscape gardener, and taken a computer course – collecting a huge amount of trainee and work experience, but never lasting till completion.

Several of the projects that we researched were organized in ways that explicitly took into account this tendency towards low endurance amongst a substantial part of the young adults involved. In Germany, for example, the acknowledgment of their volatility was an important consideration in the creation of highly individualized training programs in the project of the *JobXchange*, where individuals were only employed for short periods – between three hours and two days – as a day laborer in transport, renovating, baby-sitting, work in restaurants, and so on. The Belgian project *FlexiJob* also assumed a lack of patience and 'discipline' among many of the participating young adults and only provided short-term employment or training: '30 Days Max'. The immediacy of financial needs took priority over lengthy training. They were eager to start as quickly as possible in any job and earn the money required to meet short-term needs.

Projects such as these pandered to young people who adopted this stance, with the consequences that work was turned into a regularly interrupted flow of fragmented episodes. The individual young adult was not expected to develop any commitment to particular norms or values, nor to a formal organization or workplace community. In one respect this organization of work experience seemed to match the working-identity these young adults sought to develop.

Yet, at a deeper level, this type of stance in relation to the labor market was driven more by the imperatives of survival rather than choice. But these survival needs also suited the requirements of companies who sought lowly skilled, short-term, just-in-time labor as the pathway to economic competitiveness. Yet, some of the young adults also noticed how in this way feelings of isolation and extreme individualization were created or reinforced and they expressed the fear that it would contribute to a further disintegration of their already shaky sense of coherence.

However, endurance is not the only thing that differentiated these young adults' working-identities from the ones who are closer to a more traditional wage earner identity. Many of them resisted relationships with authority figures such as employers, teachers, foremen, and officials. This can be understood as a learned response to perpetual educational failure, with the consequence that by the time they are placed in 'activation projects' they tend often to react spontaneously and emotionally (often aggressively), without much consideration for the context or the situation they are in. They find it difficult to 'decode' the rules and reactions they meet in projects:

> *I left school in the sixth grade. I'm 24 years old and no schools want me It's many years I've lost with school, and why should I sit with my pencil and put my hand up to a teacher. I wouldn't be able to stand it. I would explode... . Never Because I couldn't stand it. I would explode if a teacher said to me· 'It's not your turn'. I would go crazy because I'm not used to it I'm not used to people snarling at me. Do you know what I mean? It makes me angry. But really what do you want me to do? It's too late for me I don't care about education Do you know what I mean? I just want my own business and to earn a lot of money' (Martin, participant, Denmark).*

Apart from the very low level of tolerance vis-à-vis authorities, this statement touches upon yet another aspect that makes the working-identity stance of these young adults different from those who adopt a stance of 'tenacious duty' in relation to the labor market. The latter are motivated to work for money and connect this to the role of 'breadwinner'. For these young adults, however, money from work is connected to consumption. As Marc said:

> *Then I could work out and I could become a removal man, couldn't I? Then I could buy anything I wanted. I could buy clothes for 5000 DKR. I could...I like New York...baseball clothes, I like that, not really wide pants, more the jackets and so, you know. That Glommy costs 270 DKR and then the shirt. It is 500 to 600 DKR. I just had a look (Participant, JobXchange, Germany).*

From the perspective of this working-identity stance, work is not the road to earn the money that is needed for the production and reproduction of the family unit and social status. Instead, work is the necessary vehicle to earn the money that enables short-term consumption. For many of the young adults involved, achieving material symbols that signal a 'valued' lifestyle has become the parameter by which one's value and position can be ascertained.

What can be easily missed amongst the young adults, who adopted this stance, is that their desires and aspirations were relatively clear and well formulated. They did know what they wished to be and who they wanted to become, if the possibilities were only there. However, the paradox and sometimes severe dilemma for this group of young adults was that their inner pictures of 'how things should be' and what kind of work would suit them, was contradicted by their actual lack of competences and stamina to make them come true. In other words, they adopted a working-identity that they were unlikely to realize in practice.

We noted on many occasions how their dreams, expectations, and orientations, in comparison to their real life abilities and attitudes, hinted at a serious overrating of their personal possibilities, certainly in the eyes of many professionals who worked with them. In a way they become caught in a 'subjective expectations trap' that captures them as much as the structural restrictions they encounter in the world of labor.

The 'unrealistic' dreams of these young adults not only included expectations that they could easily attain high incomes. They also foresaw themselves as capable of leadership or self-employed positions in the labor market. In a way they seemed to create a 'plastic world' that they could model at will in their minds. This was used as a shield against the restrictions that superiors and authorities in general imposed on them. This stance was typified by the words of this youngster:

I want to be self-employed. I don't want to . I'm not working for anybody Somebody is going to work for me instead I want to leave when I want to, you see Come when I want, right. Close the shop when I want. So that's the best You see, when I see the friends I know who drive around in their cool Mercedes and cool shops and Copper Locks, I tell him: 'Would you look after my shop, because I have to do something'. You see, it's like you do something but not as hard as your pupil over there, in your shop, he does more than you do, you just come there to do the books and get the goods and then go home again and relax. And then you go back and get your money and then you leave. It's the best, it's what I like anyway, and it's just what I want to continue doing, right (Participant, House of Keys, Denmark).

The dream of being self-employed for young adults like this one holds that income, independence, and prestige are easily attainable. They perceive these as the surplus values that accompany work. It will conserve the lifestyle that they highly appreciate – a life without many responsibilities, and certainly without all those forms of authority they are not able to 'decode' and to cope with. Their working-identities are consistent with their perceptions of success and status. In other words, in the projects, they act as if they are already their own boss although they are unemployed. In turn, they project this possibility easily onto the worlds of work they yearn to inhabit.

In the inner logics of many of these young adults, such desires are not unreal fantasies. To them, 'dreaming' oneself into reality is a perfect way to cope with an often marginalized and pretty hopeless situation, even if that implies that their dreams become a caricature of normality. In their eyes there is nothing wrong with the statement one of them made about his expectations of participation in a project:

And now the plan is to get a job, get an apartment, and a lovely woman. Everything that you dream about, right?¹ (Participant, House of Keys, Denmark)

Many of the young adults who are oriented to a working-identity of 'instant satisfaction', however, often collapse beneath the load of demands to take on an ever-increasing personal responsibility for their own life situation – a demand that is also crucial for socialization into the world of work nowadays. In their personal narratives, permanent negotiations about issues of responsibility are paramount. By negotiating, they try to absolve themselves from the failures and disappointments that many of them have experienced in relation to school and the social security system. They readily blamed their social environment for their difficulties. As Sean stated:

Well in the municipality...there are 13 schools that don't want me Is that my problem? But that is also ..that's how they start; 'but that is your problem' – as a 13-year-old – my problem¹ 'It's his fault'. I mean it's not 'his' fault, because 'he' can't stop, so 'he' has to go to a private school or something. But they never did anything like that So ..it's not my problem. It's their problem actually (Participant, Advise First, Belgium).

Similar to this example, there were many other instances where participants tried to 'negotiate themselves out of the responsibility' for their own actions. To them the narratives of the outer world seemed fragmented and incoherent. Their inner logics project the responsibility for their actions onto the surrounding world, which, in their own minds seems consistent and justified. As a Dutch professional observed:

The students attempt to seduce you to send them away (Professional, Netherlands).

In doing so, they clear themselves from any responsibility, because:

you have sent them away, so they can't be blamed for it (Project professional, Netherlands).

Thus, the inner logics of these participants contribute to a self-fulfilling prophecy, that to them confirms their accusations that life is unfair and rules them out. The clash between the inner logics of many participants and their sense of injustice resulting from engagements with the labor market figures in a situation that was described by another Dutch professional:

One of my students at a work placement, worked at the renovation of a house. In one of the cupboards upstairs he found something interesting to read and started reading Unfortunately, the owners of the house found out He was fired immediately. His response was: but I didn't break anything, nor did I steal, I just read the book and put it back (Project professional, the Netherlands).

No wonder then that for a number of the young adults who carry this type of 'instant satisfaction' career-identity, the real and imagined discrepancies that are inherent in the world of labor and training for work seem too complicated to grasp, much less bridge. These are the ones who can soon give up any hope of making their dreams come true. Some content themselves with just 'keeping things going as usual', whilst being stuck in the system – wearing their work-clothes to their activation project. They have given up trying to find an education or struggling to move on. To some, the fear of failing again has come to dominate over their courage and the will to attempt to change their situation. The solution that they 'choose' turns out to be a situation of inertia or social immobility because the status quo seems preferable to the risk of yet another defeat. One of the professionals used the following phrase to capture something he kept encountering amongst those in his charge:

When I grow up I want to be nothing (Project professional about project participants).

For him, this described the ultimate desire of this group of disillusioned participants. Some of the young adults themselves uttered future wishes like:

... Then I just WANT to be unskilled...
.. Then all I want is a driver's license..

Others just drop out and since they are increasingly ineligible for benefit when they do so, retreat out of reach of official statistics. Some of this group, however, consciously seek the realization of their instant satisfaction dreams in the illegal market. This can lead to them becoming 'new numbers' in a different set of statistics, such as 'first time offenders'.

Those who assumed a working-identity stance of 'instant satisfaction' in relation to the labor market and life generally, were the most heartrending we came across in our research. The gap between their inner logics and the outer logics of the world of education and labor appeared impossible to bridge. Consequently, young people who took up this stance were most strongly at risk of being excluded and marginalized even more than before. Their participation in the educational provision especially created for them, turned into just another failure to improve their situation.

Disorienting Freedom

> ... Then I did not bother doing that any more .
> .I really do not know what I want, I have no idea.
> .. There were so many options I was interested in, so I could not decide ..

> Then I began a plumber's education That was all right, but only after a month we got to the stage where we were allowed to cut in sheet metal Then we did that for a couple of months but by then I did not bother anymore and I quit. Afterwards I had to work on an engine where I earned a lot of money. But then I stopped and did nothing for a year. Then I got on as a temporary worker for three months That was a bit boring so I stopped and did nothing until I started here [on the activation project] (Project participants)

The young adults who developed this working-identity stance differed from the ones who figured in the previous sections. They expected to find a job that would be personally fulfilling. In their eyes, work should be a source of animation and motivation, and contribute substantially to a sense of meaning and direction that had been lacking in their lives thus far. Their problem was that they were hardly able to sense, let alone formulate, what they would really like to do within the frames of actual possibilities provided. When confronted with an overwhelming range of possible options, they lacked the focus and the ability to decide which corresponded best to their interests and capacities. Many of those who assumed this working-identity, therefore, only knew to phrase their freedom of choices in negatively colored statements. They often explained and justified their choices and rejections by using an expression like:

> . to bother or not to bother...

A Dutch professional described their condition in the following way:

They are not used to knowing what they want; they usually do know what they do not want (Professional, Netherlands)

The tension these young adults experienced between their expectations of a fulfilling job and their inability to determine whether one job or direction might be more meaningful than another, was partly caused by a lack of knowledge about the world of labor. But it was as strongly connected to their confusion about what meanings and values they should attach to work. It was not at all clear to them what work should be about. Was it to do with something fulfilling? Was it to make money in order to support oneself? Was it doing something that would be appreciated by others? Did it mean you could still have a good time? What priorities should be made and what perspectives were there?

To a certain extent their confusion and disorientation as to what work should be about, makes them more vulnerable than young adults who more or less orient themselves to variations on the rather clear-cut and familiar model of the traditional wage earner. The young adults who were stuck in this stance had no identification whatsoever with a working-identity from the era of industrialization. They had nothing at their disposal to create a clearly developed alternative working-identity to guide their explorations into the labor market. Without such support, it was not surprising that amidst the abundance of experiences and options that were made available to them, they experienced serious problems in making decisions about which ones really might be interesting and fulfilling to them. They were confronted with the paradoxical situation that their 'subjectivation' of the late modern process of phasing out traditional wage earners, not only created cultural liberation but also cultural disorientation. This disorientation represented, to some extent, a non-existing working-identity: what we might refer to as actively assuming no stance.

This disorientation drives the participants into desperately seeking to balance coherence and meaning with experiences of an 'engulfing freedom'. They sometimes gave shape to this search through trying out endless numbers of jobs, and education and training opportunities. Similar to many young adults in the previous section, the ones who so intensively experiment in their quest for meaning, in many cases also show a serious lack of endurance as well. They exhibit the hyperactive restlessness of youth in late modernity that, according to Ziehe (1992), favors a rapid scratching at the surface of diverse fields of knowledge, rather than the tenacious exploration of a specific field of interest.

When we also take into account other life domains of these young adults, the need and gravity of their endless search for meaning cannot be ignored. Their disorientation seems to have permeated almost every dimension of their existence. Whether it concerns the decision of when to wake up in the morning, or the choice between attending this training program or another, or far reaching decisions like whether or not to drop out of school, or to leave a job – every time the core of their considerations is constituted by the possibility of detecting something that might help them, or getting a feeling that 'something matters'. Life to them seems to have turned into an ongoing process of decision-making and endless justification.

In their daily lives, the postmodern condition of uncertainty and cultural liberation from tradition becomes very specific and concrete. As a consequence, internal deliberations about decision-making permeate all levels of their being, including minor issues like what to do the next day or the next hour. Everything is to be discussed and all arguments are to be taken into account. All perspectives matter and nothing matters – all at the same time. This general reflexive tendency of late modern society is pushed to its extreme with these young adults, who predominantly live outside structured institutions like schools and organizations, and therefore have little to support them in finding a different kind of stance in relation to education and work.

These participants are caught up in highly demanding processes of identity-formation. Although they may experience themselves as liberated from their social and individual backgrounds, they have no access to 'naturalized' meanings of labor that might help them in finding a clear-cut working-identity. The globalizing economy provides them with little to hang on to. Consequently, the processes of clarification and decision-making that are expected as part of education for work become so psychologically challenging and demanding, they can exacerbate their sense of disorientation at a profound and existential level.

When asked to consider choices for education and work, these young adults are on a slippery surface in their development of a clear working-identity. This in itself is sufficient to give rise to further confusion and disorientation. But it is a different matter when we see behind this crisis in working-identity, their more general disorientation in life and their difficulty in coming to a decision about whether and how to situate themselves in relation to the labor market. We are thus confronted with young people who are living with permanent insecurity about what is meaningful and what makes sense at all. In this situation, we would argue that providing support in processes of working-identity orientation and formation becomes more important than labor market orientation per se.

The projects that we researched bear witness to this complicated challenge of reconciling education for labor market participation with this more general disorientation and uncertainty with regard to meaningful career decision-making. In most projects, many young adults who were trapped within this dilemma found it difficult to navigate through the apparent impenetrable chaos of expectations, hopes, and options that advisors, counselors, and professionals tried to offer them. In spite of attempts to find a solution within the frame of a training course or activation program, many experienced ambivalence as they alternated between their fear of remaining in a marginalized position on the one hand, and their need to be guided out of their present situation by professional support on the other. Others seemed to give up trying to deal with this lack of direction and orientation. They tried in whatever way to withdraw from those engagements in life that demanded any endurance or longer-term obligations. They tried to prolong their 'youth phase', almost as if they could make it permanent. To them life had turned into a matter of 'which party to go to next'.

A number of young adults, in the last resort, even experienced each and every choice and decision as merely coincidental, other-induced, or accidental due to circumstances and events beyond their control. Such a perception often coincided with an almost complete emotional and normative indifference, where nothing seemed more important or valuable than anything else; an attitude which inclined some young adults towards socially destructive behavior, like hooliganism, criminal activities, or vandalism. In the words of another young man:

> *It's all the same to me (Project participant).*

Activation projects set up to guide this group of young adults into the labor market in many cases seem to be doomed to fail. In the daily practice of the projects, practitioners often were unaware of the profoundness of the young adults levels of disorientation and the emotional and practical difficulties they experienced in successfully navigating the many options they were faced with. At the same time, practitioners were faced with the dilemma of how to effectively engage young adults whom they assumed to lack motivation and the ability to take responsibility for their own lives.

On a more structural level, this group seems to have fallen victim to the fragmentation and volatility that has penetrated every domain of life in late modern society. Their inner disorientation reflects the hazards of a life that can no longer be constructed around fixed and stable blueprints, models, and working-identities. The liberating effects of this may benefit the *joie de vivre* of those who are able to grab whatever chances come along for new choices. However, the young adults who had adopted this stance exhibited the backfiring of late modernity and the immense social and biographical consequences of living in societies that make an icon of the possibility of 'infinite choice'.

Self-expressive Ambition

> *... The main thing for me about work is enjoyment...*
> *..It is not really like skills and qualifications that bother me, the main thing for me is to enjoy it...*
> *...I will only do it if I enjoy it.. (Project participants)*

Raina, from England, relates some of the story of her life:

> *I've signed on before and been stuck in jobs I don't want to be in and I could've done factory work, but I actually wanted to find something I was interested in so I wouldn't be back here in six months. I don't want to go into a job I don't want. You've got to be happy in what you've got. I mean I was doing an office job for a year and I'd just see people that'd been there 25 years and thought, they're happy with their little life, but I couldn't do this Until I find a job that I'm interested in, I don't think I ever would get settled properly (Raina, participant, England).*

For Raina – and other young adults like her – work is clearly about enjoyment, about living out interests, finding happiness in life, self-fulfillment and self-expression. These young people place emphasis on inner experiences of meaning in relation to work, over and above external incentives such as financial rewards or status. This type of inner logic deviates from the traditional wage earner identity and represents the construction of a new orientation to work that itself, paradoxically, is shaped by discourses of ultimate choice.

This stance is closely related to the logics of a knowledge-intensive society. In particular the better-qualified young adults in our research experimented with an identity marked by a flexible juggling with opportunity structures in the labor market. They tended to rank their personal development with the growing production, innovation, and profit of the organizations they wanted to get involved with. Self-expression for this group of young adults was closely linked to the process of acquiring more general qualifications and specific competences that would enable them to survive and benefit from the fast changes in current practices and situations they met.

The working-identity they seek is one of becoming a 'chaos pilot' – someone who, mindful of the importance they attach to personal growth, feels self-confident about how to live from one incident to the next.

In most of the countries involved in our research, the projects in which this category of young adults participated were perceived to provide them with ample opportunities for a job or for further education after terminating the project – but many of them were not motivated to take them. Raina's quote above was representative of others who felt like her. She did have a job in an office for a year, but quit because she was bored – the job could not offer her the other needs she expected to be met through work, such as for creative expression or meaningful relationships. Consequently at some point she 'chose' unemployment. She and others expected something more than just an average job. In the logic of the working-identity of 'self-expressive ambition' routine jobs were a 'non-option' – illustrated by another young English woman, Elaine, who stated:

> *The worst thing is to get a warehouse job .. I'm not going to be stuck in that just shuts off your mind really...become a robot (Elaine, participant, England)*

Rather than being trapped in an 'unbearable, routine job' many of these young adults prefer to take the risk of being unemployed for a while, and to spend time on their search for a job with 'style'. The challenge for activation projects in dealing with young adults who adopt this stance is not so much a matter of how to overcome insufficient qualifications or a fundamental disorientation in life, like with many other participants. Indeed, a considerable number of the young adults who are oriented to a working-identity of 'self-expressive ambition' are relatively highly qualified and socially and emotionally well enough equipped. The first question to be answered therefore, is why they are to be found in these kinds of 'activation' projects at all, given that the institutionalized logic is to support young adults who are unable to help themselves? To this question, we suggest several answers.

One reason in some of the countries is the lack of suitable jobs from which such young people might choose. For example in the former GDR, where our German case studies were situated, the number of qualified young people was far higher than the number of jobs available on the labor market. But there were other reasons. For instance in Belgium we found some relatively highly skilled young adults, who could have easily found a job that matched their qualifications, yet a number of them remained unemployed. We came across the same situation in Denmark where, at the time of our research, youth unemployment was still an issue, despite a situation of almost full employment.

For some of these young adults, being unemployed for a while is a kind of 'time-out' – a stop on a flexible route to an unknown destination. They can perceive this self-chosen interruption as significant for the development of their 'self' as a formal education or employment trajectory. A description of how these participants see themselves was given by a Belgian professional:

> *A highly qualified person who succeeds in building a career, while making use of several short assignments in close connection with his/her personality and individual agenda. The alternation of periods of work and non-work is for instance exemplified in the trend to travel around the world for a couple of months (Project professional, Belgium)*

During the writing of this book, we encountered in England a young man, aged 25, who described himself as a 'career job tripper'. In other words, he took pride in being able to take up a diverse range of working-identities (from chef to salesperson to guide to grape-picker) interspersed with periods of travel. Another had completed his degree in Business Studies, but concluded that he would work on making it as a singer. He cited racism as one factor in this decision, having decided that the odds were against him in ways he was no longer prepared to tolerate. But, although he would keep trying to get demonstration records accepted by the music world, he meanwhile would raise enough money to get to a Caribbean island and help his friend run a bar from time to time: when he needed money.

Another answer as to why young adults with a working-identity of 'self-expressive ambition' are to be found in projects for the unemployed refers to the high demands they make with respect to the kind of jobs they are looking for. They expect work not only to serve their material well-being but first and foremost work should contribute to their need for fulfilling self-expression and meaningfulness. In many cases they therefore identify with prestigious professions – often with explicit cultural and aesthetic connotations, such as becoming a musician, scriptwriter or TV producer.

This group's stance towards work reflects a tendency that is clearly to be found in studies of mainstream youth (Ziehe, 1989; Nielson, 1993). For these young adults, work has an increasingly important role in compensating and replenishing the loss of meaning that many experience in a life under late modern conditions. Obviously the expectation that self-actualization, education, and work should be closely connected is not confined to the higher and more privileged parts of society. Nor does it belong merely to those young people who can be expected to make these aspirations come true, due to the extent of their cultural capital and formal qualifications. Instead, a significant number of young adults who – voluntarily or against their will – are clients of projects for the unemployed, have also internalized such a working-identity.

Yet another resemblance can be identified between the orientations we found in these participants and more general studies of youth. Their 'self-expressive ambitions' seem to fit perfectly in a more widespread discourse among young people that might be labeled 'you can become anything'. This discourse reflects the huge number of opportunities that, in their experience, open up to them when they think about their future life. In contrast to young adults who are oriented to working-identities of 'tenacious duty' or 'instant satisfaction', the reality of this discourse for 'self-expressive ambitionists' is not questioned by subjective feelings of failing capacities and qualifications, lack of endurance or missing confidence. The specific paradox they experience is the, as yet, failing correspondence between their ambitions on the one hand – for instance to become an F16 pilot, as one Dutch guy dreamt of – and the required circumstances to bring out fully their innate personal competences and abilities on the other.

To this group of young people, to achieve their desired working-identity, that can be seen as the equivalent of a 'self-actualizing professional', is just a matter of finding or creating the proper conditions to enable them to make their dreams come true. However, in seeking to balance inner dreams and capacities with outer circumstances they can easily lose track of reality. In the words of a Portuguese professional, these young people:

> *usually do not have any correspondence to reality (Ines, project professional Portugal).*

A professional in one of the UK projects described how:

> *Some are inclined to overestimate themselves. They can be managers, only it has not happened so far (Harry, project professional, UK).*

In general there seemed to be serious disjunctions coming into play at the boundary between professionals exhortations and reality testing, and the young adults desire to assume a stance of self-expressive ambition. We often encountered the young adults' very different constructions around the notion of realistic choices and the management of expectations. These young adults were deeply convinced that – even when formal qualifications are indispensable – eventually a person can become anything if they have the talent and the endurance to persevere in believing dreams are possible.

What was worrying was the extent to which the majority of the professionals represented a contrary expectation of a working-identity. They were certain that these young people simply had to get rid of their 'silly' ideas and to become more realistic about what they might expect from work. In their view, it could only benefit the well-being of the participants themselves if they became aware that people who have developed only a few skills, and who furthermore could show no qualifications or employment records, should not dream about becoming scriptwriters, film stars or professional footballers.

Consequently, in a number of projects a strategy of 'dream-crushing' was employed to bring participants down to earth. Depending on variations in national context and in the organization of projects, however, this strategy was applied in various ways, relating to different options and policy priorities.

For example, in the UK *New Deal* many professionals perceived it as a priority to direct young people specifically toward jobs and careers where there were vacancies. In this context the desire of a large number of participants to become a car mechanic was deemed 'unreal', as there were relatively few jobs available in that branch of the labor market. In other countries we found a more open process of clarification that coupled a strategy of 'dream-crushing' with a process of self-clarification among the young adults involved, without pressurizing them into a pre-structured range of limited options. A Dutch counselor described an example of this approach:

> *In the clarification process I make their dreams – like becoming a F16 pilot – realistic by taking them very seriously and then referring them to the information desk to find out what qualifications they actually need to fulfill their desires; usually this puts them off and then I can continue the process (Counselor, Netherlands).*

Juggling while Navigating Shaky Ground

The identification of different working-identity stances set out here shines a light on the diverse situations of unemployed young adults. However, we need to consider the ways these different stances are experienced and played out in young adults lives – and the challenges this poses for professionals. The latter group also seeks to find meaning in their responses to the situations they confront within activation programs. These considerations cast a dark shadow on possibilities of constructing effective activation strategies in late modernity.

The various working-identity stances we have constructed from our research findings, as mentioned earlier, are not to be understood as fixed or clearly delineated. The orientations that characterize young people's trajectories exist in all kinds of mixed and often contradictory combinations and none of them can be exclusively associated with one particular group of young adults. Actually, we found features of several types among almost all participants of the projects that we visited. What we are trying to convey here is the complexity at play in the lives of unemployed young adults to which policy and practice are tasked to respond.

The 'inner logics' around work and identity that are evolving in Late Modernity are often in considerable tension with the inner logics of professionals and projects. We thus believe it is of value to our purposes here to map the various meanings that these young adults ascribe to work and to what it means to be a worker for two reasons. First, even if hardly any of them perform any of those working-identity stances in a 'pure' form, we could nevertheless discern clusters of orientations. For example, some young adults clearly adhere more to the traditional wage earner identity, whereas others foster much stronger 'self-expressive ambitions' in comparison with the majority of their companions. Staying questioning about these differences in the inner logics of participants, and seeing them as stances open to dialogue and inquiry rather than as 'labels' challenges professionals and policy makers to develop a wider range of creative strategies and interventions. Moreover, they are challenged to be more reflexive about the assumptions they implicitly or explicitly bring to their practice, and how these may be working against, rather than with, the young adults' inner logics.

Secondly, by distinguishing these different working-identities on the one hand, and at the same time understanding how the distinctions between them are blurred in the actual lived experience of these young people on the other, we are able to gain insights into the possibilities and limitations of options for constructing working-identities under late modern conditions. In other words, traditional orientations such as suggested by a stance of 'tenacious duty' have not 'melted in the air', to be dismissed as 'modernist history'. Rather, they are partly relativized, partly mixed with other possible kinds of working-identities, and partly eroded yet without being replaced by solid alternatives. Consequently, the act of constructing working-identity stances that might have meaning in both one's own life and on the labor market has turned for many of the young unemployed into a hazardous quest for stability and certainty, without the support of well-defined outer standards and signposts. They encounter a plethora of contradictory demands, barriers, and opportunities. For young adults who are coping further with homelessness, racism, additions, the hopeless inadequacy of standardized 'choice oriented' strategies becomes more apparent.

The construction of working-identities, like so many other aspects of late modern life, has turned into a highly individualized enterprise. It requires many strategies to navigate and grasp possibilities and ambivalences that may interrupt and paralyze the search for work as a source of meaning. Insight into the various working-identities that young people see as available to them may enable professionals to better identify the pitfalls to which they might reflexively attune alongside their clients. What is equally challenging is how to offer these young adults some 'bearings'.

Emerging Paradoxes, Pitfalls and Possibilities

We now wish to highlight some of the most striking features of late modernity which young adults and professionals are now confronting. These are not easily labeled, but each of them, for us, suggests the simultaneity of paradoxes, pitfalls and possibilities.

Individualization and Marginalization

Most of the young adults in this research shared expectations and perceptions of the possibility of a unique and individualized pathway leading them towards the labor market. Individualization has become such a pervasive discourse, that they accept it as a faithful description of how the world really is (Cieslik and Pollock, 2002). They hardly sense the constructed nature of the images and stories turned into practice by the discourse of individualization.

In general, they understand individualization as a change in social and cultural conditions that enables and stimulates them to make free and specific choices in an ongoing process of identity formation. Along with their feelings of an increasing range of possibilities and choices, goes a strong belief in self-responsibility. This is being induced by both external discourses and internalized expectations. They firmly stick to ideas of a personal accountability for one's choices – no matter whether the choice is about educational trajectories or about pizza toppings.

While the young are immersed in this discourse, the demands on individualization that are made by peers, relatives, and friends are reinforced and widened in the options that are provided and the qualifications and competences that are demanded as imperatives, by the educational and the labor system. The widening of possibilities for a personal meaningful life-course by making the 'right' choices with respect to education and work aggravates the pressure that they feel in every corner of their lives: that is, to take personal responsibility for making the right choices and benefiting from the chances they meet. To many of the young adults in our research, this pressure evokes feelings of uncertainty, lack of confidence, stress, resignation, resistance, despair, and so on.

While some seemed to benefit more easily from the advantages that may be implied in processes of individualization as well, others find blame the easier pathway. These findings bear witness to the truth of Bauman's statement that individualization does not affect the lives of young people in an equal way and that there are huge differences between them in their ability to benefit or lose by it (1999). A core feature of these differences seems to be the variation in competences to juggle with and navigate between a mix of the different working-identities the young unemployed are faced with.

The four working-identities explored above, reflect the dilemmas, tensions, and contradictions that participants encounter when attempting to perform this stance in actual labor market conditions.

The partly completed replacement of a robust traditional labor or career-identity with a range of more or less hazy notions of alternative working-identities may in fact trap young people in a muddle of contradictory expectations, aspirations, and perceived opportunities. This may deepen their social marginalization rather than enhance their social integration.

To escape this doom, they need a highly developed sense of agency and capacity for reflexivity, relating to when and how to assume a particular working-identity stance, and when to detach themselves from it.

We were struck by the considerable number of young unemployed we met who still identified with at least particular aspects and symbols of a traditional wage earner mentality. This was gendered in its performance, with mainly young men assuming this stance. Many of them still valued wearing traditional working clothes, looking for well defined specific tasks and instructions, making a sharp distinction between working hours and leisure time, conceiving work as the key to social normality and integration, and so on. At the same time, however, they experience both the relativity and the limits of this same working-identity. This is evidenced in its eclipse by the emerging labor market and in increasing demands for young people to take the initiative, to cooperate, to be innovative, reflexive, and flexible. It is not only the young unemployed who find it hard to reconcile and integrate these 'new' competences with their expectations of work.

The traditional hierarchically organized work environment, where the worker is required to adhere to operations clearly defined by his or her boss, paradoxically then, becomes a 'pipedream' for many of these young adults. Yet, paradoxically, the majority of them would hardly be able to function adequately within such an organization. Just as they have problems in adjusting to late modern demands for self-management, reflexivity, having a spirit of enterprise, and so on, they also resist authority and attempts by others to 'tell them what to do'. But working-identities and life-identities are not so easily separated. Their dreams about a 'normal' traditional job can be understood as part of a wider search for an idealized normality that includes a traditional family, wife, children, and house. They also communicate their dreams to have their simple wish fulfilled – to be respected by and to become part of society at large. Performing the identity of having a regular and permanent job in the classical sense – even when they are locked into an activation project that is not in the least remotely connected to work – is for them a first step in making such dreams come true.

But the tragedy is that their wish to enter a 'normal' situation implies a dream that is the exact opposite to the conditions in which a vast number of them currently find themselves. Every domain of their lives – their unemployment, their often poor housing conditions, their often strained relations with family, friends, and partners – may be dashing their dreams against the rocks daily. Nonetheless, they still cling to their dreams of a traditional wage earner, even if they are hardly able to cope with its demands. This is so, even when they know and experience the insignificance of this kind of working-identity in actual organizations of today and its remoteness from the worlds they inhabit.

What we may be seeing here is the need for these dreams and their implied illusions as a survival strategy. In other words, it may be enabling the young people to deny a present that, if realized in its entirety, may paralyze them altogether. They may feel forced to modify and reinterpret their perception of the outer reality, as a 'strategy' to create and sustain a coherent inner logic that sustains the hope of escaping from a depressing existence. But this inner need to 'dream on' stories of a normal life without facing the serious challenges that come once a job is secured, is exactly the reason that in many cases causes these young people to come into conflict with wider cultural codes of 'normality'. Their self-images and mental mappings of reality outside reinforce them into further socially marginalized positions.

At the same time, the paradox is that a number of them gradually lose the belief that they will ever succeed in making their dreams come true. They are inclined towards expressions of disappointment and rudeness while often remaining the toughest judges of themselves – often unbeknown to the professionals who work with them. They experience themselves as not being able to carry through any education. They seem to 'prove' over and over again to themselves that they are unable to succeed in accomplishing anything important in life at all. In their view, they perceive themselves as having had chances, but as failing by their own shortcomings to make the most of these. To them, the pipedream of a wage earner identity in many cases comes to a dead end and turns into a hopeless succession of unskilled and uncertain 'flex-jobs' or into a 'career' into the social security system – at least as long as they manage to stay aboard.

So what seemed to make a difference, compared to those young unemployed people who – either by dreaming or by failing – assumed (variations of) a traditional wage earner identity? The young adults in our research who seemed in the stronger position to prevent or escape (further) economic and social marginalization and to benefit from the new chances that an individualized society provides, were the ones who succeed in performing different working-identities. They transform their biography into a kind of social laboratory, where they experiment with the best that can be extracted from each new option. Postponing or switching between concrete decisions concerning their working-identity, they alternate their involvement with unemployment, work, and the educational system. In so doing they prolong the traditional adolescent phase, literally turning their life into an experience of 'life long learning' – though not necessarily through the forms of participation and expectations of commitment envisaged in policies under the same name! Yet they see trying out possible options, as a means of improving their competence to survive in ever changing situations. They perceive 'working at their personal growth' also as another viable strategy for surviving, and indeed thriving, in the labor market.

These 'strategies themselves, though, carry particular risks such as when the young person adheres too exclusively to the construction of a singular work-identity, as was illustrated in the section on the identity of 'self-expressive ambition'. The capacity to juggle with different options and working-identities clearly distinguished those who were fairly successful in finding their way out, from the ones who were hopelessly floating in the disorienting chaos of late modern demands and chances.

For that reason, learning the biographical competence of juggling and navigating the range of possible options and orientations in a way that reflexively suits the ongoing story of one's life might be a critically important focus for activation work. Yet, the integrity of such an ontological standpoint can come into conflict with policy agendas concerned with the instrumentality of welfare to work imperatives (Dwyer, 1998; Finn et al., 1998).

In a society where looking backwards for traditions and models to guide future options and decisions has become counter-productive, yet remains compelling; where looking forward creates a sense of disorientation and a fear of being tied down to irreversible (and enticing) choices, other strategies become required. In this perspective, the competence of being able to identify oneself as a skilled juggler that can keep balls in the air and two feet on the ground despite changing circumstances might be the most prominent one to develop and support in activation projects.

Thus, the professional's role could be reconstructed as helping the young person to actively search – in non-linear ways – towards forms of economic, social, and cultural participation that have some meaning in their lives – and simultaneously develop capacity for 'juggling' and re-inventing working-identities in relation to opportunities that both arise and that they too help to create.

Individualization and the Blurring of Inequalities

The second set of pitfalls, paradoxes, and possibilities we see professionals and young people confronting is how the individualization of social life on the surface seems to level and yet exacerbate former inequalities, reinforcing dividing lines in the options and life courses that are open to different social groups. In the words of Du Boys-Reymond, pre-structured life courses seem to have been transformed into 'much more open models' (1995, p. 79). In line with this, Furlong and Cartmel (1997) observe that all young adults have more choices and opportunities nowadays, but at the same time are exposed to growing uncertainty and risks as well, irrespective of the social category they belong to. The *impression* might easily be created that traditional indicators of social inequality, such as class, gender and ethnicity have a decreasing significance, because decision-making and responsibility with respect to life chances and life courses are more and more ascribed to individual agents. Consequently, it is the individual who is praised or blamed for the success or failure to shape a meaningful and respectable life and work pathway. Yet, unemployment remains disproportionately higher among certain groups, such as Black and minority Ethnic groups.

The majority of the young adults we met in our research had internalized the discourse of individualized opportunities and responsibilities. Even if some of them point to the responsibility of external institutional circumstances and persons, almost all of them in one way or another primarily blame themselves as deficient individuals, who have been filtered out by the ruling laws of the market.

Blaming themselves for their shortcomings, these young unemployed can sink even deeper into the marshland of frustrated expectations and crushed hopes. Not only are many of them objectively marginalized because of the failure to create themselves an acknowledgeable position in the world of education and work. Their self-image justifies their position at the fringes of society and continually defines their identity as a 'loser' – one who lacks the fundamental ability to 'make it' in normal life.

Only a small minority of the participants perceive themselves as part of a specific class or of any other identity-supporting collectivity. Those who do can be seen to be better off, because this perception at least enables them to consider the more structural mechanisms at work that contribute to their failure to benefit from available opportunities. A collective identity can shield them from the dramatic shattering of self-confidence that can drive others into perpetual resignation.

Although new social discourses attempt to deny specific differences based on poverty, poor housing, race and ethnicity, and so on, (traditional) social indicators of an uneven distribution of life chances and lifestyles are as valid as ever, even if their impact is reduced and transformed, compared to some decades ago. As Furlong and Cartmel observe:

In the modern world young adults face new risks and opportunities. The traditional links between the family, school and work seem to have weakened as young people embark on journeys into adulthood which involve a wide variety of routes, many of which appear to have uncertain outcome. But the greater range of opportunities available helps to obscure the extent to which existing patterns of inequality are simply being reproduced in different ways. Moreover, because there is a much greater range of pathways to choose from, young people may develop the impression that their own route is unique and that the risks they face are to be overcome as individuals rather than as members of a collectivity (Furlong and Cartmel, 1997, p. 7).

Their observation points at the significance of looking explicitly at patterns in the life chances and life courses of young people on the one hand, and identifying social categories like class, ethnicity, and gender on the other. Individual choices and decisions are not made at random, but remain strongly influenced by the (multiple)-identities individuals live through.

The dominant thesis in late modern discourses is that traditional structures have been replaced by a flexible market place of individualization and risk. This seems to suggest that in 'pre-late modernity', young people in a particular social class all followed the same predictable route into the labor market and were able to assume a fixed career or labor market identity. Yet, the implicit (and often unchallenged) assumption seems to be that within the previous modern age there were jobs for life, predictable labor market transitions and unstinting social affiliations. The idea that 'life then' was simple, uncomplicated and lacking the need for individual and social reflexivity, warrant deeper questioning.

Indeed given the continued pervasiveness of structural inequalities we have witnessed in this research, there appears more merit in understanding changes in the dynamics of youth transitions consequent upon globalization, post-industrialization and the onset of the risk society less in black and white terms and more in more nuanced shades of gray.

Working-identities across Countries and Cultures: Paradoxes of 'Progress'

Our intention in this research was to gain deeper insights into the diverse experiences of young people across Europe. In this section we bring to the fore some generalizations from the cross-national outcomes of this research and relate them to some studies of young people in general. We invite readers to consider these in the spirit of working hypotheses.

By and large, we discerned that the lower qualified the participants were, the stronger they were oriented to the various forms of a traditional wage earner identity. They were the ones who rarely ever completed any educational trajectory. Their working experiences – if any at all – were mainly in unskilled jobs like cleaning, cashier, and such like. This was true throughout all six countries researched, although the specific circumstances they met might vary strongly and their problems of entering into the labor market consequently had different origins and prospects. In the former GDR and Portugal, for instance, there were numerous projects to increase their skills, but little hope that a substantial number of jobs would be available to them in the near future. This made their frustration of not fulfilling the dream of securing a wage earner career-identity different from similar frustrations of young people in those countries where near full employment existed, but where simultaneously the traditional wage earner working identity was increasingly hard to express in the labor market.

In general it can be observed though, that the more a country bears the characteristics of a late modern economy, the more this group of young adults is in trouble when they try to secure access to the world of labor. In such countries, low qualification jobs are, to an increasing extent, to be found in the service sector, where there is less call for the qualifications of the traditional laborer, than for the competences that traditionally relate more to middle class and feminine cultural capital (Andersen, 2000). Such skills include social skills for cooperation and flexibility, instrumental demands for computing, the ability to express oneself clearly orally and in writing, and personal qualifications with respect to acknowledged appearance and style. As a result, both in terms of qualifications required and of their own inner logics, the lowly qualified unemployed aspiring wage earners find it hard to find a suitable job and therefore risk remaining unemployed.

The failure to keep up with changes in the labor market and to adopt new working-identity orientations has different implications in the various countries, due to specific national and contextual circumstances. For example in Portugal we found that a number of the young adults, who took part in this research, expressed pronounced fears of leaving their ghetto-like social environment behind them. They unambiguously fostered the wish to disrupt their cycle of poverty and exclusion but simultaneously were afraid to be separated from the familiar symbols and atmosphere of a lifeworld where they felt acknowledged, valued, and confident. To these young unemployed, the culture of the ghetto seemed to represent and express soothing 'rituals of resistance' towards the relatively unknown world outside, where the rules of an increasingly capitalistic labor market and discriminatory social order dominated. These Afro-Portuguese youngsters were not so much bothered by the changing vocational nature and demands of a traditional identity, but had trouble in coping with the loss of social stability and security that traditionally were related to the status of a wage earner.

The problems that Danish lowly skilled young adults met when they pictured themselves as a wage earner were quite different from this. They faced a situation of nearly full employment, work was available to a vast majority of people who wanted it and qualified labor was increasingly in demand. Indeed, a discussion was going on about the importation of labor from abroad, to solve specific shortages on the labor market. However, there was a growing tendency amongst lowly qualified young people to stay away from the kind of jobs they could actually obtain – a well known phenomenon in other late modern societies like the UK also. They were put off by the changed vocational qualifications and the demoted social status of the traditional working-identity in such jobs, and were unable or unwilling to accept this.

Broadly speaking, it can be observed that, although inner and outer market mechanisms vary across southern and northern countries, all over Europe the globalized labor market tends especially to marginalize lowly-skilled and unskilled men and women. This is (not only) due to 'objective' factors like rising demands that can only be met by an ongoing process of updating and increasing qualifications, summarized under the call for lifelong learning (Dupont and Hansen, 1997; Sennett, 1999). Young adults – particularly young men – who are oriented towards a traditional wage earner identity find themselves in an increasingly marginalized situation. Their internalized images and expectations of such an identity do not correspond to the actual changes in the content and the new social embedding of this same identity. Therefore, to interrupt such processes of marginalization, activation projects cannot merely seek to pressure or 'equip' these potential employees to adapt to the labor demands of employers.

Working-identities that make a better match with the changes of late modernity and globalization were found throughout all the countries we researched. But the extent and the impact of such working-identities, not surprisingly, were greater, the clearer the post-industrial nature of the country's economy. Therefore, these working-identities were more evidently present among a number of the young unemployed in the UK, Belgium, Denmark, and the Netherlands, than in Portugal and the former GDR. This observation is in line with evidence from other research projects that show that the turning away from a traditional labor identity is most widespread in the northern parts of Europe (Baethge, 1989; Furlong and Cartmel, 1997; Simonsen, 1998).

The rise of new working-identities is not, however, solely influenced by national or regional differences. Throughout all countries, our findings clearly point to a relatively higher level of education and a more privileged class affiliation with the young adults who assume more flexible orientations. Most of them had a record of a relatively intensive and long school attendance, even if many had never succeeded in obtaining any formal certification after primary school. Furthermore, a number of them originated from family and class backgrounds, where they had experienced more or less the same 'language' and 'codes' that constitute the cultural capital of teachers, counselors, and instructors as well. To think and act in terms of autonomy, in other words, to make their personal choices and decisions in accordance with personal feelings and preferences, was understood in the same terms as the professionals they met in the projects. Therefore, communication and co-operation between them and the professionals was to a certain extent easier than between professionals and those young adults whose background has provided them with a different vocabulary and 'habitus' (Bourdieu 1985).

Consequently, challenges and problems between professionals and participants also differ in terms of class and cultural background. With the group of young unemployed who are prone to relate their working-identity to new demands of the labor market, there is not so much of a contradiction between their own attitudes and the 'right' values, norms, and attitudes that pertain to work and the development of a working-identity today. Their main problem consists of the level of expectations and ambitions as to what kind of work they are capable of. The main challenge is how to support them in redefining and assuming 'more realistic' trajectories. However, such processes of clarification are grounded in understandings that are implicitly shared between them and the professionals.

These 'activation processes' may need to be approached delicately, as they often involve some kind of 'dream-crushing': in other words, discouraging these young people away from of choices that are not quite realistic, yet all the same still dear to the young adults involved. However, in many cases such 'switches' can be constructed in ways that stay reconciled with notions of autonomy, choice and self-expression. These figure prominently in the 'lifelong-learning discourse' to which both these participants and the professionals adhere. These young adults thus can do relatively well in the activation projects that are targeted at them as 'likely to succeed' (and simultaneously exclude those who are not). Therefore, many of them can eventually succeed in finding their way.

With the participants who lack this cultural correspondence with the professionals and who predominantly are oriented to a traditional working-identity, processes of education, training, employment, and guidance functioning as 'activation' often turn into a hopeless series of battles. Moreover, these often feel little different from their earlier experiences of school. The teachers' 'disciplinarian' purposes meet the 'resistance' of the young adults striving to preserve some sense of identity in the face of those who threaten to control or undermine them – especially now as 'older' young adults. In those situations there is no common frame of reference, no shared language of work and identity. The self-referential discourse of lifelong learning and self-deployment falls flat. Desires for stability and/or consumerism cannot be assumed in the same way as with other young people. Nor do professional interventions provide a soothing antidote against feelings of radical disorientation either. The resulting miscommunication can generate intense feelings of frustration, boredom, alienation and aggression between both parties. Research by Law et al. (2002) shows that strong feelings are aroused when career development:

- is linked to, or separated from, some important need or value;

- is applauded or rejected by significant others;

- confirms or challenges prior learning – taking people into or out of their personal 'comfort zone' (Law et al., 2002).

In the case of one group, feelings are positive and reinforce implicit social identifications and aspirations; in the case of the other group, the same projects that were meant to provide them with new chances and opportunities, can turn them into even more angry and cynical 'losers', feeling neither able nor prepared to take even this 'last chance' that is being offered to them. Or they can become resistors who will make their own way on the streets and in rebellion against what they perceive as coercive and restricting mainstream systems.

Conclusion: Motion and Commotion

In this chapter we have offered glimpses of disturbing contours within shifting landscapes of the unemployed in Europe. We have brought into closer view some of the changing 'inner logics' that are influencing the stances that 'socially excluded' and more privileged young adults may take up in relation to the labor market. We have distinguished a number of tensions around both assuming and relinquishing different kinds of working-identity stances, both for diverse unemployed young adults in Europe and the professionals who work with them in activation projects. We have explored some of what may be entailed in preventing and turning upside down the processes of marginalization that a considerable number of these young people experience. We have tried to represent something of the picture of working-identities 'in motion' and also 'in commotion' that our research revealed to us. It clearly does not suffice to see activation as the provision of specific facilities and projects. Moreover, the potentially distorting effects of standardized output criteria and performance indicators are perhaps more apparent.

Our exploration of working-identities in commotion suggest the extent to which policy makers need to support the social construction of a far more differentiated and engaged 'encounter space' between professionals and young adults that can support the possibility of some kind of experience of learning as transformative and collectively constructed. As Wenger argues: 'One needs an identity of participation in order to learn, yet needs to learn in order to acquire an identity of participation' (1998, p. 227).

We would argue that activation projects' impact can be curtailed by a failure to work with the inner logics of young adults who are making their own sense of working-identities and participation in late modern and postmodern conditions. At the same time, while we wish to support the development of 'possibility spaces', at the same time we stay cynical and cautious about the extent to which education, training, employment, and guidance can help young people to overcome the conditions that produced their social marginalization in the first place.

At the very least, however, within the opportunities for education, training, employment, and guidance that are offered, there should be ample time, space, and freedom to attune to and acknowledge the inner logics of the young adults involved. Activities, rather than being approached as technical means to an end, may need to develop opportunities for more reflexive dialogue and insight into inner logics that interweave (or not) with the various outer logics that impact on their lives and work possibilities in different conditions of labor and life.

As in the research carried out by EGRIS (2001), we have encountered some of the hybrid working-identities and strategies that are evolving on the part of young adults in response to their encounters with what it means to navigate the ambivalences that mark life in a late-modern society. Understanding the implications of these for empowering very diverse young adults to experience a sense of agency and competence in relation to changing social and economic conditions is of great societal and political significance. EGRIS (2001) argues that we need policies that can take account of these transitions that so strongly dislodge standardized notions embedded in many activation projects.

In the chapter that follows, we look specifically at how the various activation projects studied impacted (or not) on young adults' sense of competence and agency in relation to having to juggle and navigate their way through a terrain where their own working-identities and those of the labor market were in perpetual motion and commotion.

Chapter 7

Agency, Empowerment, and Activation: Balancing Contradictions

Empowerment: For Whom and on Whose Terms?

In the previous chapter, we considered different ways that young unemployed adults perceived themselves and their choices in a changing labor market. We used the notion of 'working-identity' to convey the idea of young people engaging in plural, complex, fluid, hybrid, and contingent processes. Giddens speaks of identities as 'continually revised biographical narratives' (1991). To perceive young adults' identities in this way confronts us with the question of how processes of identity (re)formation might be constructively influenced by different forms of relationship and social practices:

> A coherent structure of self can, no longer be directly derived from the social environment. And so the individual comes under increasing pressure to develop an identity through the reflexive processing of life's experiences (Law et al., 2002, p. 432).

In this chapter, we explore further how various activation projects responded to young adults 'identities in (com)motion'. Implicitly, and explicitly, we are increasingly bringing to the fore questions such as whether and how funded projects aimed at reducing social exclusion and unemployment seem to be effective in influencing young adults':

- capacity to reflexively process their life and work experiences;

- development of a greater sense of possibility and choice;

- competence for different forms of social and economic participation;

- capacity to engage in social learning, around the contradictions and disjunctions they experience;

- capacity to exert individual and collective agency in response to changing social and economic conditions.

For example, we suggested in the previous chapter that the capacity to juggle and construct hybrid working-identities in response to different social and economic situations is a strong characteristic of young people who managed to shift out of unemployment. The young people who could take up different working-identity stances in relation to changing situations seemed better able to survive in conditions of late modernity. They may be less inclined to resort to criminal or self-destructive survival strategies, or indeed to blame others for their situation. But we would suggest that this capacity for fluidity and reflexivity does not happen through unmediated experience alone – and especially amongst young people who are multiply disadvantaged and burdened by more than the challenges of unemployment alone.

In this chapter, we therefore will explore how the fostering of activation and the fostering of agency might be working against each other. We wish to open up further conversations about whether, how, and to what extent, the researched education, training, employment, and guidance projects in Europe that target young unemployed adults seemed to foster young peoples' sense of empowerment as potential labor market participants and their capacity for competent social and economic actorship in late modern societies. Or does the concept of 'activation', as it is being constructed by particular social policy discourses, imply a contradiction in terms with respect to notions such as 'empowerment' or the development of young peoples' agency? Empowerment, as defined by radical educators such as Freire (1993) and Lather (1991) is conceived as what people learn to do for themselves; however in many constructions of 'activation', it seems to be undergoing a radical transformation in meaning. We now hear a great deal about how employers, the state, and projects will empower young adults: in other words, about how they will do it for the latter on the former's terms. What currency do ideas such as empowerment have in a late modern and postmodern society?

Activation Projects as Communities of Practice?

Before looking further at specific projects and practices, we wish to begin this consideration of specific projects and dimensions of competence, empowerment and agency by drawing on insights from Etienne Wenger's social learning theory (Wenger, 1998).

Wenger starts from the position that there is no such thing as individual learning. Instead, he regards all learning as social and as mediated by social practices and relationships. A key concept in his work is the notion of a community of practice. He is concerned here with people who work together, pursue more or less the same objectives and are concerned to create a shared language, common rituals and codes to guide their engagement around a 'joint venture'. The validity and viability of the notion of a community in late modern conditions are topics beyond the remit of this book. However, we might argue that some of the most successful activation projects we studied do foster communities of practice.

Wenger (1998) has elaborated four dimensions in his social learning model, which itself has been derived through a study of work related learning:

- *Community* (through which the process of belonging becomes a learning experience).

- *Identity* (which is produced through learning, and involves negotiation and 'journey' embedded in history yet in movement).

- *Meaning* (generated through negotiation, out of experience and through participation in its co-shaping).

- *Practice* (enabling engagement with a joint enterprise or activity).

From this perspective, it is not possible to separate out meaning, learning, identity, and enterprise, since all are being mutually shaped and influenced within the various communities of practice to which we belong. Viewed from this perspective, identity, and learning are inseparable. Identity is a person's source of meaning and experience (Castells, 1997). It is also the process and product of learning.

What we want to focus on here – as a relevant prelude to what follows – is Wenger's theorizing around the theme of belonging. This may be a generative notion in considering notions of competent actorship in activation projects. As we pointed out in the previous chapter, one of the most challenging tasks facing professionals and practitioners involved in education, training, employment, and guidance schemes is not that of skilling-up young people for jobs. It is creating in them some sense of identification, some sense of possibility and connection with the labor market.

Wenger identifies three modes of belonging in communities of practice that he argues create the possibility for competent actorship. In fact, he introduces the concept of 'identity forming competent actorship'. In other words, he does not regard the processes whereby we learn to identify and then act as a linear process. Instead, it is through (inter)action in communities of practice that we learn to identify with a sense of competent actorship and possibility in ourselves and in relation to others. He suggests the following three dimensions of belonging as integral to the development of competent actorship.

Imagination

Wenger emphasizes the importance of 'playing' with the work experiences one acquires. Imagination enables participants to look at their work choices with the eye of an outsider and to consider the intended and unintended impact of particular daily practices. He sees the fostering of imagination as a pre-requisite for developing a future perspective. We see his use of this term as another way of understanding the process of reflexively looking at past and future experiences and experimenting with biographical re-construction. In other words, what possibilities and alternative routes are available to me in my present reality? What can I/we influence and what do I/we need to accept? Imagination can also take account of intuitive forms of knowing and experiences of unfolding into 'what seems right' in the context of a person's biography and lifeworld.

The very process of imagining can help young people envisage themselves in the role of actors in their individual and collective experienced life stories. They can play with various visions for how they might engage with not just the labor market, but other forms of economic and social participation. Need they feel driven into one route, with all their dreams crushed along the way by professionals who think they need to be more realistic? In other words, they can experiment with situating themselves at different crossroads of what is and what might be.

Engagement

The second mode of belonging Wenger identifies is that of engagement. His research showed how participating in a community of practice can develop one's ability to influence and contribute substantially to the interactions that take place. But this capacity to influence that of which one is a part is highly dependent on the quality of one's involvement in the communication flows that go on. On the one hand, we might imagine that for young adults to stay engaged in learning from experience in work settings they need experiences of being 'included' – feeling accepted and acknowledged, being 'heard' and taken seriously. On the other hand, engagement relates to the ways actors express personal attitudes towards feeling responsible for both the objectives and the fortunes of the community as a whole. We would strongly distinguish this from that of 'emotional pawing' and pseudo therapy cultures that we encountered in our research. This leads us to wanting to ask:

- To what extent do activation projects discourage and encourage such identification?

Genuine engagement implies for Wenger, a dedication to adapting, sustaining or altering interactions, on behalf of the shared interests and joint aims of the community. Learning how to gain respect and recognition on the one hand and how to connect a sense of personal responsibility, accountability, and agency to a social 'enterprise' on the other, might thus be regarded as an indispensable competence then for young adults who intend (future) participation in (labor) communities. The scope for generating communities that can themselves create enterprise is another way of understanding such a strategy in the context of 'activation'. But we suggest that such aims cannot be imposed: they need to be grown in partnership, so that their meaning is jointly constructed.

Alignment

Wenger talks about alignment as the development of the competence to skillfully and reliably perform tasks and activities integral to one's specific role and function in a community of practice. The knowledge and skills that enable an actor to know how to act – and to learn how to act well – in the performance of a job, can provide a sense of 'ownership' as to the practices of a community. Feeling the 'right person in the right place' becomes essential for one's identification with the group or organization in which one participates. However, for Wenger, alignment does not only imply the development of 'technical' know-how for the performance of a particular job. It pertains also to adequately anticipating and meeting demands and expectations and learning how these are connected to the rules, attitudes and codes that are judged to be inherent and appropriate for the work at hand. These are likely to represent not only a mix of specific, community-bound rules, but more general and more widely applicable ones as well. In this way, being a skilled worker in a certain community can become experienced as connected to a broader field of communities. These may be perceived as both inside and outside the world of labor.

Wenger's development of this concept aligns, for us, closely with the key concept that guided the funding of our research: fostering capacity for wider economic and social participation. The concept of alignment enables us to consider the performance of instrumental competences as providing the opportunity also to challenge actors to question the validity and justification of community-bound rules, codes and attitudes in a wider context. They can express their agency through participation in the dialogues with other workers about the construction of hybrid working identities to support a sense of belonging. We might argue, like Farrell (2000), that they can learn to become not merely adaptive, but rather more reflexive about their choices as to whether and how to navigate the contradictions and paradoxes that all workers encounter in labor contexts. They too can begin to imagine themselves as active participants in the 'sites of struggle' that are forming in relation to imposed constructions of working identities in globalizing companies (ibid). They can make more informed choices about whether, where, and how they engage in these struggles and in so doing, foster their own sense of agency and empowerment in relation (and in reaction) to the discourses that form them.

Seen another way, experiences of learning to become a competent actor in an 'activation' based community of practice may help to promote processes of identification, imagination, engagement, and alignment. These in turn may support young unemployed people in developing an alternative sense of possibility and connection in relation to the labor market. At the same time, giving life to notions such as imagination, engagement, and alignment in actual contexts of practice requires further competences in negotiation as well.

All three modes of 'belonging' entail learning about the efficiency and meaning of different options, questioning vested routines, experimenting, with unknown or as yet peripheral pathways, expressing discomfort with oppressive habits and circumstances. Yet these are firmly rooted in a social, rather than individualized, learning context. In this way, developing competences for meaningful participation may simultaneously address issues relating to the identification of young adults with wider communities, while also helping them to clarify their own interests, desires, possibilities, and so on.

Balancing Competences?

When we began our research, we were interested to explore projects that were committed to developing biographical, social, and instrumental competence and to exploring possible integrations of these. As discussed in Part I, we anticipated that projects doing this would be the exception, not the rule. We assumed 'mainstream projects' would tend to favor the development of instrumental competences. We believed that those projects that were committed to 'balancing competences' would be more successful in helping young adults to develop their capacities for reflexive processing and agency and to broaden their imagination about what might be possible in terms of economic and social participation.

We will now lightly hold this original framework and that of Wenger's as two additional templates for our exploration of this shifting landscape of activation. They will help us to consider how and to what extent the researched projects promoted young adults' competences within communities of practice.

We shall focus on three different cases, one of which we introduced in Part I and to which we now deliberately return here. We shall also thread in findings from other projects to show, in particular, how some projects prepare participants only for a restricted mode of 'belonging' in (labor) communities. As a result, they can develop a reduced scope of agency and contribute to young people experiencing further social exclusion through the activation project itself – a powerful theme in previous chapters. We shall bring into clearer view more of the possible unintended consequences of well-intended choices of practice on the part of policy makers, program designers, and professionals.

Practicing Imagination and Re-vis(ion)ing Biographies: The *Bridging the Gap* Project

As described in the 'pen portraits' of the case studies in the Appendix, the *Bridging the Gap* project houses homeless, unemployed young adults 24 hours a day, seven days a week. In the chapter that introduces Part II, we considered this, alongside the Portuguese project, to represent an example of socially situated learning that itself was offering opportunities for transformative learning.

More than any other project we visited, this one functions as a kind of community in itself. It provides a framework for young people to develop life skills in the context of their daily lives, such as buying and preparing food, washing, budgeting, observing appointments and coping with interactions in the group. The culture of this project is explicitly expressed in empowerment terms:

> *Empowerment is the cornerstone of our philosophy, whereby we create a community where things can get better for them (Staff member, Bridging the Gap, England).*

The 'philosophy' of 'success through empowerment' is the driving force behind the different activities that are deployed in the project. Its roots lie in a commitment to understanding the complexity, patterning, and heterogeneity of the participants' needs. Therefore, success is not narrowly defined in terms of measurable outcomes like finding a job or achieving a certain qualification. The focus of interventions is on long-term objectives of helping young people to support themselves in the world rather than on short-term outcomes. This approach is considered to be directly useful and relevant by the young people themselves. It not the same as a 'needs knee jerk response' approach.

This is reflected in the kind of activities that are promoted. Basic is the provision of the young unemployed person with a safe, secure, and supportive space, to create some 'respite' in their lives – to sort themselves out and to achieve some stability. Building up confidence and self-esteem in daily interactions is coupled with challenges to reflect on their own values, actions, choices, belief systems and perceptions of their circumstances. Billy, one of the participants commented:

> It's just money for sorting your life out really. It's an incentive for sorting things out It's brilliant, I'm just glad the opportunity rose to me (Billy, project participant, Bridging the Gap, England)

Apart from this, the young adults in this project are provided with opportunities to gain new experiences by engaging in a range of activities. These are meant primarily to build confidence but also to grow new skills and knowledge. Such experiences can be work-related, but in the case of this project are more likely to be connected to a 'survival journey', or to performing successfully in an activity that is perceived as directly pertinent to the young person involved.

As a result, the empowerment that is implied by the *Bridging the Gap* project centers on the development of biographical competences through strengthening the imagination of the participants as to who they might be, could be and may wish to be, in future, in relation to both who they are and who they do not want to be in the present or future. The UK researchers expressed it thus:

> The individuals are provided with the opportunity to reflect on their own behavior, take responsibility for their actions and, with the help of the worker, consider alternative ways of being (Researchers, Bridging the Gap, England).

The young adults are thus strongly encouraged to look for the meaning of their present activities in the perspective of what they want with their lives. They are thus being trained in competent actorship through engaging in reflexive biographical work.

The project is perceived, both by the professionals and by the participants, as a link in the chain of growing both the autonomy and the social connectedness of these young adults – a 'next step' on the road to having choices and being able to enact them with greater confidence. As Sean, one of the youngsters, observed:

> It's like giving you a chance to try things out and see how things go...facing up to reality, learning different things, life skills etc. I've got an incentive to do that and that will make me more determined Helps you to be an individual. That's what I need more than anything (Sean, project participant, Bridging the Gap, England)

Compared to other projects we visited during our research, the *Bridging the Gap* project was not unique in its emphasis on promoting biographical competences through imaginative and reflexive activity. However, it seemed the most innovative and successful in realizing its objectives. For instance, it offered a considerable contrast to biographical work in the Danish *House of Projects,* as introduced in Part I. This project aimed at guiding young unemployed to the labor market or the educational system as well, while training them in 'life skills'. It also dealt with young people who, in their current situation, were deemed 'unfit' for the labor market. However, the Danish project seemed to fail to strengthen the biographical imagination of the youngsters and the 'skills development' felt Kafkaesque, on the part of young people and professionals. In other words, it was insufficiently aligned to any grounded sense of actorship in the world. As the Danish researchers observed, the participants seemed unable to identify themselves with the project, nor to make any connection between their present situation and their future prospect of getting a job.

What marks the difference between the two projects for us seems to be related to the extent to which the young adults are systematically encouraged and supported in explicating and negotiating their experiences and experimenting with different ways of thinking and acting in their presents and in relation to their future. However, in contrast to the *House of Projects* in Denmark, the primary objective of *Bridging the Gap* was to enhance the agency of young people as individuals and as an effective community, rather than merely as potential labor market participants. The *Bridging the Gap* project workers worked hard, individually and collectively, to stay attuned to the meanings that the participants attached to their experiences and knowledge. They took these as their starting-point to explore with the young people alternative or unknown options, to challenge taken for granted assumptions and to develop new competences and ways of being in relation to their challenging lives. Young people often expressed considerable relief at this approach, comparing it to their former experiences with schooling and training. This is witnessed in this statement by Bob, one of the *Bridging the Gap* participants:

> *Different sort of environment not like school. I went to [another training course], I went down there and all you do is sit in front of a computer all day. Was just boring. I was thinking 'what am I doing here?'* (Bob, project participant, *Bridging the Gap,* England).

In the Danish *House of Projects,* on the contrary, the experiences of the participants and the meanings they gave to them, were often perceived as deficit experiences, or as signs of obstinacy, de-motivation, and inadequacy. These were seen as things that had to be overcome or rectified by the professionals, rather than as offering opportunities for reflexive learning and competence development. Thus, the whole project became a source of frustration, both for participants and for professionals. The young adults formerly expressed concern with not being taken seriously; the professionals tended to feel humility, resentment, and disillusionment. The professionals could soon conclude that there was little prospect of helping these young adults to create a more 'healthy' perspective or to overcome the marginal situation they were in.   The self-fulfilling prophecy becomes clear: therefore, they are 'unskilled' and 'unemployable', fit only for short-term low level jobs, if that.

What was also distinctive about the *Bridging the Gap* project was how it seriously sought to integrate biographical competencies with the promotion of engagement. The project functions more or less as a community of practice and as an ongoing action inquiry (Percy-Smith and Weil, 2002, 2003). The participants are systematically challenged to 'negotiate' views and implications of their own actions and choices in the perspective of their responsibility for the well-being and the future sustainability of this 'community'. But this is not the *raison d'etre* of the project, it is just something they have to do to make the community they live in work. In learning to communicate about interactions and the role of themselves as participants within it, they are both invited to voice their personal opinions, intentions, and feelings and to listen to and acknowledge the views and meanings of others.   These high levels of engagement tended to foster some sense of belonging and aspiration.   Given the scale of problems that individuals in this project face, most of the work is done one-to-one, with staff meeting regularly to reflect on what they are experiencing, both separately and with the community members.

On the one hand, we can regard *Bridging the Gap* as fostering a community of practice of sorts, which contains young people (by keeping them off the streets, off drugs) and simultaneously provides space within which alternative constructions of their lives can begin to be imagined and authored. Learning to perform the tasks and functions that align them to this wider community of practice can enable identification and engagement, as well as feelings of pride, 'ownership', and critical reflection.

Bridging the Gap may seem to be focusing almost entirely on biographical and social competence. On the one hand, this may be justifiable, given the harsh realities being worked with there. These included homelessness, failed family backgrounds, drugs, prolonged unemployment, and other serious social and personal problems. Getting young people to experience any form of continuity, sustainability, and self-discipline were major achievements – although more instrumental policy makers may regard such achievements as 'by-the-by'. The question, 'But did they get a job?' could all too easily obscure the considerable effort entailed in fostering new forms of participation that is invested every single day, every moment, in such a project.

At the same time, the acknowledgment of instrumental competences that challenge and develop the interests and capacities of young unemployed is also integral to empowering them fully for participation in (labor) communities of practice.

A key tension in a project such as this is the desire to keep such multiply disadvantaged young people in their comfort zones of familiarity. This may be supportive to a point, but how do workers stay critically reflexive about when they may be unnecessarily diminishing these young peoples' sense of agency with respect to wider social and economic participation? The UK researchers express these tensions thus:

> *Alex liked animals and reptiles and chose to spend his hours doing a project about them. On the one hand, this gave him an opportunity to follow a course of action that was appealing to him. On the other hand, the question arises about whether following this interest is really moving him forward, or just keeping him trapped in his situation of being unskilled (Researchers, Bridging the Gap, England).*

Tougher and more blunt edged targets will never change this situation. They may only lead to young people and professionals dropping out even more.

What was most powerful was how *Bridging the Gap* exhibited ways in which meaningful learning could be embedded in a 24/7 'life-generated' curriculum. It functioned as a community of practice dedicated to keeping kids off the streets and helping them to become empowered to explore alternatives. Staff took every opportunity available to create possibilities for learning – without neatly distinguishing biographical, social or instrumental competence.

- At what cost might such projects become coerced to operate more explicitly and instrumentally?

- What could 'balancing competences' also mean in the context of *Bridging the Gap*?

Missed Possibilities: The *Female Electricians* Project

As described in the 'pen portrait' in the Appendix, the project *Female Electricians* was an innovative initiative within the general framework of Germany's regular vocational training system that was targeted at young unemployed women who wished to become electricians. The project aimed to integrate theoretical knowledge and practical skills and consisted of practice at the school's workshop, theoretical lessons in the part-time vocational school and a period of trainee service outside the school. Most of the time, however, students stayed at the workshop, where professionals encourage self-supportive learning in groups as the primary educational approach.

The workshop made a strong appeal to the young women to develop their technical skills and their willingness to engage in collaborative learning. As a group, the participants were faced with problems and challenges that were clearly focused on the common goal of learning how to be an electrician. These could only be solved through cooperation and mutual support. As a result, they developed technical competences through being engaged in a common practice of learning through interdependency and mutual responsibility. In this way, we could see an alignment of social and instrumental competence development with opportunities to develop a more traditional labor- or career-identity as an electrician.

However, the promotion of self-reliance and confidence in learning the vocation of an electrician was also perceived as a *group responsibility*. Each participant was challenged to contribute to the tasks and problems the group met during the workshop sessions. Thus, these young women were stimulated to exchange and share knowledge and to use individual abilities and knowledge to support the group in mastering the given assignments. At the same time they were encouraged to acknowledge and value differences in competences and opinions, to explore alternative options and to speak up for themselves to the other group members.

The professionals, when interviewed, commented that the young people came to prefer their peer discussions about alternative proposals and possibilities for solving a problem, to seeking such responses from an instructor or project leader. Overall, the young people felt supported by the instructors in a way that was experienced as safe yet stimulating. The workshop challenged participants to deploy their abilities, while simultaneously being embedded in:

the shelter of a warm nest (Researchers, Female Electricians, Germany).

They were also provided with diverse opportunities to develop hands-on the skills and knowledge that were required to become a qualified electrician. This helped them to gain a sense of identification and 'ownership' in relation to the vocation they were trained for and a sense of alignment with the broader world of labor and vocations. Being made responsible for the progress and collaborative achievements of the group, promoted their engagement and involvement. So, both on the instrumental and on the social level and in particular through the interweaving of these two, the workshop clearly fostered the capacity of these young adults for wider social and economic participation. At the same time, the significance of negotiation and experimenting was assured through an approach that favored team discussion about problems and alternative ways of responding to the social and technical challenges that confronted them. The meaning of a learning process that evokes experiences like these was expressed by one young woman, who stated:

It [the project] makes you know that you are needed (Project participant, Female Electricians, Germany).

The further development of the young women's sense of competence and agency occurs through a period of traineeship. The young women spoke to the German researchers about their feelings of astonishment, challenge, and surprise from realizing they could take their learning from the workshops into a real-life setting:

The period of practical work is the most enjoyable...this is a totally different dimension. . I have learnt a lot (Project participant, Female Electricians, Germany).

The traineeship provided them with first-hand experience in the labor market and challenged them to make sense of the codes, rituals, and mentalities that were at play in electrician communities of practice and the larger labor context they were part of. As a result, this process of activation became more concrete, meaningful and substantial, through their participation in actual practice outside the workshops.

However, there was yet another dimension to the real life experiences of these trainees that might explain their enthusiasm about the meeting with a real labor community: the biographical one. The period of practice in the real world helped these young women to imagine their future life and to find out, in a more concrete way than before, what it would be like to be a female electrician in a male dominated vocation. This closer look at their potential labor market participation helped them to develop reflexive capacity to imagine, with their peers back in the workshop, how they would meet, challenge, and change dominant norms in the profession. They could imagine possibilities and different working-identity stances. Being a trainee thus helped them clarify their own individual aspirations and desires about how they might imagine themselves as a future worker and the directions in which they might further develop their skills and knowledge:

> *The young women develop specific professional plans for their future that meet their wishes such as working with solar or alarm systems. They do not all intend to work, like most of the men, in a construction site (Researchers, Female Electricians, Germany)*

This biographical dimension certainly appeals to the participants, as it gives them a clearer picture as to their own desires, options, and limitations in the vocation they are being trained for. However, the development of biographical competences is highly arbitrary – a side effect – of their real life practice and it is left to them if and how they want to work it out. Biographical competence is hardly an explicit issue on the agenda of the project. At the same time, as discussed in Chapter 5, these young women had been carefully selected for this project, on the basis of the likelihood of their success.

Yet, the project potentially offered enough room for a deepening of biographical reflection that might further empower them to take agency both within this profession and indeed to make choices in other directions. The theoretical part of the project that was provided in the part-time vocational school might very well serve this function. For example, insights into gender and power relations in the workplace might be opened up, as a prelude to supporting them in discussing the questions, confusions, and 'breakthroughs' they experienced during their traineeship.

During our case study work, this theoretical part was by far the least interesting and least meaningful for the participants. The German researchers also observed an atmosphere that was more characterized by resignation and routine than a real interest in the experiences and knowledge of the young adults on the part of the teachers. They also noted an apathetic attitude on the part of the participants.

Theoretical issues did not succeed in capturing the imagination of the participants and promote their engagement. Neither did they seem to make much sense from the perspective of their life course, career-identities, and their lived experiences as electricians through the project. As a result, the young women tended to view the theoretical classes as a plight – obligatory but of little significance in enabling them to make connections with their group and individual practical experiences and emerging questions.

Opportunities were thus being missed to find a dialectical interplay between instrumental, biographical, and social learning on this project. Overall, we concluded that the vocational school was failing to maximize its potential for balancing and integrating different forms of competence development. They were missing opportunities to foster the agency of these young women for competing in a field that would be technically and socially challenging, yet highly challenging with respect to the discrimination they could face – and indeed were facing while participants in this project.

Yet we can also see the potential for this project to function as a community of practice, where social, instrumental, and biographical competence development is embedded in all aspects of the learning process, held throughout by the clear focus on electrician training. We can also imagine that successfully achieving in a specifically focused project such as this would support the transfer of a sense of agency and competence to other choices for labor market preparation and participation.

The Dutch project *Community College* also failed to realize opportunities that were available within the remit of their funding and structure. This initiative was similar to the German one in its objective to provide vocational training for a specific professional field (administration). It too focused on the development of instrumental and social competences. Here, however, more than in the *Female Electricians* project, the training program was predominantly located in a school setting, with little opportunities for practical experience in the field.

As a consequence, the participants experienced even more problems than their German counterparts in developing engagement and imagination or experiencing a sense of identification and alignment with a wider world of labor. They shared hardly any common practice, or any sense of community and found only scanty clues about how to 'play' with the meaning of the instrumental knowledge and skills in view of their own working-identities and the field they were meant to enter. The participants longed for more training in practice and enjoyed the practice-oriented lessons above the theoretical ones. Professionals regularly sighed that:

> *The curriculum could benefit from a more profound integration of theory and practice (Project professional, Community College, Netherlands)*

Like in the German case, however, none of the actors had a more or less clear notion of the reasons behind the failure to make theory work for practical experiences and vice versa. There was also little reflexive dialogue about this situation. In general, participants became captured in a construction of theory and practice that saw them as worlds apart: as if they represented two different outlooks on reality that were hard and probably impossible to reconcile.

Without simplifying the inherent tension between theoretical and practical forms of knowing, in our perspective the key lies in the gap between the two: in an approach that is more inclusive of biographical and social dimensions of learning. The practical experiences, knowledge, questions, doubts, and so on, of the participants could be transformed more systematically into starting points for reflection and theoretical exploration. In this way, the instrumental and social competences that are learnt in practice could be turned into more comprehensive and transferable insights and skills. But as importantly, participants may be helped to understand the inherent normative and value-bound character of what is currently being presented as a purely instrumental and functional training for a specific vocation or job. Equally, such an approach neglects the operation of theory in everyday life; in other words, participants are not challenged to be reflexive about implicit 'theories of practice' in specific contexts of action. As a result, opportunities for social and biographical learning that can build capacity for wider social and economic participation are yet again being lost.

A gender-based perspective on the vocation of electrician illustrates this point further. The class atmosphere of the vocational school in the *Female Electricians* project was characterized by mutual disapproval. The male and female participants tended to speak and act from the prejudices with which they entered the project. Males frequently made scornful comments to the female electricians. But, surprisingly, neither these stances and behavioral choices, nor the women's' reactions, were ever publicly questioned within the workshops. Nor were they explored from a wider perspective, such as the young women's possibilities for agency and competence in responding to such challenges. These tensions between the women and men could be turned into explicit starting points for discussing and 'negotiating relevant theory', such as the gender basis of all vocations and its implications for biographical and social reflexivity and agency.

The German researchers suggested that the young females in the project would benefit considerably from a pedagogical approach in which issues like these were turned into a subject for theory-induced arguments, biographical, and social learning. This would not only connect practical experiences and personalized opinions to theoretical debates and insights but moreover, it could increase their imagination and sense of competence for skilful actorship. They could relate participation in this specific community of practice – electricians – to participation in wider communities of practice that would involve men and women working together. The issue of gendered working-identity and questions and their counterparts are all simmering under the surface, ready to be used as springboards for activation that would have meaning for the young people involved. In this way the young females might be better prepared and be in a better position to make personal choices as to whether and how they were to make their entry into the wider community of electricians in Germany.

Situated Learning for Social and Economic Inclusion: The *Cultural Mediators* Project

As explored in some depth in Part I, the objective of this project is the training of cultural mediators. It targets young people aged between 17 and 28 years old who live in a ghetto-like community of migrants from the former Portuguese colony Cape Verde and who have finished at least nine years of education. The vocational training for cultural mediators is meant to enable young adults to mediate professionally between this community, to which they belong, and the wider Portuguese society, as well as at cross-cultural boundaries within the community, such as between teachers and students, parents and children.

We deliberately return to this case study, since it enables us to fold in, at this stage in our book, further considerations of agency and empowerment from the perspectives we are specifically exploring here. The specific nature of this project provided opportunities to balance the development of biographical, social, and instrumental competences more than any other we encountered. It is in this context particularly that we re-visit it in this section.

On the one hand, the participants had the opportunity to apply their learning immediately in concretely located practice. But unlike the *Female Electricians* project, this practice could be undertaken within and on behalf of the community to which participants, on the whole, already belonged. This context strongly facilitated their identification with the project, in that it enabled the participants to relate their experiences directly to questions about who they were, socially and biographically. As Izelda commented:

> *We learn things that are connected with us (Izelda, project participant, Cultural Mediators, Portugal).*

The engagement of the young adults certainly was eased by the fact that the project was situated in and aimed at the benefit of the community they belonged to. It also arose out of needs and problems that were affecting the wider social welfare of the community. It did not result from an imposition of some formula to get the 'socially excluded activated'. At the time of our research, funding was also not stringently tied to externally determined performance indicators, nor to the monitoring of instrumental target achievement.

But these factors in themselves probably would not suffice to give the participants the feeling that they had learned very much more in this school than in others. What seemed to be critical were the organization and the culture of learning that gave rise to the practices they met. The professionals viewed the encounter and the dialogue with their trainees as a process of building a learning community that essentially contributed to the empowerment of the wider community in which it was located. This view was expressed and transferred to the young adults in the practices that were developed in the project. This project can also be seen as taking Wenger's notion of a community of practice into new, hitherto largely under-explored and under-researched domains for social learning with socially excluded young people.

On the one hand, the project placed heavy emphasis on creating a safe, secure, and supportive atmosphere and building relationships of mutual trust between professionals and participants. To re-capture the words of one of the young people:

I use to say that this place is like a family and that is very important (Project participant, Cultural Mediators, Portugal)

The feeling of 'belonging' expressed in a statement like this, was not only promoted by the mutual interactions of the participants, but also by the joint challenges and commitment to learning that occurred daily amongst the participating professionals and between the professionals and young people. The sharing of common objectives, assignments, and 'rituals' was commonplace. This seemed to generate an excitement about collaborating in and sharing the responsibility for an innovative 'joint venture'. The Portuguese researchers observed that the participants clearly felt supported and enriched by their companions, with whom they learned and worked for the same cause.

The professionals also systematically reinforced this feeling of shared responsibility for a common enterprise. They involved the participants in decisions concerning the content and the progress of the project. In this way, the young adults learned to negotiate their views, actions, and preferences in relation to their personal and social objectives. They remained motivated to turn the project into 'their own case'.

This implied that they felt encouraged to speak for themselves and to present openly their questions, doubts, and worries. They also felt able to point to contradictions between professionals' espoused values and how they experienced these in practice. They felt no embarrassment in doing so, because of the sense of equality and 'partnership' they experienced from the side of the professionals. The following statement from Paolo represents the sentiments of many young people on the project:

The teachers let us speak. We don't feel intimidated to ask something Doubts just come out. Besides, we both are part of and contribute to the training sessions (Paolo, project participant, Cultural Mediators, Portugal).

The setting and culture of the *Cultural Mediators* project thus seemed to spark the imagination of the young adults easily and they felt empowered to take their own agency in 'grabbing' possibilities for social and biographical learning from the project. They perceived the project as 'a niche' that gave room to explore who they were and what they could be, in terms of issues of bridging and belonging individually and collectively. In other words, how they could relate where they came from to a meaningful working-identity. Coming to explore the realities and possibilities of several options and scripts for their future, the prospect of becoming a cultural mediator offered a meaningful and promising alternative to dreams that predominated in this community, such as being a famous football player, a musician, a top designer or simply a bus driver. A wider range of alternatives were being jointly constructed and enacted, relating to how they could work with others to interrupt the cycles of poverty and social exclusion that characterized their community.

Remarkably enough, this 'playing' with diverse imaginings of themselves in a wider future, worked in two ways. It seemed to open up new perspectives while simultaneously creating a growing self-confidence. On the one hand, they pictured themselves more in terms of being a social asset than of dreaming about individual 'stardom'. The Portuguese researchers reported:

> *They are keen to imagine themselves going to support others coming from the same background as they themselves do (Researchers, Cultural Mediators, Portugal).*

At the same time, they are helped to gain a deeper understanding of the thoughts and acts of others and to abstain from hasty judgments and conclusions:

> *Sometimes I felt anger when I heard about something and I used to react by saying. 'Hire a bunch of boys and beat them up', but now... We have to think things over; we have to understand the reasons why people act like they do... I believe I am learning very much (Project participant, Cultural Mediators, Portugal).*

The development of instrumental skills and the learning of the practical knowledge needed for their future vocation took place in the real-life setting of the community they lived in, as well as in their project modules. This form of competence development, therefore, easily made sense to them. It provided them both with experiences as to how things worked for real in life 'out there' and made them feel participants in a wider 'community' of socially acknowledged workers.

The very nature of the project aligned them in an 'organic' way to the world of labor. There was nothing formulaic or mechanistic about this project; and yet it did offer a clear structure and concrete ground for learning, that helped these young adults find their own bearings. The targets were internally derived rather than externally imposed. Contrary to other projects that were practice-oriented and founded on 'learning-by-doing' as well, the *Cultural Mediators* project aligned young adults to the real world of labor.

In the Belgian project the *Farmhouse Shop* young women went through a one-year training for the sales and distribution branch. They, however, met problems in sustaining their motivation because they felt their assignments to be artificial and not connected to the real world of sales and distribution. The young women eventually came to call the training 'occupational therapy' and to doubt its significance in the wider world. In this way, in contrast to the Portuguese case, they did not feel equipped sufficiently to face the world of labor that awaited them after the training was completed.

Summarizing, one may conclude that the Portuguese project united the best of the two projects we described before in this chapter. Like the *Female Electricians* project it promoted alignment through engagement and like the *Bridging the Gap* project it provided participants with sufficient opportunities to develop their imagination and biographic competences. Moreover, it succeeded in balancing these different kinds of competences fairly well, without 'economizing' these in instrumental ways. As a result, this project genuinely strengthened young adults in becoming agents of their own lives, committed to the development of their own and others' social and economic empowerment to the benefit of the (labor) communities they were part of.

Over and above developing agency among young adults, this project is also exemplary in terms of structural restraints and pressures. The *Cultural Mediators* project stands apart from even good education, training, employment, and guidance projects, in facing these challenges in various respects.

The first concerns their attention to the social background and position of youngsters involved in programs for social activation and participation. As indicated in the chapter on identities, many young adults in such projects have experienced social exclusion in their own lives and those of their families and communities. They have relatively little social and cultural capital at their disposal. They therefore have little sense of their possibilities as an actor in the wider labor market and a constricted sense of what is possible in terms of their choices for social and economic participation. In the *Cultural Mediators* project, this was reflected in the insecurity and diffidence the participants experienced when confronted with the actual world of labor after training that was limited by funding for only eight months. Despite the intensive preparation during this period and the active fostering of competent actorship in all respects, the Portuguese researchers referred to:

> *a certain immaturity on their part and a perception of the world characterized by a victim perspective, resulting from their past experiences (Researchers, Cultural Mediators, Portugal).*

The young adults in this project were used to looking at themselves as 'victims' of the system and were accustomed to developing 'survival strategies' in coping with issues of how to find a place to live in a society that they experienced as saturated with racism in diverse forms. Now they were being prepared for a role in the labor market where they could act as 'winners' or as actors who would have the self-confidence and knowledge to make things happen in accordance with the ideas and the interests they represented, both to themselves and to others. They were constructing an individual working-identity that was simultaneously collectively and socially situated.

However, activation projects cannot overcome the power relations, structural barriers, prejudices, and pasts that will be embedded in any engagement of these young people with the labor market. When combined with deep seated feelings of being a 'loser' that have been shaped through encounters with schools, social workers, and other authority figures, the professionals can feel it is nigh impossible to close the gap. This metaphor itself becomes delimiting but is integral to the social policy and power discourses that will also influence these projects. The question arises:

- Given this wider social, cultural, and historical context and the realities of a changing labor market, what qualities of actorship and possibilities for wider social and economic participation can be generated within the limited time and resources of a single initiative or training scheme?

• What if projects were empowered and funded to engage and develop from within actual communities, rather than being required to engage with individuals?

• What other kinds of success and evaluation criteria might encourage projects such as this one to take risks and be more creative around ideas of social and economic empowerment?

The professionals often lamented that eight months was just not long enough to help these young adults over the boundary. We are inclined to add that no education, training, employment, and guidance project by itself could solve this challenge, even if the available time were multiplied. If the world outside does not provide opportunities to strengthen the feeling of actorship among these youngsters, what can be achieved through any activation project will always be limited. At the same time, a market for this work was being created, and as Portuguese society becomes more diverse, was potentially sustainable.

The second structural limitation is the actual number of available jobs after finishing training for meaningful participation on the labor market. In this case, as discussed earlier, the 'profession' of an intercultural mediator was created out of a community need and the imagination of alternatives. Although the first group that finished the training did find employment in various schools, extension, and continuity of this vocation could not be guaranteed. The professionals were also working at other levels of society to have this profession not only acknowledged within their own community but also by the world outside. Yet, at the time of the research, the outcome of their efforts was still very uncertain. Since the trainees were very willing and eager to find jobs as mediators, they thus ran the risk of being seriously frustrated when this expectation could not be met; a risk that was even more real as long as their alignment to the world of labor was confined to just this one specific future perspective of becoming a mediator.

At the same time, these young adults were being 'trained' to learn from uncertainty, complexity, and challenge. How might processes of institutionalized racism result in other potential employers denying and discounting the value of their 'activation' learning experiences?

This question leads into a third structural limitation: whether and how participants in this project may be implicitly or explicitly encouraged to conform to dominant White middle-class cultures in order to be successful in school and in life' (Bernstein, 1977, 1986; Solorzano, 2002). As a result of this research, the professionals on the project began to engage more reflexively with this question.

These structural limitations point to the true tragedy of life in late modern society for young unemployed people: the alienating economic, political, and cultural forces that dominate all domains of social life. Having overcome their own unrealistic dreams of meaningful work, they now are faced with the shortcomings of a society that fails to create meaningful work possibilities to which they might belong.

These young adults have shown the creativity and endurance to seek a qualification for work that, without doubt, would add to the quality of life that grows ever more complex and multi-cultural. But they have had to discover that in the age of globalized capitalism, society is not very inclined to promote labor opportunities that do not transform into calculable profits and products. The frustration and resignation that can be evoked by this state of affairs, is another problem that only can be attacked if educational projects are integrated in much more comprehensive, multifaceted policies for social activation and participation, and poverty alleviation.

Conclusion

In this chapter we have opened up tensions and possibilities related to widening young adults' choices for social and economic participation. Taking Wengers' social learning theory, and particularly his concept of belonging within 'communities of practice' as a starting frame of reference, we drew on our case studies to reflect critically on approaches adopted by our researched projects. We considered whether and how projects develop young adults' capacity for more reflexive agency and related to this, some kind of balancing of social, biographical, and instrumental competence development to support economic and social empowerment.

We used Wenger's three dimensions of belonging – alignment, imagination, and engagement – to reflect further on whether and how these concepts may matter, in terms of the espoused aims for activation projects: to decrease unemployment and reduce social exclusion. We glimpsed the value of using participants' experiences of contradictions arising from their own engagement with labor market preparation and participation as starting points for learning. We saw how activation projects functioning as communities of practice with such commitments, can bring the realities of the young adults' lifeworlds and the pressures they confront as potential actors in a labor market, into new forms of relationship. As such, they can open up possibilities for situated learning that can indeed enhance young peoples' capacity for more competent individual and collective actorship. At the same time, we challenged the assumption that activation initiatives alone can make a difference in overcoming social exclusion and unemployment. If anything, these projects are more at risk of exacerbating experiences of social exclusion, if an instrumental approach prevails and is all that is rewarded by those who exert influence from outside the project.

We have found our metaphor of 'balancing competences' to be generative in thinking about these issues. By this we imply firstly that participants are helped to reflect critically and creatively on their personal biography.

- How can they be encouraged to 'play with' different meanings and options for developing knowledge, skills, and practices – in the short- and in the long-term?

- How can the re-presentation of present dreams and the imagining of future options in dialogue with others become valued as valid and important 'labor work'?

Social competence can be understood as the dimension evoked by situating learning in a community of practice whereby the shaping of common goals and mutual taking of responsibilities occurs in a safe atmosphere. At the same time, it takes account of the critical importance of approaching learning through engagement with contradictions that relate directly to young adults' actual lives and experiences of labor market preparation.

By instrumental competence we suggest the development of relevant know-how, skills, and hands-on experience, in working practices that help young people to gain meaning both in their personal lifeworlds and in the wider world of labor.

We suggest that projects that reflexively attend to balancing and interrelating these different dimensions of preparation for more competent actorship can be more effective in creating a sense of possibility and choice for socially excluded young people in relation to the labor market. Such initiatives cannot undo conditions of poverty, social exclusion, and multiple disadvantage. But they may be able to inspire alternative approaches across Europe to understanding possibilities for reducing unemployment and social exclusion within actual communities, and supporting such developments through more innovative policy and project governance initiatives. We return to these issues in Part III.

We have opened up questions about the unintended consequences entailed in approaching competency development as something that can be formulated generically, and approached as a linear 'list' of things to do. We suggest that curricula to support economic and social participation, in way that are to have life and meaning for those involved, cannot be pre-determined externally. We ask these questions:

- At what cost do we detach learning within activation projects from the lifeworlds of the young adults involved or the world of labor? How can it be 're-attached' without falling prey to instrumental rationalities?

- What space and time discourses, metaphors, and practices can support the development of alternative notions of 'activation' that interrelate social, biographical, and instrumental competences to individual and collective agency in social and economic participation?

- How, in not so doing, might we risk further exacerbating socially excluded adults' detachment and alienation and therefore their social exclusion?

Our research leads us to understand better why so many of the projects insufficiently succeeded in achieving such a balance, despite the best of intentions. This is not so much a matter of 'deficits' in the specific target groups with whom they are working, or deficits in the approaches of professionals. Instead, the main tensions may arise from unclear concepts at policy and practice levels about what empowerment and agency might entail in 'activation' projects and what it may mean to create alternative communities of practice that support and work with situated learning processes. We have seen how easily educational projects can turn into 'pseudo-communities of practice', representing a reality of their own, disconnected from (labor) communities in the world 'out there' and thus serving to further disconnect young people. The consequences of such approaches for young people who are already socially excluded deserve closer policy and practice attention.

Furthermore we see more and more education, training, employment, and guidance schemes being transformed into individualized just-in-time, off-the-shelf 'packages' of activation skills, advice, information giving, and knowledge. The competence lists get more and more sanitized and decontextualized. Metaphors for such activity also become increasingly mechanized. We hear talk of 'delivery', 'packaging', and 'targeting' as if interventions with socially excluded and unemployed young people could be neatly reduced to linear, pre-specified, and functional processes with technically definable means to ends, irrespective of who is involved – the young people or the professionals and the different communities they are navigating.

Perhaps projects may aspire to 'produce' competent actorship for (labor) communities of practice only, if they succeed in providing the participants with an environment that catches their personal imagination, promotes their social engagement and aligns their instrumental skills development to wider practices of labor and social participation. However, is such a strategy appropriate for all young unemployed people, including those who have experienced failure at every turn? We suggest that we have to do more than this. These projects have shown us that this is possible, if we can widen the narrowing remit of social policy discourses and governance practices, and invest simultaneously in tackling the structural limitations that sustain poverty and inequality.

- At what cost does the EU pour more and more money into activation as a set of practices governed by particular policies that may increasingly contradict the possibility of persuading, much less empowering young people, to imagine and pursue the potential of their social actorship in relation to demanding social and economic conditions?

In the chapter that follows, we shift the lens onto the professionals involved in such initiatives. We share what we have learned from their experience of the present, shifting, social policy landscape and what light this sheds on our inquiry into tensions and possibilities for activation in Europe.

Chapter 8

Re-vis(ion)ing Professional Practice with Young Unemployed Adults

'Getting Inside' Lifeworlds

This study has shown how getting 'inside' lifeworlds can open up alternative ways for understanding, approaching, and appreciating the challenges and complexities of professional practice in education, training, employment, and guidance projects targeted at young unemployed adults in Europe. Although the scenarios we have offered up thus far are not exhaustive, they provide examples of a broad spectrum of professional interventions encountered in this research. Yet, despite this diversity, common to all interventions in activation projects is the reality of mediating tensions between social and economic participation objectives. Herein lies the core dilemma of professional practice.

Our aim here is not simply to switch the focus from youth to professionals. Instead, we wish to examine the tensions and possibilities in the 'communicative action space' between young people and professionals – a concept to which we shall return later in this chapter. Drawing on empirical data, we shall begin by identifying five dilemmas that we encountered again and again. Each of these relate to the nature of professional practice and the role of the professional working with unemployed youth in changing social and economic circumstances. We shall then inquire into whether and how professional interventions might benefit from 're-writing' the notion of educational professional practice as co-interpretive practice. We shall consider the implications of this reconstruction for opening up new forms of communicative action space between professionals and young adults.

We focus on these dilemmas on the basis of our concerns about mainstream constructions of the adult professional on an 'activation' project strategy (whether referred to as advisor, trainer, teacher, or facilitator). Current policies and practices seem often to assume and reinforce:

- The legitimacy of power imbalances.

- The superiority of professional norms in determining what constitutes effective performance and participation.

- The deficiencies in young unemployed persons, and especially those who are socially excluded.

139

Our research has suggested risks entailed in imposing normative expectations and obligations on young adults without taking into account their specific lifeworlds, biographies, and the impact of social, cultural, and economic forces on their trajectories and identifies. This work has shown how failure to attend to these dimensions can result in missing opportunities to extend their economic and social participation.

We were struck by the extent to which current policy discourses construct the professional role as a simple functionary in a linear process of instruction meant to get a young person out of unemployment into employment. In late modernity, we would expect the role of the professional advisor or educator to involve a far greater diversity of practices. They need to operate at the boundary of policy formation and policy implementation while staying attuned and responsive to young adults who are growing up in a world that may be as bewildering for the professionals also. What is entailed in such a role is not reducible to a list of generic competences – formulated at a distance from the 'swamp' of everyday practice.

In this chapter, therefore, we wish to open up the dilemmas that professionals face in their roles on activation projects. We explore the risks in perpetuating an assumption of, and adherence, at both policy and practice levels, to taken for granted expert roles. We consider other forms of expertise that may be demanded by the circumstances within which professionals now work.

The Unsettled Professional

Throughout this study, we were struck by the extent to which the education, training, employment, and guidance projects professional is experienced by young adults as a dominant influence in their experience of 'activation'. Young adults frequently made reference to professionals, without being prompted to do so. Surprisingly, their perceptions and expectations of what professionals 'should do' in the projects corresponded more or less with how professionals themselves conceived their task. Yet, in practice the 'espoused ideals' for the professional encounter are not always realized. This is because professionals have to mediate between the complex and often contradictory needs young adults present and the demands of social policy and the labor market which strongly frame the intervention.

Against the backdrop of different economic and socio-cultural contexts, organizations and programs, we observed a number of recurring tensions in the projects we studied. Each raises issues about how both professionals and participants experience encounter and intervention, what they might expect from each other, what kind of difficulties they are faced with and how these are addressed in different contexts. Drawing on data from interviews and participant observations with both young adults and professionals, five practice dilemmas capture a great deal of the complexity at play and the patterns that often recurred:

- The dilemma of individual choice and social obligation.

- The dilemma of young adults stopping still and moving on.

- The dilemma of pedagogic care and the constraints of performance.

- The dilemma of mediating structural and biographical complexities.

- The dilemma of competence and deficiency orientations.

Individual Choice and Social Obligation

For many young adults, choosing a career and navigating a way out of unemployment and into the labor market can be a troublesome task. Hopes and aspirations are often diluted by the reality of opportunities open to them and obligations enshrined in the social policy discourses that influence specific projects. For many young adults, the practicalities of engaging in the labor market can also seem a daunting prospect, as a result of a perceived and/or real lack of skills and confidence.

At the same time, as explored in Chapter 6, young adults can be immobilized by indecision and a 'state of not knowing' as to how they might best engage in the labor market. The balance of biographical, social, and instrumental competence seems critical in influencing the capacity for young adults' engagement. The task for the professional may therefore be to hold this balance in a way that empowers and enables the young adult to make informed choices for participation in work or training.

In essence, the task within the encounter space provided by an initiative can be understood as one of negotiating between young peoples' lifeworlds on the one hand, and the social obligations of active labor market participation on the other.

The following comments from an educational professional in Belgium illustrate how this dilemma can be played out in practice:

Sometimes people without children are living on unemployment benefit. They could work if they wanted, but they don't I have problems with that. I do not show it, but I find it difficult that they come here and tell me several times that they want to work. When I give them a job, they don't go. Towards the society I feel responsible to report them at the employment office and tell them that they have to stop the unemployment benefit. On the other hand I find it difficult to do that, because it will bring the people severe problems (Educational professional, Belgium)

The implicit assumptions underlying the use of state-induced sanctions like withdrawing welfare entitlement, are often that unemployed young people can be socially irresponsible, inclined to abhor work and seeking to develop a 'career' on public benefits (Dwyer, 1998; Percy-Smith and Weil, 2002). A young person's passivity can be interpreted by professionals as indifference to their social obligations.

Across the EU, long-term unemployed young adults are becoming constructed as a group unlikely to take up employment or training opportunities by themselves. The direction for policy and practice, therefore, becomes one of motivating them by providing external inducements that will overrule their right to benefit and 'force' them into their social duties. Yet the *limitations* of the fundamental assumption that motivation is 'the problem' are seldom the focus of policy evaluation and monitoring practices.

Young adults in this situation can feel misunderstood in such situations. In turn, they can react against the exercise of such punitive authority. Those who experience multiple problems may feel misjudged or that their needs are not being recognized. They can dismiss what is happening to them as familiar: yet another clash with authority figures that try to assume control over theirs lives, yet another failure seen as 'their fault'.

Decisions can all too easily begin to get taken by professionals on behalf of young adults to ensure conformity to the social policy imperatives that shape the project. Paradoxically, for many professionals, this may be preferable to a more open dialogue and the complex issues that are likely to emerge. Alternative forms of engagement may only surface the wider problems young adults are facing, leaving professionals working within an ever-narrowing educational remit and feeling disempowered themselves.

Inherent in many education, training, employment, and guidance projects therefore, is a distinct tension between individual choice and social obligations. In many situations, this becomes treated as if it were a dichotomy, rather than a dilemma to which there are no easy solutions. Seeing alternatives to this dichotomy, such as approaching identity, community, meaning, and practice – or biographical, social, and instrumental competency development – as core and fundamentally interrelated, as suggested in the previous chapter, seems outside the frame of dominant practice. Those professionals, who try to work with these tensions differently, can see themselves as very much working against institutionalized norms.

On the one hand, increasingly in 'activation policy' the promotion of employability is seen as requiring individual commitment, a client-centered approach and the building of trust between professionals and participants. In this respect the espoused objective seems to be the empowerment of young adults as active citizens. On the other hand, professionals are expected to be key social actors in enhancing labor market participation and reducing unemployment figures. They can therefore feel compelled to overrule the freedom of choice and right to self-determination of young unemployed people when they do not comply with expectations and prescriptions that are made integral to many activation initiatives. Moreover, failure to comply carries consequences. Project funding is becoming more and more dependent upon success in achieving clear project 'outputs' from specified inputs. This language, and the assumptions embedded within it, has little meaning when working 'in the messy swamp of practice'!

What happens is that young people can feel that they are losing control and the right to self-determination. Interventions may appear only to be concerned with disciplining them into the duties and demands of labor market participation. Moreover, this becomes defined in very restricted ways.

We encountered this tension in projects across all six countries in this study. In each case, professionals are caught in the dilemma of how to empower young unemployed people in ways that acknowledge their lifeworlds and economic participation as a social learning process, whilst simultaneously complying with the disciplining imperatives of labor market policies. Further, we found many professionals to be driven by moral obligations of welfare and justice. In many cases, these were integral to their personal justification for working with young people who were at risk of social exclusion. At the same time, they were subject to strong political influences that required them to punish young people for transgressing the prescriptions and obligations that were 'written into' a project – or they too would be punished.

No wonder that many of them felt trapped by these often contradicting sets of appeals. How could they earn and maintain the confidence of the young unemployed, if they were simultaneously required to act as representatives of a disciplining regime?

Stopping Still and Moving on

Many of the young people we encountered had lives that were characterized by emotional disturbance, low self worth, and social disorientation resulting from neglect, social stigmatization, a lack of security, and little identification with 'mainstream' social markers. Many of the young people we encountered could be seen as being 'not work ready'.

Take Bob for example, an apparent 'gentle giant' carrying the burden of a lost childhood – in and out of care homes, a mother that couldn't cope, a father he did not get on with, an unsuccessful school career, low self-esteem, and a life of emotional turmoil – and at the time of our study, homelessness too. Whilst Bob had many skills and aptitudes, he had a problem engaging with 'life out there' – outside the project. In this situation, coaching Bob into the hard realities of labor market participation and the threatening loss of benefit would not give rise to any sustainable solution to the social exclusion that characterized his life. Nor would it help him in getting or keeping a job. Instead, in cases such as this, a period of non–engagement may be more productive. This can help the young person focus on what is required to bring about stability and build up their own capacity for social and economic participation.

This poses a dilemma for professionals in knowing how far they should honor the young person's need to stop still and when they should support the young person in moving on, as illustrated in the previous chapter with the *Bridging the Gap* and *Cultural Mediators* projects. Most professionals are well aware that this specific group of young people-at-risk are in need of specific care and attention, and that many of them simply are not ready (yet) for clear cut choices and for adapting to the disciplining impact of the world of work. This tension is also expressed in the stories of professionals in the Dutch project *Right Match*. They are strongly committed to the well-being of the youngsters they work with and understand their biographies as a struggle to achieve some stability in their lives:

> *These kids need a lot of care and attention and need to be approached positively.. You shouldn't exert too much pressure; after all they have plenty on their minds (Wendy, project professional, Right Match, Netherlands).*

Therefore, providing a safe, secure, and supportive environment may enable them to take some 'respite' from their plight, sort themselves out and achieve some stability. This might be more important than sending them along the shortest track to the labor market:

> *We should realize that we already demand much of these students, some probably are better off if we don't immediately send them to work (Wendy, project professional, Right Match, Netherlands)*

Time spent on such a 'respite from daily life' is referred to by Edwards (1999) as 'soft time', 'being time', in other words, a creative time for personal regeneration, 'living without goals or purpose'. She contrasts this with 'hard time', during which the individual is 'driven by duties, goals, obligations, and tasks'. Enjoying soft time, individuals are temporarily freed from the demands of the world outside and enabled to focus on building up confidence, 'chilling out', taking stock, regenerating, staying still, and reflecting.

For a considerable number of the participants in the projects we visited, this seemed to be exactly what they needed to get even close to being able to deal with issues of labor market opportunities at all. In contrast, in the eyes of policy makers and the inherent formal project objectives and evaluation criteria, hard time was what activation was about – whether a program was called education, training, work experience or guidance and counseling. Participants were meant to be challenged to take action and make decisions concerning their access to the labor market. They had to stay busy enhancing their qualifications, getting experience and learning to accept rules, boundaries and the obligations of citizenship – even I it felt, as in Denmark, that they were busy doing nothing.

Soft time seems to be the privilege of 'better off' young people who are expected by their parents to have a 'gap year' as a right (such as between school and university). Time off, time at home, time to travel are often perceived as central, not peripheral to becoming 'ready' to take on the obligations of the labor market. But with long term unemployed youth, soft time in current ideological environments can be seen as skiving and getting away with something to which they have no right.

The dilemma of finding an appropriate balance between hard time and young peoples' need for soft time was a major preoccupation for professionals in all projects and countries we researched. They were alert to the contradictions and differences between the stance they might take as *in loco parentis* and that which they were meant to assume as an 'activation professional'. There was little space to consider alternative roles between these two poles.

A common anxiety was also focused on the risks of tipping the scale too far toward soft time. What if this only creates and reinforces feelings of dependency in the participants? Their staying captive within the protective shell of the project, without actually moving on and finding themselves a meaningful place in the world 'out there' thus becomes perceived as both a dilemma and a risk. Professionals in projects like *Right Match* are well aware of the danger that a one-sided focus on creating a pleasant atmosphere and on minimal rules and demands, might have in reducing young peoples' willingness to deal with unknown and uncomfortable challenges. Although there is acknowledgment of the need these young people still have to 'mess about':

They are still very young and should be able to horse around a little (Wendy, project professional, Right Match, Netherlands).

Yet, they are also approached as adults who should take responsibility for their own choices. Interestingly, participants at the other end of the employment ladder, senior managers at *Shell* are being taught to 'play' with possibilities for choice and 'action arising from' and to learn from a wide range of scenarios. This process of experimentation and improvisation is seen to be integral to developing effectiveness for planning in an uncertain globalizing market (De Geus, 1997).

From an 'activation' perspective, the 'point' of the policies and ideologies that guide such initiatives is to empower these young adults to gain access to the labor market. But:

- How can protecting them from the frustrations, tensions, and boundaries of different realities – as it can be seen – help them to find their bearings in dealing with the 'real' world and its demands?

- How can their being expected to be merely instrumental and goal focused build their capacity for navigating multiple worlds, without going under?

Most of the professionals we encountered did indeed feel pressured to build in hard time to their projects and to maintain a clear focus on achieving qualifications and developing attitudes for participating in labor communities. Hard time involves stimulating participants not to eschew disappointments or obstructions, but to deal with them in a 'positive' goal oriented way. As mentioned in the chapter on working-identities in (com)motion, this may also involve professionals in challenging young people's perceptions of what is realistic and unrealistic with respect to their participation in the labor market.

But projects such as the *Cultural Mediators* project in Portugal urge us to question these professional stances as givens, and to open them up to deeper scrutiny and challenge. Genuinely respecting young adults and taking them seriously is not at odds with being honest with them and holding out no false hopes and exploring realistic prospects. Like one of the professionals in *Right Match* stated:

I usually draw a 'ladder'. I make them clear that the top is only gradually reached. It's still a long way to go (Project professional, Right Match, Netherlands).

Yet also, who decides what is 'top'. What of young adults like Stefan from Chapter 1 who leave university and enter corporate worlds, but who soon decide to downshift into different lifestyles before they are downsized or devoured by corporate demands? How many middle class children shock their parents with their determination to do something that seems anything but realistic – and yet succeed in the labor market in their own time and on their own terms? Tipping the scale too far toward hard time can shift the professional into an authoritarian role and knock the interaction into a strictly 'parent-child interaction'. Rebellion rather than empowerment can all too easily ensue.

Need hard time be merely about disciplining participants and ignoring their own capabilities and wants? Or can professionals interrupt the operation of these dualisms within which they and the young people are equally entrapped? How else can challenge and boundary setting occur, whilst simultaneously maintaining an 'adult–adult relationship'?

Being respected and involved in the process of decision-making is of vital importance to these young adults. When professionals achieved this, in ways that did not require them to abandon their own expertise, but to feel free to use it differently, we often saw relationships that flourished. We witnessed young adults shifting into new stances, both with the adult professionals and the labor market. Such experiences helped them to experience and imagine alternatives to the often negative experiences they had had in the past too often. This meant school teachers, employment advisers or employers looking down upon them and treating them in ways that made them feel as if all unemployed young people are unwilling, incompetent or trying to get an easy deal.

Across the EU, young adults (and not only those who are unemployed) hate to be treated like school kids or students. Many demand that professionals see them as adults with their own experiences and agendas, and as capable of making their own decision. As a young woman in the Belgian project *Farmhouse Shop* remarked:

> *They have to value you like you are, not because you have a lower degree in school, because you did not attend the university. We have the same rights as people with a qualification They have always excuses, like about me being slower Maybe I am slower in thinking, but not with my hands (participant, Farmhouse Shop, Belgium).*

Pedagogic Care and the Constraints of Performance

Beyond the challenges of mediating between the different needs of young unemployed adults and social policy imperatives, professionals experience considerable constraints in what is realistically achievable:

> *One tries to find a balance between what we can do and what we are aiming to do, but this balance causes a little frustration which is in danger of becoming a big frustration, so one tries to do things with professional dignity and with a pedagogical sense (Teacher, Cultural Mediators, Portugal)*

This quote surfaced a third dilemma that we found many professionals having to cope with in their practice – that of the gap between their pedagogical concerns on the one hand, and the reality of being confronted with young people who they perceived as being deeply de-motivated and suspicious with respect to the projects in which they were jointly engaged, on the other hand. The majority of the professionals we encountered genuinely tried to respect the young adults they met, to raise their motivation and self–confidence and to help them get involved in 'appropriate' programs for training and intervention. Yet, in many cases professionals too become despondent when they confronted the ambivalences, cynicism and chaos of the participants in their charge. The time, energy, and good-will professionals invested in these young adults were often repaid with indifference, resignation or unreliability. The efforts professionals took to discuss and counsel about the young people's options were often met with a bluntly expressed demand for a job that brought money or meaning. This recurrent tension between their pedagogical ambitions and the limitations they faced in the reality of daily practice, and the jobs that were actually available to project participants, was, for quite a number of professionals, as frustrating and demoralizing as the structural restraints and the organizational pressures they experienced.

The reaction of Martin, from whom we first heard in Chapter 3, exemplifies the attitude of a number of the young unemployed people we encountered, where project participation was low, and where professionals were unable to overcome feelings of ambivalence and indifference:

Martin: *Well, the first week it was ok, fun, but afterwards* [makes a snoring sound]... *Sleeping! Do not bother!*
Researcher: *What did you think about when you woke up this morning?*
Martin: *That I did not bother* [laughs].

In this particular project, *House of Projects*, participants and professionals alike expressed dissatisfaction with the lack of activity and the very low attendance, which led to each day being unpredictable, since nothing could be planned. The professionals felt deeply frustrated by the distant and indifferent response of the young adults to this situation. Neither party succeeded in transforming this mutual frustration into a more inspiring and productive educational experience. The despair this evoked in the professionals was expressed by one of them in the sigh:

I do not care whether it is frustration or aggression, just as long as they engage themselves!! (Project professional, House of Keys, Denmark).

The tensions professionals experienced in working with lowly skilled and lowly motivated young adults, sometimes made them give up illusions of being able to help the so called 'very weak' or 'hard-to-help' ones. They could lose all confidence and switch to the opinion that, whatever pedagogical intentions and methods are brought into play, these youngsters just would not come any further. They assumed that they just were not going to open up for contact and support – this being sometimes the very least they felt empowered to offer. The tendency was then for the professionals to begin paying less attention to these youngsters and to concentrate more on those who were more compliant and willing to be responsive to support and advice. Yet, those who they 'excluded' from their attention and energy were the ones least able to find their way to the labor market without support. Professionals therefore became complicit in reproducing the very conditions that were integral to these young adults' social exclusion.

Feelings of disempowerment among professionals were further provoked by organizational and structural pressures and constraints. At the organizational level, they had to deal with pressures to comply with formulaically presented pedagogical and didactical approaches, increased bureaucratic monitoring, and evaluation, and limited material facilities, support and service systems. Each one of these pressures alone might have given rise to frustrated pedagogical ambitions. When they came on top of working in a project that was difficult to experience as any kind of 'community of practice', professionals could feel caught in fragmented and often contradictory set of relations between different factions: too often, 'piggy in the middle' and seldom an 'eye in the storm'. Many would resort to protecting their own agendas and interests and, as a result, these blockages drained all energy and hope from the situation. In such contexts, pedagogical ideals appeared to be perishing in the often bureaucratic and competitive 'warfare' between different stakeholders in and across different projects. Moreover, all different local projects were competing for the same limited funding. The result was a confrontational system rife with tensions. In such a context, the scope for building social and economic capital is also being fragmented and undermined. This choice is in fact disappearing from view, as discourses for activation become more and more individualized.

The frustration of a professional in the Dutch project *Right Match* about the lack of a shared pedagogical vision is representative of professionals in projects in other countries:

> *In general the pedagogical idea behind Right Match should become clearer for all . I think the instructors should receive more pedagogical support They, after all, do see the students on a regular basis and monitor their behavior and attitude (Project professional, Right Match, Netherlands)*

Another source of frustrated pedagogical ambitions was the structural situation on the labor market. Professionals were well aware that the competence of the young people they worked with in many cases would still be relatively low after finishing the project. This tension was felt more acutely in projects that were short-term and have youngsters-at-risk as their target group – a trend that was starkly apparent to us during this research. All their professional efforts and ambitions seem to no avail, since all that happened was to support access to poorly paid and pretty boring jobs, with little chances for promotion and further self-expression. And sadly, the young adults only choice is to begin yet another 'activation project'.

In such a context, the black economy could have compelling appear. Here, young people could see the risks of generating money and power in a very short time, as less onerous than the demands they had to face in an activation project. . This 'reality', well understood by all participants, confronted many professionals with a sense that their pedagogical interventions hardly 'made a difference'. They could feel that they just could not compete with the choices these young adults were being confronted with on the streets. They knew that without the kind of systemic and policy learning and change that might support them in alternative ways, the tensions between young people's lifeworlds and the reality of the labor market would only increase.

Mediating Structural and Biographical Complexities

For many of the young unemployed, their experiences in an activation project were strongly influenced by a biographical background that is perhaps best characterized in terms of multiple disadvantage. In addition to facing unemployment, they were simultaneously struggling with serious personal and social problems, due to (a mix of) various social and economic circumstances. These significantly influenced the levels of energy, commitment, and skill they might bring to any project meant to help them discover alternatives for economic and social participation.

Among the young unemployed we met during this research, the following problematic experiences and situations were mentioned regularly:

- Peer group influences that gave rise to abuse of drugs and alcohol and/or to involvement in criminal activities.

- Broken families/problematic relationships with (step-)parents.

- Poor upbringing.

- Single motherhood.

- Mental and/or physical handicaps.

- Bereavement of a meaningful adult.

- Negative and/or fragmented school records.

- Ethnic-, gender-, race-, or class-induced discrimination and deprivation.

- Emotional turmoil.

- Low self-esteem.

Brussels may speak of overcoming social exclusion and economic disadvantage through education, training, employment, and guidance initiatives. However, just one story amongst many – in this case, that of a young woman, Lisa, in the English *Bridging the Gap* project – gave us a glimpse of some of the complexity with which young people and professionals are jointly struggling:

> *My dad went to the pub one night, spent all his money and he came back and decided that he didn't want me anymore so he leathered me and threw me out. I had had an argument with my ex–boyfriend because he had dumped me for my sister I started arguing with my dad again and he just started on me again so I walked out. He had been beating me up since I was about one so, I have been in and out of my dad's home for the last year or so. I moved out when I was fifteen and I went back home on my sixteenth birthday and I moved out again a week before my seventeenth. I was staying in Towcester for a couple of months, then up to another supported accommodation*

center in town, but I got picked on   I was only there three weeks (Lisa, project participant, Bridging the Gap, England)

But how might this notion of 'multiple disadvantage' become a construction that itself begins to limit young people's opportunities to engage with the 'outside world' in different ways? Before we rush to label or presume, we need to recall alternatives. For example, the young people in Portugal are labeled by a wider system as ethnic minorities. This can soon escalate to authorities further labeling them as socially excluded and unemployable. Yet, in the *Cultural Mediators* project, these young adults were being treated quite differently from the young people in Denmark, who had been written off as 'hardcore' unemployable – with radically different effects.

Young adults' 'starting points' for engagement in a project both influence and can be influenced by attention to biographical, social, and instrumental competences. Yet, professionals have to mediate what it means to balance attention to young people in ways that feel meaningful in terms of their disadvantage and trajectory, with attention to structural complexities, restraints, and possibilities. Yet, recent changes in the labor market have created specific requirements that cannot be ignored in professional practices for activating the unemployed.

A striking trend is the increased demand for 'flexibilization', understood as the willingness and ability to permanently shift jobs, functions, places, and time-schedules in accordance with the demands of labor organizations. At the same time flexibilization implies requirements for new qualifications that raise individual's economic and cultural capital. The demand for flexibility also implies a rearranging of time and space that opens up new perspectives on the life course (Jessop et al., 1997). We are being socialized into perceiving that temporary and part-time employment are offering the opportunity to alternate between periods of work and non-work and to connect personal agendas (such as the desire to travel, or the want of leisure time for family life) to options on the labor market. Yet, the hidden curriculum is that of accepting permanent instability in one's working life.

However, as explored previously, many of the lowly qualified young adults, are severely disoriented with respect to the development of working-identities. They are often dependent on unemployment and other social benefits. Temporary work to them mainly means fast income and a material base that helps sort out problems in the short term. It is an enticement neither for self-expression, nor for sustained livelihood. As mentioned by Jans in the Belgian project *FlexiJob*:

> *With temporary jobs, they always send me to different places and in the end I don't know any more what I am doing That is the problem. Everything in my life is mixed up. I can do a lot of things, but everything is mixed up (Jans, project participant, FlexiJob, Belgium)*

Labor market and employment policies significantly influence the action space in many activation programs. Professionals are increasingly being urged to orient many of 'their' young unemployed to 'flexijobs' – short-term and temporary vacancies. They are encouraged to accept 'bottleneck jobs' in sectors where there is a need for unskilled or very lowly qualified workers. When the impositions of performance indicators include clear outputs, these are the only choices for professionals if they are to continue to receive funding for 'delivering' a project. These are what are available to promise a successful 'output' in the terms that are taken as given. The pressure to choose this road to 'success' is even heavier, as it can be perfectly justified in view of their formal obligation to help young adults off benefits and into work, and to make them adapt to the rules and demands of the labor market. If young adults refuse or quit the jobs that are offered, this may endanger their benefits. Moreover, they can internalize the perception of themselves as irresponsible and non-cooperative in finding employment. This can lead to a conscious choice to opt out of any form of mainstream social and economic participation altogether.

So while young adults are saturated in a market-oriented society that celebrates the ethos of individualization and the discourse of free choices, their choices are minimal. 'Economic participation' facing such young people and professionals comes to signify poorly paid, unskilled, and leftover jobs that others who have the possibility of 'real choice' (however illusory this may be) do not want. This vicious cycle can leave professionals feeling complicit in reinforcing an attitude of dependency and indifference, rather than promoting feelings of agency and empowerment.

Rudd and Evans (1998) speak of needs for 'structured individualization', with which we concur, but the tensions at the boundary between the activation project and the labor market can make all involved feel as if they are keeping busy going nowhere. For both groups, this can feel like an irresolvable dilemma, to which escape can seem the only 'real' chance to exert one's sense of agency.

Competence and Deficiency Orientations

Youth has traditionally been regarded as a transitional stage in between childhood and adulthood, in which the young person has to finish his/her studies, find a job and secure an income to support independent living (Bell and Jones, 1999). Until these transitional tasks are accomplished, the young person stays dependent on parents and/or other adults.

Today, these definitions do not seem to suffice anymore for characterizing the stage in the life course called youth. On the one hand, an increasing amount of young people are prolonging their studies until they are well past twenty, staying longer with their parents and postponing their entry on the labor market. At the same time they spend a great deal of their time with peers, seeking to express their own preferences for particular lifestyles (Miles 2000). Short-term employment and weekend jobs may allow them a considerable amount of financial independence and a relatively high level of consumption. They may enter into relationships that vary in duration, with or without children, as the idea of a stable family life becomes increasingly de-stabilized.

New notions of young adulthood are being constructed, such as 'post–adolescence' or 'extended adolescence' (Klein, 1990). Notions like these signify that those young people are sexually, psychically, juridically, and politically defined as 'grown-ups'. However, they have not yet made the transition to a labor career and a stable family life (Ter Bogt and Meus, 1997). Coinciding with these changes, the transition of youth to adulthood has become increasingly more individualized and de-standardized, in the same ways that working-identities are being de-stabilized and re-constructed as hybrid and complex forms. Young people may be firmly inscribed in the discourse of having the opportunity to be the 'author' of their personal lifestyle and life course. However, they are also regarded as being personally responsible for the failures and successes that result from the choices they make (Buchner, 1990; Giddens, 1991; Beck, 1992; du Bois–Reymond, 1995; Furlong and Cartmel, 1997).

This 'new normative' view of an 'extended adolescence' has given rise to shifting notions of their rights and competencies for participating in affairs and issues that have a direct impact on their choices and activities. In general, traditionally adolescents were seen as yet too immature or deficient to be involved in discussions and decisions that touched upon their own future. The young adults of today are more often conceived as competent actors and authors of their own lives, 'active citizens' who, to a large extent, are entitled to autonomous decisions, opinions and preferences. The social policy rhetoric speaks of them as 'essentially equals' who may need support to realize their potential, but who are sufficiently accountable and capable of serious discussion and deliberation as to their opinions and wants about desired outcomes.

This changed social construction of young adults, is another structural pressure that influences the action space of professionals and participants. They cannot hide from the expectations and demands that originate in this general notion of 'extended adolescence'. The young adults in the researched projects experience themselves as sufficiently mature and independent to expect a serious and respectful approach by the professionals. We also encountered professionals who worked to mediate the power imbalances and to ascribe to the participants sufficient discernment and responsibility and to expect an engaged and dutiful attitude towards the program.

However, professionals struggle with the extent to which connotations of 'competent extended adolescence' can apply to young adults who have experienced many years of economic, social, and educational disadvantage and hardship. This notion seems to apply to young adults with relatively high standards of education, who have had possibilities to experiment with time, money, jobs, and so on. These are the kind of young adults who might be these professionals' own children.

What is at issue for us here is not so much the debate about extended youth, but rather the emphasis of new discourses of childhood and youth that construct young people as active agents: who have a 'right to say' and participate in decisions that affect them. This is reflected in many policy imperatives now, and in the UK, all government childhood and/or youth programs stipulate that young people should be participating in the design and implementation of service delivery.

What is crucial here is how these discourses influence the perceptions and choices of professionals. Do they see and treat young adults as passive incompetents in need of socialization or as competent actors?

Of course, young adults who leave school early in many cases are immediately facing all the problems of adult life – like finding housing and money to survive, struggling with the governance of bureaucratic and other authorities, facing pressures to become involved in drug and crime cultures. They are often the most vulnerable and disoriented in life, having to deal with complex personal and social problems, apart from being unemployed. They are all too easily experienced as deficient, and fundamentally lacking, rather than competent and in transition.

The structural barriers that urge them into poorly paid, unskilled, and temporary jobs – or an ongoing experience of activation projects – can reinforce positions of dependency and indifference, rather than promote a sense of empowerment and agency. The dilemma confronting professionals is that, guided by dominant notions of youth participation and perhaps values of equal treatment (for instance, what if this were my son or daughter?) they feel that they should approach the participants from a competency-oriented perspective. They seek to respect them as individuals with unique biographies and potential that is waiting to be realized. However, the realities of their encounter with young adults' and their performances of resistance can easily lead to them being judged as deficient and irresponsible rather than competent expressive social actors. Such a judgment, in its turn, perpetuates relationships that reinforce power imbalances and normative imperatives for behavior that further a culture of deficiency orientation. These young adults, in a clearly targeted EU category of 18-25, begin to be treated as immature, as if they were under-aged and first need to learn discipline before their participation in discussions and decisions that are related to their own learning and future options can be 'allowed'. Perhaps one or two individuals stand out and are successful as a result of their more appreciative demeanor in attracting the energies of the professionals. As a result, yet again, the cycle of social exclusion for the remaining young people is reproduced and individual culpability for failure reinforced.

The action space of projects is seriously influenced by the everyday enactment of this wider tension. Obviously a number of professionals can become frustrated and disillusioned to the extent that they give up hope of motivating certain of these young unemployed people to take responsibility for their own lives. They may content themselves with applying the formal rules, prescriptions, and options that are inherent to a project and 'given' from above and beyond. Complying with the formal objectives and the required outcomes of a program, and blaming these for the limitations on what is possible can lead to them not to bother much about the lowly skilled and poorly paid routine jobs that appear the only future option for these participants.

Other professionals, on the contrary, try to stick to their image of working with potentially competent and responsible young adults. They are the ones who do accept and respect even the 'weakest' youngsters they encounter, trying to build up relations of mutual trust and to use the very stuff of everyday life as the indispensable basis for learning how to engage in mutual meaning making and action taking. They try to take seriously the need to involve participants in deliberations and decisions concerning their future options, however meager, and the possibilities they can *jointly* construct for the activation project in that context. The action space of a project in their view should be employed and widened in order to include whatever opportunities emerge for young adults to explore and develop their inherent potential for active participation and commitment, both in this program and in future (labor) communities. To them the discourse of 'competent extended youth' should not be reserved for 'privileged' youngsters, but be used as an incentive for the promotion of agency with the disadvantaged ones as well.

The following excerpt captures something of the flavor of this dilemma that professionals and young people jointly face. Nine participants on the *Bridging the Gap* project went off to a residential week in Wales: a project that did not involve their staff. On their return one of the lads recounted his experiences:

> *It was crap for the first two days because they treated us like 12 year olds. But the last three days I didn't want to come home... Going away brought out team spirit – how to help people – it was what the week was about. We did a challenge wall – 16 planks high! Obviously I couldn't get over but I managed to help others over. It was about real life stuff It's difficult to say what it was exactly it is just about doing it. Caving was wet and cold but brilliant and the zip wire in the dark was amazing It challenges you and builds you up as a person and you get a certificate at the end of it... It changes something inside .boosts your self-esteem ..achieve goals you didn't think were possible If it wasn't for the residential I would still be like I used to be. .lazy and not giving a fuck .but now I feel I've sorted my life out a bit, it brought out something in me (Jason, project participant, Bridging the Gap, England).*

For these young homeless people, the familiar routine of their life was challenged. Meeting new experiences and activities through teamwork unleashed a new sense of self-esteem in the mutual respect and responsibility with their peers. They had fun in solving unknown problems and mastering new skills during the process. Yet, at the same time the clearly structured program met their need for security and certainty.

So, is this 'hard time' or 'soft time'? Or does this story suggest the inadequacy of this dichotomy into which so many are squeezed? This example suggests how organizing the action space in activation projects in a way that gives pleasure and a sense of meaning to the participants, has nothing to do with an unjust 'fun reward' to problematic youth, the familiar sneer of public opinion. Rather, it can be the indispensable condition to empower these youngsters in making small but significant steps that widen their repertoire of choice and action for meaningful social and economic participation.

Opening up 'Action Space'

Tensions and Possibilities in the Meeting of Structures and Biographies

In almost all instances the action space for practices of education, training, employment, and guidance is strongly dependent on national policies for bringing young unemployed people to the labor market. There were clear differences between the six countries that were involved in this research. However, all were having to cope with the European trend towards demanding more and more calculable 'output', more invasive bureaucratic monitoring and evaluation of performance, alongside reduced funding that limited personnel, material, and time resources. On top of this, clear prescriptions about sanctioning participants who failed to meet their obligations were becoming more and more common, despite the supposed emphasis on more advice, personalized guidance, and 'choice'. Consequently, these wider discourses and prevailing cultures of governance easily urged professionals to standardize procedures and collude in the game of 'measuring the immeasurable'. They seem often to acquiesce to the time pressures, lack of resources, strict prescriptions, and compulsory attendance requirements.

It can seem easier to adopt a practice that deals with young adults as a homogeneous group and act 'as if' they can be handled in a fairly similar way, applying similar objectives and standards. Such an organization of the action space appears to justify disjunctions experienced between biographical and social needs, and instrumental demands for successful activation. They can more easily rationalize that the young adults seem to need security, stability, and a clear structure in their activities. The prevailing assumption is that this will help them to overcome the chaos and disorientation of their daily lives. But this choice of response to the external environment can serve the function of seeming to protect professionals from the overwhelming anxiety of 'losing control', feeling undervalued, and losing hope. Adhering to well-fixed standards, rules, goals, and methods becomes a surrogate form of taking control and exerting agency. Again, we find the pitfall in the polarity.

When you are in up close, it can seem to be a generative strategy. But as became apparent in our research, when viewed from other perspectives, this restricted course of action can seem anything but, in terms of wider policy goals, to reduce social exclusion and empower young people into social and economic participation. What was quite disturbing to us was the extent to which many of the professionals seemed to rely on some form of 'coercive' strategy to keep these young adults aboard of a project. Perhaps this is unsurprising given the constraints of the systems within which they work. But we wonder what changes to systems and programs in organizations are needed to support professionals working in more creative and less constricting ways?

The exceptions in which the action space could interrupt the constraints were those projects where there was a clear collective commitment to creating a culture of empowerment that built on whatever strengths and opportunities presented themselves. But to enact this espoused aim in everyday practice required ongoing reflexive learning from everyday experience and new forms of dialogue and co-inquiry between professionals and young people (Percy-Smith and Weil, 2003). It required freedom to operate at, across and outside boundaries, and to follow and strengthen the threads of possibility for new forms of economic and social empowerment as they emerged and were jointly constructed.

Coercion was not a major issue in projects where there were genuine attempts to balance competency development and interrelate processes of meaning making, identity formation, social learning, and practice learning. Processes of setting boundaries, learning from the creative and difficult tensions in doing this, and working with contradictions and emotions were integral to the culture. In the case of the *Bridging the Gap* and the Portuguese *Cultural Mediators* project. Wenger's 'community of practice' idea seems to have been given life beyond that which he envisaged, based on his own research in work circumstances that were far away from those being experienced here. What was also apparent was how difficult it was for individual professionals within a more coercive and restricted *modus operandi* to shift less willing colleagues in a different direction. The justification of an alternative form of action space for activation needs to reside in the wider culture and systems if alternative communities of practice are to be encouraged.

Communicative Action Space

What we are opening up here are questions about the extent to which the creation of alternative action spaces is possible. Here we wish to draw on the concept of the 'communicative action space' (Kemmis, 2001). We quote at length here, since this passage brings together a number of ideas that have been implicitly and explicitly present and explored in this book until this point. Kemmis, working from the ideas of Habermas, uses the term communicative action space to signal a particular quality of reflection and discussion that comes through interrupting:

> *what we are doing (generally a technical or practical action) to explore its nature, dynamics and worth.. The theory of communicative action includes a substantive theory (the theory of system and lifeworld) which offers a new way of construing many of the problems...which arise for participants in a setting when the personal, social and cultural processes that sustain the setting as a lifeworld collide with processes which characterize the setting as a system (the means-ends functionality of systems oriented to outcomes or* success) (Kemmis, 2001, pp. 97-98).

Kemmis' work in educational settings over many years has evolved from his conviction that, despite challenges from postmodernists and poststructuralists, Habermas' theory of system and lifeworld still provides a valid framework to consider changes in education, in that it offers a way of understanding participants' perspectives as structured by the contrasting, sometimes competing, imperatives of social systems and the lifeworlds participants inhabit. As a co-researcher with others one could, on the one hand, explore with participants how they were engaged in three kinds of lifeworld processes in the settings they daily constitute and reconstitute through their practice:

- The process of individuation-socialization (by which practitioners' own identities and capacities are formed and developed).

- The process of social integration (by which legitimately ordered social relations among people as co-participants are formed and developed).

- The process of cultural reproduction and transformation (by which shared cultures and discourses are formed and developed) (Kemmis, 2001).

Alongside this exploration, one could also investigate how practices in the setting enmeshed participants in systems functioning – the exchanges and transformations taking place to yield outcomes of interest to those involved, to the systems of which they are part, and to the wider environment beyond. In his recent work, Kemmis re-constructs these ideas with a view to critical action research, whereby we can explore interconnections and tensions between system and life worlds as they are lived out in practice.

Within the limitations and possibilities offered by our research design, this is in essence what we have tried to do. Practice choices are inevitably influenced by the interpretations and sense of agency professionals bring and discover (or not) in the face of the structural restrictions and opportunities they face. We have revealed in this research some of the relational and practice choices they make, and the extent to which these choices succeed in reconciling their own biographical and pedagogical orientations with the biographical needs, desires, and expressions of the participants. But our exploration of the metaphor of the 'action space' provides us with a different point of departure for considering ways of stretching professionals' conceptions of what is possible in the thick of it.

In other words:

- What further repertoires for generating mutual insight may not seem immediately apparent?

- How might engaging in collaborative inquiry (such as around tensions and contradictions as lived out in the context) generate possibilities for collaborative action and learning alongside project participants and reveal alternatives for choice and action?

- What other 'ways of being in relation' are available to us in such circumstances?

All structures offer both opportunities and constraints, and the chance to author alternative biographical and social stories – to the detriment or betterment of those involved. These notions themselves are contestable. We believe that these tensions are worthy of further exploration and need not be equated by critics with falling into a false romance with technologies of education.

On Re-creating Action Space

We see professional practice as not only a matter of working within but also of working on a given action space. Moreover, remaining co-inquiring in relation to what emerges through interactions within one's environment, itself offers opportunities to glimpse and co-create with others new 'action spaces' for social learning.

Such ideas sit uneasily with technical–rational, means–ends understandings of activation and require the adoption of different ways of being, seeing and knowing that reside in the fluid space that opens up between holding an intention lightly (such as to work with young people as competent actors) and learning from emergent processes in specific contexts and conditions of practice. This approach can open up possibilities that reside in the very contradictions and paradoxes that are revealed through the dynamic intersections of professionals and participants' lifeworlds and the system in everyday practice.

The notion of 'action space' is also related to the structuration theory of Giddens (1979). This starts from the assumption that professionals and young unemployed are not determined by the structures that delimit their practices. As actors they actively (re)produce the structural context in which their meeting takes place. Therefore they are involved in the permanent (re)creation of the conditions of their encounter, not just as passive performers on a pre-given stage. This requires the courage to remain critically reflexive about the practices and systems of which we are a part, not apart. In other words:

- How can we engage in social- and practice-based learning from the contradictions between our own naming of the 'Other' (for example a social policy discourse) as the source of our disempowerment and our own collusion in (unintentionally) upholding the very status quo against which we rail?

- How might we objectify the 'Other' in ways that make us blind to new communicative action spaces within the contexts we already inhabit? (Weil, 1996, 1998; Percy-Smith and Weil, 2002; Percy-Smith and Weil, 2003.)

The main question becomes how professionals and young unemployed adults learn together to continuously (re)create their action space in the specific circumstances and context of activation programs:

- How can the dilemmas and tensions of professional practices be interpreted as expressions of the often contradictory appeals that are implied in the various 'narratives' of the actors involved, and as presenting a diversity of potential options for the mutual development of competent actorship; a co–created sense of possibility regarding our agency?

The Interpretive Professional

Adopting the metaphor of action space has at its heart challenges to the concept of the professional as a 'technical' expert. The possibility of providing standard solutions and applying uncontested stocks of knowledge is fundamentally dislodged. The scope for outcomes remains, but any formulaic prescription of success and effective performance contradicts the very possibility of success. When professional practices essentially are located on the cusps of various and contradictory 'stories', we need a new and more flexible concept to describe and reveal professional practice.

These ideas are not new. They relate to the notion of the 'discursive turn' in particular theories and practices of adult education and learning today: for example, in 'the pedagogy of (dis)location' developed by Edwards and Usher (1997), or the theory of a 'constructivist adult education' elaborated by Arnold and Siebert (1997). The critical constructivist and social learning dimension to such theories brings into prominence the different discourses that are interwoven with specific educational practices, and identifies critical and creative reflection in and through action on such discourses as the most integral challenge to the professional.

Wildemeersch (1999) in his exploration of social learning refers to the notion of the 'co-interpretive professional'. With this, he too signifies possibilities for a professional practice that creates the conditions for understanding and critically reflecting out of the 'situatedness' of learners, and the concrete material, aesthetic, socio-cultural and economic conditions in which all are jointly embedded. As with Schön's (1983) concept of the 'reflective practitioner', co-interpretive professionals also ground their 'state of the art' in a disposition towards 'knowing and reflecting-in-action' that supports learning from the heart of uncertainty, instability, uniqueness, and complexity. In a co-interpretive practice, professionals and participants continually interpret and negotiate individual and collective possibilities and limitations for young unemployed adults, against the background of a changing labor market and the pressures of current social and labor policies.

Interpreting and negotiating in this perspective constitute an open-ended process. Professionals use the information coming out of boundary tensions between their own and their participants' lifeworlds and those of the system, by staying critical and creative about the choices that cannot be seen except through new forms of dialogue, inquiry, and action research in practice (Lave and Wenger, 1991; Percy-Smith and Weil, 2003). In other words, this is a process that cannot be prescribed in technical–rational terms and has no meaning except in concrete conditions and specific contexts and communities of practice. Learning, as situated in this way, becomes a never-ending task of supporting the search for new answers and new solutions, for each particular young adult and for every specific situation. For example, drawing on research in the UK, the imperatives for 'policy learning' include:

> ...the need to develop a genuinely more client-centred and less bureaucratic service, in which social and biographical considerations central to young peoples' lifeworlds can be balanced with youth policy objectives. This requires a built-in critical reflexivity to enable continuous practice learning and the *development of the system itself* (Percy-Smith and Weil, 2002; emphasis added).

Secondly, interventions need to become more responsive to the problems of disaffection and multiple-disadvantage that many unemployed young people experience, but which currently remain untouched by *New Deal* and other such projects. Thirdly, because of options often being seen as inappropriate or unattractive, there is a need to broaden the range of opportunities to better meet the career aspirations of all young people. Finally, inter-personal relationships between advisor and client are crucial as to whether interventions are successful in making a difference to young people's capacity for social and economic participation.

There is therefore a need to provide a space for empowerment in which young people (and professionals) have a greater degree of autonomy in choice-making and choice-taking on programs such as *New Deal*. This requires new approaches to professional intervention practices.

In the remainder of this section we aim to explore to what extent our findings in the researched projects highlight some of the criteria and ways of being in relation to young people that might constitute a co-interpretive practice.

Holistic Approach

> *The approach is flexible and holistic, based on recognition that the needs of young people are complex, variable, and heterogeneous. The culture and ethos are also based on the assumption that if one area of an individual's life is out of balance then this will affect other areas of their life. As a result, success is not necessarily prescribed in terms of the hard outcomes required by government or funding bodies (such as finding employment or achieving qualifications), but instead is interpreted according to criteria that are meaningful for the individual   the most important thing is to deliver what the young people need, regardless of whether it meets government objectives or not. The investment in the young people is about long-term objectives of social inclusion, not short-term outcomes that may not be useful or relevant to the young person (Researchers, Bridging the Gap, England).*

This extract summarizes the 'philosophy' of the professionals involved in determining the nature and objectives for a new approach to dealing with homeless young people in Northampton.[1] By choice, they did not seek external funding for the project's set up – lest the philosophy and the opportunity of a truly innovative project be compromised.

The espoused culture and ethos, from the beginning, had the intention of functioning holistically. In other words, the professionals started with the presupposition that the imbalances these youngsters had to deal with were multi-dimensional and therefore could only be re-mediated by working with different areas of their lives simultaneously.[2] In line with this view, the staff team as a whole took responsibility for working with every resident to construct opportunities for their personal development. It is obvious that professional practice as conceived here did not pivot upon merely matching unemployed young adults with vacancies or just training them in the skills required for a particular job. The more holistic approach enables them to address these problems from a very different set of assumptions about 'what works'. First, the problems these young people face in getting a job coincide in many cases with a jumble of problems across diverse areas of their private life.

Besides having a need for skills and knowledge, the majority of the young unemployed who populate activation programs face challenges in other life areas as well. These can seriously interfere with the development of their capacity for some form of sustained labor market preparation. Failing to recognize this can give rise to the further alienation of young people as Jimmy, whose story we heard in Chapter 1, stated:

I mean I'd just been made homeless and they expected me to continue this Environmental Taskforce option...rather than sort my life out (Jimmy, project participant, New Deal, UK).

Activation programs that focus so clearly on skills training targeted exclusively at specific jobs miss opportunities. It is this very clarity of focus that becomes the problem, although this appears to be the solution. An alternative way of understanding competing tensions and priorities is to focus on the wider 'social ecology' of the participants' lives, and use opportunities for learning arising from these to equip them to cope with physical, psychological, emotional, relational, and financial challenges. 'Training for flexibility' is not approached as an instrumental target. Instead, developing the capacity to juggle, for example, identified earlier as associated with success in the changing labor market, is not imposed. Nor does it become the basis of some formulaic standardized format. Instead, the development of flexibility arises organically out of a professional engagement with these young adults' social ecology. Biographical, social, and instrumental opportunities for learning emerge and are approached in ways that remain fundamentally dialogic and relational. They are not immediately 'instrumentalized' into an objective that has no meaning within the young person's life.

This is in fact what began to happen when the *Bridging the Gap* project accepted external funding and they could not entirely escape accountability pressures to demonstrate progress in linear and technically rational terms. (Earlier, we identified tensions that subsequently arose from the introduction of external funds that were 'tied into' prescribed instrumental performance setting objectives.) The disjunctions between an emergent approach and an instrumental process threatened to undermine the entire authentic attunement. It threatened to undermine the complex responsive processes through which opportunities for learning emerged at the cusp where lifeworlds and the wider system met.

- When we couple social exclusion objectives with those of reducing unemployment, how else can any meaningful participation in the labor market be fostered?

- How can facilitating participation not be combined with developing competencies to cope with peers, family, authorities, 'leisure time', and so on?

In recognizing the vicious cycle from competency to deficiency that can arise and threaten young people's ability to survive, much less thrive, we should equally recognize the positive counter-balancing effect of gaining one experience after another of meaningfully stabilizing their life – even if only for a moment at a time – and helping to strengthen the inner resources required in work and life.

Returning to points made earlier, activation programs that focus merely on the training of functional skills for a narrowly defined job, can so easily neglect (or instrumentalize) the development of social learning capacities that are significant for sustained economic and social participation. Balancing the development of instrumental, biographical, and social competencies in a holistic or ecological perspective seems to open up new communicative action spaces for fostering successful actorship.

As the *Bridging the Gap* case suggested, applying a holistic approach requires re-conceiving professional practices as a co-interpretive practice that requires constant (re)attunement to patterns and particulars, as well as to the insights of other professionals. All of our individual knowing is only partial. Therefore, it involves teamwork, rather than individual professionals 'getting it right'. Such teamwork entails systematic cooperation and consulting between professionals and requires support processes of ongoing mutual and critically reflexive learning. Multi-dimensional perspectives on multi-faceted problems and strengths of multiple disadvantaged youngsters can be maintained and constantly re-formulated. Different forms of knowing are encouraged, such as through play, everyday tasks, structured activity, drama, and other forms of artistic and expressive performance. There is a constant appeal to the diversity of expertise and facilities that can help in creating new forms of communicative action space to support the young adults' development.

Trainers, counselors, teachers, supervisors, trajectory guidance officers, and others all offer insights to overcome the tensions and differences that are inherent to the development of competent actorship. Promoting co-operation between a diversity of professional and peer expertise requires commitment to opening and sustaining regular channels of communication up and down and across the organization of a project, and reflecting on how to align and engage organizational policies and daily practices to the benefit of the specific and diverse social, biographical, and instrumental trajectories of these young adults.

A more holistic perspective on professional practice also requires ongoing critical reflection on the notions of success that are being used and how they support or get in the way of intentions or are dysfunctionally influencing everyday practice. Again, contradictions, disjunctions, and experiences of displacement (Edwards and Usher, 1997), can be seen to offer up a curriculum for professionals, participants, funders and policy makers alike. From an ecological perspective, success can no longer be conceived in dualistic terms such as 'hard' and 'soft' outputs. The 'hard' outputs demanded by government or funding bodies – like the number of filled vacancies or the level of achieved qualifications – can be differently understood and approached. The success of a project can begin to be interpreted in accordance with criteria that are meaningful for the situations in which professionals and participants are jointly embedded, and to which policy makers can become committed to understanding better. Social learning can begin to flow up and down and around the system.

The *Bridging the Gap* project showed consistency in its 'philosophy' in these respects as well, since it had to influence the new external funding body or go without the possibility of its funding, in order to ensure that its approach, previously so successful, was not to be compromised. The objectives of the funding body were simply expressed in calculable outcomes. The governments' objective was for 85 percent of 21 year olds to reach NVQ level 2 or equivalent by the year 2003. The explicit target was to make a prescribed number of young unemployed who entered the program pass the test. For the staff of the project, however, the priority was to provide the participants with what they needed, irrespective of this government objective. Mutual mediation and learning become essential for funder and project personnel to co-exist in the service of the young socially excluded and homeless people for whom such projects are originally intended.

Co-learning

> There isn't only one part learning and one part teaching, but the apprenticeship process is made together by the two parts and at the end each part has gained an added value. This is clear, not only for professionals, but also for trainees. This is important as these young adults, most of them with low levels of self-esteem, feel valued, useful, and feel that they are playing an important role in significant others' lives. Additionally, this joint learning process makes much more sense for the integration of new ways of thinking in young adults' reference frames. One of the trainees could express it in very simple terms: 'We are making part of the training session and they are making part of us' (Researchers, Cultural Mediators, Portugal).

This extract demonstrates how a co-interpretive practice can be understood as being co-produced in a dialogue between professionals and learners. Learning shifts from a directive, teacher-centered approach to the collaborative (re)production and (re)interpretation of knowledge that makes sense in the contexts of the lives of both professionals and young adults. Mutual interpretations and negotiations of the possibilities and limitations the young adults are experiencing on the junction of their lifeworlds and the changing nature of labor markets and social policies, offer the content and focus for such dialogue. The views and outlooks brought forward by the participants are acknowledged and taken seriously, but further, they are made the focus of ongoing critically reflexive and creative co-inquiry (Weil, 1996, 1998). Interrupting familiar, established assumptions, perspectives, worldviews, and choices, and challenging them to 'move on', requires professionals posing questions, asking for facts and arguments, pointing at alternatives, exposing contexts, and so on. Equally, the professionals need to demonstrate that they too can critically reflect on their own partial worldviews and function as learners alongside project participants, welcoming questions posed about contradictions they express in everyday practice. In this way the interplay between professionals and participants simultaneously enables mutual reflection and 'ownership' with respect to the views, meanings, and interpretations that are expressed.

A co-learning approach does not seek responses or decisions from the young person on face value, but rather seeks to support the young adult in making a more informed choice by encouraging critical reflection on the implications of different choices. Such a process gives meaning to Rudd and Evans' (1998) notion of 'structured individualization' by promoting individual actorship, but supporting decision-making through the structure of support and facilitation provided by the action space. Facilitating such a process is action oriented in that it seeks outcomes in the form of decisions; at the same time it is educationally generative in terms of supporting and empowering the young person in a process of reflection and personal capacity building.

The principle of co-learning cannot only promote ongoing reflection and the ever widening of options in the face of changing circumstances for the young unemployed. Negotiating and exploring meanings and interpretations in dialogue alongside the young adults, provides professionals with possibilities for enriching and deepening their understandings as well. In a learning environment all actors involved are entitled to the mutual questioning and exploring of thoughts and acts. Professionals are freed to learn as much as they teach. As expressed in the extract above, it offers professionals both the chance for deeper insights into their own position and competence, and their implied limitations, and for greater attunement to the lifeworlds of the participants, including their problems, concerns, and hopes. Thus, a co-interpretive practice may provide professionals with learning experiences that may benefit substantially the 'art' of their choice-making and choice-taking in relationship with young people.

Juggling while Skateboarding on Waves

> *In attuning youth and demands for alignment, professionals juggle between a number of practices humor, flexibility, patience, addressing responsibility, tackling certain behavior, drawing limits, an amicable hug (Researchers, Right Match, Netherlands)*

The differing – and sometimes conflicting – objectives and demands of the activation projects, the gravity and complexity of the young adults' problems, and the permanent uncertainties of changing organizational and policy contexts for learning environments, require an increasingly more flexible attitude on the part of the professional.   They are situated somewhere on the continuum between accommodating young adults' biographies and preparing them for the labor market. Therefore, this requires them all the time to be looking for communicative action spaces that can open up possibilities for finding creative solutions to the ever-new situations presented by particular youngsters. In late modernity, the co-interpretive professional has to learn to juggle different roles, responsibilities and artful practices. Participation in activation projects is constantly appealing to the professional to be simultaneously:

- *A confidential agent* trying to build equal and trust-inspiring relationships.

- *An advocate* advising young people how to deal in a legal way with the pressures they face, like the threat of being excluded from unemployment benefits.

- *A midwife of learning* who, 'instead of giving young adults a fish, teaches them how to fish'.

- *A broker or mediator* who tries to match young adults' desires with employers' needs and employment opportunities.

- *A role model* embodying democratic and human values like tolerance, solidarity, and social responsibility, and representing what it means to survive and thrive in changing social and economic circumstances.

- *An authority* that acts as a role-model, expects respect and exerts non-obsessional discipline.

- *An expert* in the field of education, training, employment, and guidance, who not only knows the 'state of the art', but who also knows how to find ways through contradictions between existing provisions, aspirations, and bureaucratic requirements, and to devise new strategies for re-animating the energies of colleagues and young adults alike.

- *An educator* who creates opportunities to engage and influence those in the wider context who might restrict what is being found to be possible in a community of practice.

The bewildering number of appeals that are now being made to professionals shows up the limitations of becoming inscribed in just one practice. The disappearance of pre-given answers and standard procedures gives rise to a de-standardization of the role of professional and to a growing complexity and pressure with regard to the expectations that must be met. Yet, our research shows clearly that it is too demanding and ambitious to try and embody all of the mentioned roles within one individual professional – a tendency of programs such as *New Deal* in the UK where the role of the 'personal advisor' places unsustainable systemic, practice, and relational expectations on professionals working with young adults who are unemployed and socially excluded. This becomes virtually impossible to sustain.

Trapped in the ever-growing complexity of practices on the one hand, and faced with the impossibility of performing adequately in so many different roles on the other, many professionals can experience growing feelings of uncertainty, insecurity, and disempowerment. In the long run this may cause serious feelings of disempowerment and even of being 'burnt out'. Opting out can be understood as an expression of agency.

In a co-interpretive practice, therefore, flexibility should be expected not merely from the role and personal stance adopted by individual professionals. Rather, our research suggests that policy makers need to lend support to strategies of professional practice. For example, different functions and roles in relation to the participants can be flexibly distributed across a team as a whole. Time and space for learning and reflection is also required, to support the enactment of these new forms of leadership and support in the specific and complex conditions of activation projects. Moreover, the organizational context should offer sufficient elasticity to allow these teams to devise and repeatedly re-work contextually, biographically and socially attuned approaches to learning between the young unemployed and themselves. On the one hand, for example, a team might jointly allocate and rotate responsibilities for different forms of expertise, facilities development, financial management, administrative duties, and responses to bureaucratic governance demands. At the same time, the various practices and roles that are required in a specific activation project can also be shared and energies for doing so revitalized. On the other hand, a balance needs to be found between expressing cooperation and expressing autonomy.

In other words, our research has demonstrated both tensions and possibilities in accommodating the various demands of a particular project. Two vital dimensions seem to be firstly, a more fluid distribution of responsibilities, combined with ongoing review and distribution of work. Secondly, there is the need for structured space to support the systematic exchange and ongoing reflection that continuously attunes the professionals and the 'wider system' to the situated learning context, and young people's concrete experiences, results, problems and such like and possibilities that can be jointly nurtured.

But sufficient freedom for individual professionals to meet the needs of the young unemployed with creative and innovative solutions seems an indispensable condition for a co-interpretive practice. The multi-dimensional character of the challenges professionals meet requires a 'community of practice' approach and acknowledgement for the contribution that can only be made through the creativity of professionals who are doing their best to find innovative ways to reconcile social exclusion and unemployment project objectives. Ideally, rewards and success criteria themselves could be re-configured, to validate, for example, innovation, courage, and widening community participation in specific contexts of practice.

Empowering Professionals

The majority of the professionals we met in the researched projects acknowledged the significance of social and biographical learning, group work, and reflection, and tried to incorporate these into the programs they provided. However, the expertise required to enhance social and biographical competencies, support social learning in practice contexts and integrate theory and practice, in many cases, is contingent and left to the chance qualities and experiences of creative and committed individual professionals.

Overall, we noticed a striking absence of institutionalized support for professionals who were convinced of the value such approaches might add to practices of education, training, employment, and guidance for socially excluded and unemployed youth. The more that the role of professionals becomes redefined in terms of co-interpretive and contextually attuned practices, that stay responsive to individual and collective social ecologies, the more funders and policy makers need to re-think what support and expectations are on offer to those carrying this task. If this 'market' only continues to mirror that of the globalizing economy, expecting more and more for less and less, society will fail to find and keep the kind of professionals who are willing and able to take on the challenges of reducing employment and persuading the socially excluded to not 'include themselves out' by merely including themselves into other kinds of statistics, such as those of crime.

Professional development opportunities built into and around projects, need to foster the kinds of professional competences and stances we have been exploring in this chapter in an ecological approach itself. The courage and capacity to balance the opposite perspectives of young adults' lifeworlds and the imperatives of the labor market cannot be underestimated, nor, as asserted earlier, can they be reduced to reductionist and mechanistic training approaches.

Methodologically this opposition could be understood as balancing between 'voluntarism' and 'determinism'. We use the term voluntarism to refer to the inclination of some professionals to overestimate the influence they may exert through the face-to-face relations they have with the young unemployed in the daily practices of a project, to a certain extent ignoring the structural context in which the project is embedded. This orientation can easily lead to frustration when their illusions of possible success fail in the face of the harsh realities of the economic and political system, at the risk of blaming the young adults for their failures through labeling them as 'non–motivated' or 'irresponsible' or 'inadequate'.

Other professionals, on the contrary, are more inclined to a deterministic point of view. Their laborious and often discouraging efforts in motivating and engaging the young unemployed towards taking up specific jobs, and the organizational and policy pressures they bring to bear on their professional functioning, can lead them to overestimate the influence of structural powers. They can feel mere victims in an unrelenting system, and questioning the meaning and effects of their own actorship. In this case, professionals may easily resort to a coercive, overly formalized, or even cynical position, whereby they just do their work without much belief in the inherent significance of it.

There is a need to empower professionals in the 'space between' these two perspectives. Instead of being guided by either or both, they should be supported in the ability to relate their own acting both to the young adults' biographical and social needs and to the structural contexts of their professional responsibilities in working with young unemployed adults. This may support them in neither under nor overestimating the impact of their own acting. Creating space for new forms of social and policy learning from the tensions and possibilities being experienced across projects (with close attention to differences), across governance levels and between policy makers and professionals may help bring into play a greater range of professional creativity and engagement without losing sight of the personal and professional limitations of such work.

Promoting empowerment in this sense requires both internal and external support. Internal support refers to attention to the complexities and insecurities professionals experience within the daily practices of a project. This might include, for example, attention to compulsions to become more coercive in the face of their growing disempowerment. If the system can move away from its excessive reliance on standardized procedures and prescriptions, professionals will have to learn *how* to deal with diverse and multi-dimensional trajectories for social inclusion and to author different forms of accountabilities, to themselves, to funders and to the young people. We were shocked in our research by the extent to which professionals were being bombarded with more and more protocols, procedures, rules, monitoring, and performance management tools. Many of them expressed a need for other kinds of support, like for example, case discussions, search conferences or networked learning initiatives. Some of them tried to organize that kind of support themselves, through informal contacts with colleagues. However, the pressures on them to turn inwards in order to survive cannot be underestimated.

There is a clear need for supporting activities to be organized in a more systematic way. Programs and organizations for education, training, employment, and guidance projects should create time for professionals to communicate and reflect collaboratively on their experiences, ideas, and learning with respect to the problems and challenges they meet in activation projects. In such a context, there would also be room to discuss, develop, and experiment with relevant methods, that enable the holistic and flexible approach that we suggest can be integral to a co-interpretive practice which pivots on the junctions of instrumental needs and the social and biographical peculiarities of any individual.

External support signifies a necessary shift in the policy priorities that *professionals are confronted with. At stake should be the political and public* acknowledgment of the possibility of meaningful social and economic participation. Activation programs should no longer be initiated and assessed in terms of quantitative criteria like the number of filled vacancies, or the relation between 'input' and 'output' figures of participants. Policy makers, managers, politicians, and unions of employers and employees need to be convinced of the value of prioritizing the quality of outcomes over the quantity of outputs that are separated from the contexts and stories that are at issue. For example, narrative based approaches to performance review, can help to ensure social learning from more innovative approaches, and can support dialogues that can guide future policy formation, monitoring, and research. We return to these issues in Part III.

Professionals also need to be allowed the conditions, time, and finances to co-create trajectories to social and economic participation that make sense to the young adults involved. Being provided with the chance to work with young unemployed in this perspective probably will be the strongest support for professionals who genuinely seek to combat the social exclusion of young adults, and indeed for the young adults whose futures are at stake.

Conclusion

This chapter aimed at illuminating and explaining the ambivalent character of professional interventions in activation projects as currently enacted. The stories of practitioners reveal how they have to balance continuously between competing, and often conflicting, wants and desires that pervade the lifeworlds of the young adults on the one hand, and on the other, the demands and imperatives of reality as constructed in the worlds of labor and education.

We have explored five recurring dilemmas of professional practice, as encountered through this research:

- The dilemma of individual choice and social obligation.

- The dilemma of young adults stopping still and moving on.

- The dilemma of pedagogic care and the constraints of performance.

- The dilemma of mediating structural and biographical complexities.

- The dilemma of competence and deficiency orientations.

We have explored the notion of 'communicative action space' that by its very nature is a place of both tension and possibility. We suggested that attention to how this is restricted in activation projects, and for whom it is made available, may open up different concepts of choice-making and choice-taking. This notion has enabled us to re-vision professional practices as a co-interpretive practice at the dynamic intersection of structural pressures and biographical backdrops. Each of these delimit, but never fully determine discourses and options for (inter)action in relation to the young unemployed.

Adopting the notion of 'action space' directs attention in particular to needs for professionals to feel empowered to mediate the disjunctions between the diverse discourses that influence their practices and to be creative and competent actors in attempting to make some innovative contribution to reconciling what now function as competing objectives: to reduce unemployment and increase social inclusion. Activation programs locate professionals in a practice where they require competencies for challenging, clarifying, juggling, and, when possible, reconciling the implications of competing discourses. We have explored the different ways in which these may come into play, considering in particular the potential of remaining socially and ecologically attuned to the contingent, specifically located stories of young people and the wider discourses in which all are located.

We have used the term co-interpretive professional, to capture something about the shifts in professional engagement that seem important from the perspective of our research. In other words, we suggest that professionals need to be regarded less as predominately 'technical' experts and more as people who need to engage in an essentially improvisational practice. This needs to remain relationally, contextually, and structurally attuned. Contradictions inevitably arise in attempts to interrelate processes of learning, work/practice development, identity formation, and meaning making (that derive from the biographical, social, and instrumental narratives of those engaged in a specific project). However, they also offer up a steady stream of live, situated, biographical, social, and instrumental 'content', which can be engaged with to widen young adults sense of possibility and competent actorship in a world full of contradictions.

In highlighting a number of qualities that may be seen as integral to a co-interpretive practice, we suggested that participating in activation projects does not only challenge the young unemployed to engage in new forms of learning. Instead, we regard this as a mutual critically and creatively reflexive learning environment. Professionals learn as well, if they genuinely seek to mediate between structural pressures, biographical particularities, and the 'art' of professional interventions. This insight may help in understanding that activating and socially including young unemployed people require more than just tapping into their willingness to learn and to take up responsibilities. It is a process in which appeals are made to the willingness of all actors involved to learn and co-create new spaces for learning for all professionals: politicians, policy makers, project-managers, employers, and workers alike.

---

[1] At the time of the research the philosophy and approach of this project was not characteristic of the YMCA nationwide in the UK, rather it was unique to the *Bridging the Gap* project in Northampton, England.

[2] This contests other theories of how young people cope and respond to multiple dilemmas e.g. 'focal theory' espoused by Coleman and Hendry (1990).

PART III
PARADOXES AND POSSIBILITIES: POLICY, PRACTICE AND RESEARCH

PART III

Chapter 9

Making the Bridge:
Introduction to Part III

In Part I, we elaborated the intentions that we brought to this research:

- To better understand unemployed young adults' experiences of activation programs and how these may be influencing their own learning, meaning making, and identity construction with respect to their participation in the labor market.

- To learn more about diverse program approaches and practices across the six countries, and whether and how these seem to impact upon young people's social exclusion and opportunities for participation in the labor market.

- To consider how changing socio-political circumstances and labor market conditions interact with notions of pedagogy and practice, and the construction of future narratives relating to social and economic participation.

Having set these intentions in motion through our research, we have treated encounters on the ground as fractals in a larger whole. Our participatory worldview allows us to interpret tensions and paradoxes we found in the local and in the particular of encounter spaces as indicative of emergent properties in a larger complex system. We have also attempted to suggest how well intended actions in one part of a system can have significant effects in other parts. We have treated these as mutually interacting and simultaneously shaping each other. We have tried to reveal ways in which the EU might know itself differently, as a more dynamic and complex system (Capra, 1996; Reason and Bradbury, 2001; Stacey, 2001).

To make this tension concrete again, here we deepen further our thesis that activation policies are defining young people and professionals *simultaneously* as both *subjects of* and *subjects to* the practices in which they are participating. What we have demonstrated thus far is the extent to which both are being restricted in their agency to give any significant meaning to the aims of social and economic empowerment of young unemployed adults at local level. We have demonstrated how a specific project cannot be treated as somehow separate from the context through which it is being funded for specific shapes, directions, and policy/discourse legitimation purposes.

Throughout, we have kept in view the important EU aspiration to reduce unemployment without exacerbating social exclusion. As we have shown, however, when these well-intended values are translated into specific practices of activation, the repertoire of choices in local action spaces becomes restricted and the currency of the wider policy intention subject to processes of economization. We recognize fully here the impact of neo-liberal economic ideologies and processes of globalization and the pervasiveness of corporate management discourses at all levels of the system. Nonetheless, we contend that there are still policy and practice choices and interventions that remain significantly under-explored across the EU that might benefit young unemployed Europeans who are, at present, all too often easy casualties of these processes. What we concentrate on here is especially those 'manufactured risks', and the possibilities that lie in processes of reflexive modernization, rather than merely technocratic modernization (Young, 1979).

In Part III, we thus use the substance of our research as a springboard for re-visiting issues raised thus far from some alternative perspectives: European ideological, discursive/analytical and systemic/future oriented perspectives. We hope that our grounded theorizing can generate opportunities for fresh thinking and practice across a newly expanded and more diversified EU. We dread to consider the consequences of current trends being allowed to continue unabated, given their growing impact on processes of social exclusion and inequality across Europe.

We approach this section as follows. Firstly, we consider issues we have raised thus far in relation to current ideological debates in Europe. In doing so, we place center stage the EU, as a key actor in all this.

This then takes us to our main offering here: the development of an alternative theory of policy practice. We engage directly with the implications of paradoxes we have found at the policy–practice interface and dynamic systemic tensions around 'learning for inclusion'. Using the current dominant European policy discourse of 'activation', we posit notions of 'restricted' and 'reflexive activation'. We shall show how restrictive and reflexive practices emerge from particular constructions and interactions between the same three lenses above, that we found so definitive with respect to 'employment preparation' practices. The table below summarizes the tensions and possibilities we set out with regard to key paradoxes related to these lenses:

Table 9.1 Basic Lenses

Basic Lenses	Restricted Activation	Reflexive Activation
Changing labor identities	*Problematizing the excluded*	*Problematizing exclusion*
Transforming competencies	*Limited responsibilities*	*Extending responsibilities*
Shifting pedagogies	*Decontextualized practices*	*Contextualizing practices*

Reflexive activation will be discussed as a strategy that can be jointly created between young people and professionals in conditions of disadvantage and uncertainty. Rather than problematizing the excluded, we problematize the notion of exclusion. We shall suggest that 'limited responsibilities' have the potential for being reflexively transformed into social learning processes to support 'extended responsibilities' for practitioners and participants. Finally we shall point to the importance of 'contextualized activation practices' as an alternative to 'decontextualized activation practices'.

With these shifts of emphasis, we further nuance Wenger's notion of 'community of practice' (1998), introduced in Part II in relation to issues of agency and empowerment. We consider how professionals and young adults alike can engage in processes of identity formation, meaning making, and practice development that make action based co-inquiry into the concrete material conditions of young people's life worlds and contradictions at the policy–practice interface the core curriculum for developing social, biographical, and instrumental competencies. Put another way, we explore the notion of reflexive activation as itself a social learning process (Wildemeersch et al., 1998).

We hope that this analysis will open up fresh ways for perceiving, reflecting upon, and enacting alternative forms of policy and practice with unemployed and 'socially excluded' young adults. This alternative framing may also pry open a different kind of conversation about tensions and imperatives operating within the EU within the framework of its concerns to be 'different' from other global powers in not separating 'the social' from the economic.

We therefore close Part III by considering the implications of opening up spaces for 'reflexive activation' within the EU. We introduce notions such as policy learning and systemic inquiry, illustrating these through the use of a radical and rare case study from post-depression USA. We consider current techno-rational strategies of new management – and how and why these are now permeating across Europe through accountability, audit, and evaluation practices. Returning to examples from our research, we suggest ways in which such practices give rise to processes of 'restrictive activation' for individuals as well as communities, and limit learning at the policy–practice interface in the EU. We then consider what such strategies might look like in practice, if implemented across a newly expanded Europe. We look at how these might further gain from the active involvement of young adults, passing on insights from this and related research initiatives (see for example, Percy-Smith and Weil, 2002, 2003; Percy-Smith et al., 2003). Throughout this final chapter, we foreground tensions and paradoxes around governance, as we see these emerging in a neo-liberal context.

Two Caveats

Before we open up these paradoxes and possibilities further, we wish to introduce two caveats. Firstly, we see all pedagogies as subject to constraints and opportunities. We are also all too aware of how often policy initiatives shift responsibilities for solving major social and economic problems onto education and training systems and practices. Our position is that any employment preparation intervention will always have a limited impact on the socio-economic, cultural and structural conditions that are also giving rise to social exclusion and unemployment. Without other strategies for tackling social exclusion and unemployment, at best, only relatively few individuals will be helped.

As a recent summary of EU targeted Social Economic Research programs concludes:

> Recently completed European research shows that various factors inside and outside education and training cause, or at least contribute, to processes of social exclusion. They are intertwined but in different ways and at different stages of life...the underlying factors involved are much broader and deeper than is often understood by policy-makers and that *one area of social policy is unlikely, on its own, to be able to address the problem* education measures will have to be reinforced by wider social and economic reforms if social exclusion is to be seriously addressed (PJB, 2003, p. 1).

We are sharply attuned to the limitations of education in the examination of paradoxes and possibilities that follows in Part III.

Secondly, we do not wish to set up a binary between restrictive and reflexive activation practices, although our formulations here may easily be read and used as such. Instead, our intention is to open up a communicative action inquiry space between the idea of 'restrictive activation practices' and 'reflexive activation possibilities'. In other words, how might practitioners and policy makers become more critically reflexive and co-inquiring – about the unintended consequences of both explicit and implicit assumptions and practices, as influenced by wider ideological discourses and the local politics of project accountability and funding (Weil, 1996; Weil et al., 1996; Percy-Smith and Weil, 2002, 2003). We agree with Edwards et al. (2001) that processes of inclusion cannot bracket out processes of exclusion. Yet current dominant policy discourses treat inclusion and exclusion as binary opposites. A range of social policy initiatives are funded with the assumption that increased processes of inclusion will decrease social exclusion, and that exclusion can be transcended through rational means–ends strategies:

> the notion of inclusion . is conceived largely within a philosophy of identity in universalist and humanist discourses that position those who are excluded as a cause for concern. In such discourses, exclusion can be overcome or transcended by changes in social and economic policies and practices, including lifelong learning. *Inclusion conquers exclusion* However, we need to ask who is included in what? Inclusion has a 'horizontal' metaphorical sense, which is *suggestive of a center towards which everyone must be given opportunities to gravitate.* Those at the margins of the economy and society must be given the opportunity to be included, with the danger that without such inclusive practices they may be further marginalized (Edwards et al., 2001, p. 424; emphasis added).

A more systemic view is proposed by these same authors who go on to argue that, '*all* practices entail forms of in/exclusion and that this is surfaced through adopting a position within a philosophy of difference' (ibid, p. 424; emphasis added). The contradictions can never be eradicated. However, reflexive inquiry into their operation and multiple forms and levels of expression in any 'activation' situation – as itself a social learning process – may open up possibilities for new forms of local action and choice. Such strategies might help to transcend and transform some restrictions to opportunity, and open up some alternatives for social and economic participation that might otherwise have remained unexplored.

Our position is that *any* employment preparation intervention will always have a limited impact on the socio-economic, cultural, and structural conditions that are simultaneously sustaining social exclusion, inequalities, and unemployment. Without other strategies for tackling social exclusion and unemployment, at best, only a relatively few individuals will be helped (PJB, 2003). And with these caveats in mind, we continue.

Chapter 10

Ideologies and Policy Discourses: Impacts from 'On High' and 'Afar'

The EU as a Key Actor

In this chapter, we consider the wider debates that influence attempts to reconcile social and economic development in the EU. We shall discuss ways in which policy shifts towards 'activation' and towards alternative constructions of education, training, employment, and guidance coincide with influential ideological positions. These relate to questions about the place of employment and unemployment within the world economy, and responsibilities of the state to both.

We contend that the EU is a key actor in the transformation of education, training, employment, and guidance practices related to (un)employment. This is somewhat paradoxical, because due to the subsidiarity principle, education and training is a policy matter that belongs to the responsibility of the national states. Yet, when education and training are linked to labor, regional, and national bodies increasingly follow instructions and trends developed at the European level. This is especially the case since the Maastricht and the Amsterdam Treaty and subsequent summits in Luxemburg, Lisbon, and Feira (Ferrara et al., 2000). The publication of Agenda 2000 (European Commission, 1997a) set out a strategy that was aimed at social and economic cohesion. 'Brussels' was subsidizing many of the projects we researched either directly or indirectly. Think tanks such as the *European Centre for the Development of Vocational Training* (CEDEFOP) also play a very important role in directing the employment and training policies of the European Union.

In addition to the influence exerted through subsidies and policy directives, a particular discourse about education, training, employment, and guidance has gradually been introduced in which the notion of 'activation' is firmly embedded – as discussed previously. This discourse reflects a wider vision on how 'economic' and 'social' policies *should* be reconciled. It is our perspective that this emerging discourse exerts considerable power at local, regional, and national levels, despite claims within the EU regarding the 'subsidiarity principle'. Building on our discussion of governmentality, we reflect critically on whether this discourse is merely 'common sense' or 'progressive'. We suggest the unintended consequences of this non-neutral discourse on diverse young unemployed Europeans remain largely invisible to key players within the EU systems. In particular, we offer an extended consideration of how these ideological debates can give rise to and sustain 'restrictive' practices, in which the disempowerment dimension tends to be stronger than the empowerment dimension. Our intention here is to provide further contextualization for our development of notions of 'restrictive' and 'reflexive' activation in the next chapter, with respect to wider processes of EU policy development, and global influences over the last decade. But first we wish to raise some difficult boundary issues that emerged as a result of our engagement with such discourses.

Macro-micro Tensions: Challenging the Notion of Practitioner Irrelevance

In our experience, when the lens is turned towards the macro level, practitioners can easily turn off. This is not dissimilar to the tension we raised with regard to research in Part I. Practitioners may rightly ask, 'What does this have to do with the young people whom we are trying to help?'

We suggest it has quite a lot to do with it, actually. Tensions may be intuitively felt, but not understood, at local levels. Experiences may be described, but their wider signification and potentially oppressive character cannot always be explained. Discourses of power experienced at the local level can be reduced to being merely different perspectives. All such dynamics can make it difficult to sees how what 'is' is being socially constructed, not just up close but from afar. Naming some of these structuring political discourses can itself enable new forms of empowerment, challenge, and agency to be glimpsed, and in turn open up alternative communicative action spaces at local levels. Understanding issues at an EU level may also support local practitioners across Europe in recognizing that tensions and pressures that they experience, are not particular to them alone, but are indicative of wider influences. Without resource to insights beyond experience alone, things are all too easily 'particularized' and all too easily discounted as mere stories or reduced to interpersonal issues. New forms of policy learning, which we explore in the final chapter of Part III, may support practitioners and young adults in taking outwards and 'upwards' insights from their own experiences and from alternative forms of discursive engagements with young adults that challenge taken for granted assumptions. They may be legitimated in bringing into the clearer view of policy makers and others, lived difficulties of trying to reconcile social and economic objectives on the ground, and the unintended consequences of current policies.

Tensions between Economic and Social Objectives

We are acutely aware that to sketch European ideological positions is itself fraught with difficulties. It is all too easy to slip into simple binaries. The positionings and discourses we point to here are far more nuanced than suggested by the brief outlines that follow. What we present here deserves to be understood in relation to various complex social and political histories across Europe. It therefore seems important to make our intention here explicit.

Once again, our gaze is fixed on the aspiration in the EU to be different: to reconcile social and economic tensions. As in what has come before, we wish here only to heighten readers' alertness to the complex responsive processes at play between global, EU, national, and local domains. What interests us here is systemically, how these mutually influence each other, mutually constituting each other and the concrete ways in which patterns at local level mirror patterns and tensions at other levels of the system.

The Primacy of the Economic

So what kinds of macro influences seem connected to tensions and paradoxes we have found in local practices? We shall begin with a review of some key historical developments, identifying some of the conflicting views about how the economic and the social dimensions of European development should (or should not) (and might) relate to each other.

During the last decade, the European Union has increasingly tried to understand and influence the employment conditions in its member states. This has been a direct consequence of strategies put in place to redress the alarmingly high unemployment rates experienced in most of member countries at the end of the 1980s. The EU has gradually become more proactive in trying to revitalize the economic situation in the European space in reaction to the growing impact of corporate globalization (Elmeskov, 1993; Bean, 1994; Heylen et al., 1997; Jackman et al., 1997; Grubb and Martin, 2001; Calmfors et al., 2002).

Economic objectives have always been the most important driving force in the formation of the European Union. However, social objectives began to play an increasingly important role in policy debates, from the 1980s onwards and particularly in the last decade of the twentieth century. The threat of social unrest and concerns about the links between economic growth and social stability has driven these interests (Ferrera et al., 2000; Brine, 2001). Brine speaks about the shift of emphasis from the nation state to the supranational state – the social spaces *between* the nation states:

> The ET policies of the European Union relate to social cohesion and social exclusion. Social cohesion relates to the relationship between nation states or regions, and social exclusion to the socio-economic and political deprivation of particular social groups (Brine, 2001, p 124).

Our concern here is similar to Brine's – namely, the unintended impacts of funds being redistributed through to education and training policy and programs across the EU:

> the EU regulates economic competitiveness; it redistributes resources such as those of the Structural Funds; and it provides legalistic frameworks such as that of the Social Chapter (Brine, 2001).

Needless to say, economic objectives and social objectives cannot always run in parallel and are inevitably hard to reconcile. But irrespective of this tension, the question about what kind of economic and social future is desired for the EU – and the future for young unemployed adults within it – is of course, not a given. It has increasingly become the focus for major power struggles and tough political debate.

Looking Back

If we begin with an historical perspective, the European Economic Community was primarily set in place to serve an economic function: to create a free trade market in 1956. All overt tariff barriers were brought down in the six states that were then members of the European Economic Community. It was not until the 1970s that political co-operation became a matter of increased importance, especially with the establishment of the European Parliament in 1979. It was in the second half of the 1980s, and especially with the adoption by all member states except the UK of the 'European Social Charter' in 1989, that the notion of the 'Social Europe' came of age (Ferrara et al., 2000). During the last decades, the social dimension of European policy making has increasingly become part of the agenda of meetings of the European Council, like the Luxemburg summit (1997), the Lisbon summit (2000) and the Feira summit (2000).

Today, the economic, the political and the social dimensions of Europe are of central importance to European unification. However, the economic aspect continues to dominate. Proponents of a more social Europe and increased political integration often express their frustration about the fact that political and social development is lagging behind. This was definitely the case during the 1990s when most of the unification efforts concentrated upon the establishment of the European Monetary Union to support the introduction of the Euro by the beginning of 2002. During this last decade, most of the member states were also subjected to austere measures, in attempts to decrease national debts and control their expenditures. As a consequence, there was little room for the development of social policy that was not in the first place directly supportive of the market objectives of the Union (Beck et al., 1998).

The Neo-liberal Market Agenda

These historical factors, combined with the influence of particular political parties across Europe during this period, have resulted in a predominantly neo-liberal market orientation to economic development to support European unification. The economic agenda has been concentrated on removing the protectionism of individual states and dismantling bureaucratic barriers that were seen to block the free movement of goods, capital, and labor. Deregulation has been a ruling principle throughout.

The protagonists of economic deregulation – such as the Federation of European Employers (2001) – fear that 'the social agenda' of the EU will put a heavy burden on entrepreneurial freedom. They argue that social reform on the European level has involved an increasing level of legislative control within the labor market. They fear increased legislation and regulation of activities will reverse the steady decline of trade union influence at the national level. Trade unions, it is argued by deregulation lobbyists, will take advantage of this European 'social dimension' and regain their influence, thereby blocking economic growth.

In other words, European requirements to attend to issues such as social inclusion, equal opportunities, positive action and the broadening of the rights to vulnerable groups are seen to delimit corporate freedom to organize activities according to the economic criteria of effective profit-making and growth. Moreover, it is argued that the increasing amount of social legislation in the EU is placing an unsustainable administrative burden upon employers (Jackman, 2002).

Despite such effects, which have major implications for the findings we present here, the neo-liberal lobby contends that a social Europe should be restricted to the establishment of minimum terms and conditions across the EU in order to create a 'level playing field' and stimulate true competition. In short, the Federation of European Employers fears that the social agenda of the EU will weaken their competitive position in the globalized market. According to them, Europe's 700 million people have a serious choice to make:

> They can either shape the forces of unification and integration over the long term to create prosperity for the EU as a whole, or price themselves out of world markets by unreasonable, short term demands for radical improvements in working and living standards (ibid, p. 7).

The neo-liberal economic view – which continues to privilege economic solutions to complex social issues, such as equality of opportunity, social inclusion, and integration – has become very powerful during the last decade. This is both on a European and a global scale, especially since the fall of the Berlin wall in 1989. Against this backdrop, compromises that were found between opposing forces in the 1960s and 1970s about labor and employment conditions in the European Union are now being challenged. Deregulation is used as the rationale for this. There is deregulation of the classical full time employment model, deregulation of qualifications, deregulation of wages, deregulation of working time, and so it goes on. Flexibility has replaced stability in most domains of working life. We saw in previous chapters how the notion of flexibility can be distorted and perverted in 'employment preparation projects'. As Chomsky argues:

> You don't have any rights on the labour market. It's just a market. That in fact is the foundation of the intellectual tradition that is called classical economics now, neo-liberalism, and so on (1996, p. 18).

Lobbyists for a More Social Europe

This neo-liberal market agenda is counteracted by those who are lobbying for a more social Europe. These lobbyists include trade unions, social democratic parties and socially oriented academics, practitioners, and citizens. They are critical of the one sided liberal economic character of the European unification and are committed to developing more socially inspired perspectives and alternatives.

So what are some of the critiques brought to this political scene by this alternative lobby? According to Bouget (1998), the economic agenda of the EU has been inspired mainly by monetarist principles. The signing of the Maastricht Treaty in 1991 was a major step towards further European economic integration because of the decision to establish a single European currency by the beginning of the 21st century. As a consequence of this monetarist doctrine, the social is predominantly defined in terms of the economic. Liberalization of markets is expected to bring economic development, with prosperity and the improvement of the social conditions being assumed to more or less automatically result from that. The social advantages are assumed to 'trickle down' from the economic benefits. No tension is perceived to exist between employers and capital on the one hand and labor on the other. The implicit assumption is that 'what is good for the firm is good for the workers'. As a consequence, social aspects of life and of policy making are defined predominantly in economic terms:

> Social participation is reduced to economic role and status (as a consumer, a worker or entrepreneur, landlord) and is a prerequisite of social cohesion (Bouget, 1998, p. 43).

From this perspective, it is hard to imagine that a social development agenda can be defined more or less independently from – or even in opposition to – an economic development agenda. From a monetarist or neo-liberal economic perspective, social integration in the European space is perceived to require first and foremost an economic integration of different countries, aimed at improving the efficiency of enterprises that have to operate in a competitive global market. In other words, economic prosperity is assumed to beget social prosperity in a direct linear relationship.

Critics of neo-liberal market orientations have disdain for the naiveté of this view. They point to growing gaps between rich and poor, and the new clusterings of urban and rural deprivation in the US and Europe. They speak of the pernicious effects of a system that sees those who remain trapped in unemployment and poverty (or lose their jobs) as failures. The individual is perceived to be at fault, as if the system were benign, and easily overcome if only you have a bit of 'gumption about you' (Chomsky, 1996; Sennett, 1998; Osler and Starkey, 1999; Bauman, 2000; Hertz, 2002).

A Long Way from the Lives of Young People?

These ideological debates may seem a long way from the lives of unemployed young people. However, as explored through this book, these discourses are played out at local levels. For example, professionals are on the one hand meant to participate in practices that are on the one hand, meant to be responsive to individual needs and on the other, to report on failures of participation. This can provoke a sense of profound dislocation in young people.

If projects are meant merely to be instrumental in 'delivering' young people into jobs to serve the market economy, the space for social and biographical meaning making can be severely restricted. More than this, the social dimension can be positively *discounted* as having no relevance to an economic agenda, unless it can be instrumentalized. We found how easily these stances on the part of professionals can impact upon young adults, who can resent, and react against, what are so obviously such mixed messages. For young adults whose tolerance of authority figures has been previously severely damaged, such dissonances can lead to opting out altogether.

We also underestimate the impact of repeated experiences of activation. This policy driven imperative, lest they lose benefit, can make them feel as if on an officially sanctioned treadmill that goes nowhere.

Such experiences can make it all to easy for young people to reject any 'mainstream' notion of economic and social participation. They then can be labeled as disturbed, impossible to reach, whatever, or they might be understood for attempting to escape or survive unbearable dissonance and disjunction (Weil, 1986, 1989). They can also be seen as choosing to exert their agency by removing themselves from the source of continual distortion and coercion: namely, activation projects and practices.

Envisaging New Balances between the Economic and the Social

Shifting Dialogues

What we are seeing across Europe is a steady erosion of the fairly favorable and stable employment conditions that characterized times of economic prosperity in previous classical welfare states. The conditions resulting from years of negotiation and struggle are often regarded, from neo-liberal perspectives, as historical exceptions rather than as significant achievements in reconciling social and economic objectives. However, what is likely to be the long-term impact of systematic deregulation and flexibilization of employment conditions, if these are not counteracted by new collective rules that attend to the social consequences of a pure market mentality on a larger scale?

As the power of the former nation states to influence and control these increased market mechanisms decreases, the EU emerges globally as a potential radical space where alternative rules can be developed and enacted. However, more progressive theorists and radical observers perceive the European Union to be completely overruled by dominant neo-liberal forces, influenced significantly by America, and institutions such as the World Trade Organization, the World Bank, and agreements such as GATT:

> The remedies for unemployment adopted almost everywhere and recommended by the European Commission...can be summed up in one word: flexibility. Flexibility in wages, in working conditions, in systems of social protection. But not in salaries paid to top executives or returns on investments. Once this policy is accepted, the economy, the currency and the fate of the working population will all be market-led and run on autopilot (Gobin, 1997).

The progressive voices warn more and more against the consequences of this one-sided marketization and flexibilization of working conditions. They argue that some of the great achievements in Europe in the recent past were based on a synergy between the social and the economic and that there is significant historical evidence to show that there need not necessarily be a conflict between 'competitiveness and solidarity'. For example, as Bouget argues:

> Social welfare grew as a natural consequence of economic growth during a full time employment period. There was a positive pro-cyclic phenomenon, a synergy between a collective choice for reducing social insecurity and a favourable economic situation, and between the social, institutional, political and economic dimensions of social quality. According to some radical critics, the situation today is completely inverted. The predominance of economic concerns in the EU seems to involve a reduction of the public sphere and a dismantling of national welfare systems (Bouget, 1998, p. 47).

Green-Pedersen and van Kersbergen (2001) also argue that,

> For a long time, Keynesianism offered a politically auspicious way to combine the expansion of the welfare state with an effective governance of the economy. What was socially just was also perceived to be economically efficient (p. 3).

Even Adam Smith, often held up as a hero of the neo-liberal economists, was not ignorant of the darker side of an ideology that treats the market as natural and neutral. Those who labor most get least:

> In the progress of the division of labour, the employment of the far greater part of those who live by labour...comes to be confined to a few very simple operations; frequently to one or two... The man whose whole life is spent in performing a few simple operations...generally becomes as stupid and ignorant as it is possible for a human creature to become (Smith, 1776, pp. 302-3, in Sennett, 1998, p. 37).

In the 1970s, however, welfare oriented state policies came heavily under pressure. The European economy entered into a crisis, unemployment rates grew rapidly, public debts became huge, and inflation could not be brought under control. The Keynesian recipes were increasingly being criticized both by academics and politicians of the new right. State interventions in the economy with a view to sustaining welfare structures became increasingly suspicious. From that moment onwards, as a consequence of the perceived 'sound sense' and success of neo-liberalism, especially in America, there was a sustained broadening and hardening of the 'belief' in competition (Vandenbroucke, 2000, p. 28). Competition was broadened to new domains where the competition principle was considered applicable.

However, moderate observers argue that, in spite of the global influence of a radical neo-liberal discourse, the welfare states in Europe are *not* crumbling (Ferrera et al., 2000). Yet, they suggest that former synergies need to be re-invented on a larger level than that of the nation state. In the 1960s and the 1970s, this may have been a relevant level on which to operate: The point here is that there are many who believe that this historically less familiar antagonism between economic and social development in the European context can and should be reduced, and that a more positive and mutually beneficial interaction between both spheres can and should be created.

The Erosion of the European Welfare State?

From the 1980s onwards various societal domains have been subjected to the market and to competition. The UK has 'led' the way, with its so called 'reforms' of for example, the health service, transport systems, and public utilities, all of which have involved different degrees of privatization, sub-contracting, and economically determined accountability criteria. Simultaneously, global competition has become fiercer. The assumed balance to be achieved between market competition and social solidarity, which was so characteristic of various forms of welfare state systems across Europe, has been under sustained attack. It is beyond the scope of this book to engage in depth with questions and debates about the extent to which a return to the model of the welfare state – or new notions of the welfare state – are feasible today in circumstances of a globalizing economy. However, what is relevant to the ideas we wish to deepen in this and the subsequent chapters is that over the past 15 years, the expenses entailed in sustaining public services such as health, education, and social security have been considered far too high. This has generated a climate in which it can be more easily argued that these costs immobilize the normal functioning of the free market and weaken the competitiveness of private enterprises. Moreover, the forms of welfare provision that had been developed in the previous decades are scapegoated as the 'cause' of dependency, passivity, and reduced creativity. The services delivered 'from the cradle to the grave' become constructed by so called liberalizing forces as forces that take away people's responsibility over their own lives. The critics of a Social Europe continue to argue that the welfare state model in Europe has had its day and that alternative, more market-oriented state policies are now necessary.

However, some observers, like the aforementioned Ferrera et al. and Vandenbroucke, criticize the viewpoints that emphasize the disappearance of the welfare state. They argue that many of the welfare state provisions in Western Europe are not really vanishing, as might be expected when listening to the ideological debate.

> A popular view is that West European welfare states are crumbling under pressure from external competition, while the globalization of production and finance, combined with the policy constraints of the EMU, have all reduced the capacity of the state for implementing corrective remedies (Ferrera et al., 2000, p. 1).

They even argue that European welfare states have remained fairly stable over the last decades, or emphasize, as Vandenbroucke (2000, p. 43) does, that the weight of the social expenses in European countries has continued to increase, especially in the Southern European countries. This argument is supported by the observation of others that 'there is little evidence that the social democratic project of combining justice and economic efficiency has lost its *political appeal*' (Green-Pedersen and van Kersbergen, 2001, p. 5).

This more optimistic view, defended by Ferrara et al. (2000) as a form of 'social pragmatism,' accepts that despite this, the context has irrevocably changed. It is no longer possible to achieve full-employment, social protection, and equality with the same post-war welfare oriented policies. However, they do perceive a vast field for the negotiation of alternatives, whereby welfare systems might adapt themselves to the new conditions. They predicate this on the assumption that the nation state continues to be the main center of policy influence and change. According to these authors, the major challenges for a unified Europe are, in fact, placed 'at the intersection of the international and domestic economies in the area of employment' (p. 11).

The Emergence of the 'Third Way'

In order to sustain the project of a Social Europe, certain political parties and key players have felt obliged to revitalize the concept of the Welfare State and adapt it to the economic and sociological circumstances that have emerged at the end of the twentieth century. Consequently, ideological and political changes are increasingly in evidence, not only under the pressure of the neo-liberal critique, but also under the influence of increasing international economic competition. In many countries, the argument that state bureaucracies had become fairly inefficient and ineffective has been taken seriously. As a consequence there has been an emphasis on increased managerialism and public accountability in the public sector, with a perceptible decrease in accountability in global corporate structures, as mergers, flattened and diffused global structures, and the use of flexible labor forces impact upon consumers. There have also been clear trends across Europe to make certain benefits, such as unemployment support, more 'incentive compatible'.

Of course, the extent to which these neo-liberal doctrines and disciplines have impacted on concrete every day policies and practices that influence young unemployed Europeans has varied across different contexts. The UK under Margaret Thatcher and afterwards, has been much more radical in attacking traditional welfare institutions and state infrastructures than was the case in the German or the Scandinavian context of the 1980s and the 1990s.

Under the Blair government, this has been reframed as a 'Third Way', between 'the state and the market, involving an accommodation of market pressures with the preservation of social protection and consensus':

> Old-style social democracy concentrated on industrial policy and Keynesian demand measures, while the neoliberals focused on deregulation and market liberalization. Third Way economic policy needs to concern itself with different priorities – with education, incentives, entrepreneurial culture, flexibility, devolution and the cultivation of social capital. Third Way thinking emphasizes that a strong economy presumes a strong society, but doesn't see this connection as coming from old-style interventionism (Giddens, 2000, p. 73).

This Third Way should, according to Ferrera et al. (2000), be seen as having potential for creating possibilities for more socially just growth. On the one hand, social justice objectives are maintained and on the other hand, a solution is found for fiscal and policy problems that undermine economic competitiveness. Thus, according to this recipe, the revised 'welfare state' results from a policy mix that reconciles these objectives of 'social justice' and 'economic competitiveness'. At other occasions, this reconciliation is described in terms of creating new balances between 'flexibility' and 'security', synthesized in new trendy neologisms such as 'flexicurity' (Sels and Van Hootegem, 2001).

The Third Way is actually not just a reinvention of the welfare state such as we have known it in Western Europe during the first decades after the second world war. A distinctive turn is discernible, which is the result of intensive debate and reflexive processes about how social democratic principles and policies should be shaped in present day society. For the protagonists, it is more than just an economic project. It tries to reinvent the relationship between the state, the economy, and the individual. It is about helping citizens to pilot their way through the major revolutions of our time: globalization, transformations in personal life, economic, and political migration, and our relationships with the environment:

> Third Way politics looks for a new relationship between the individual and the community, and a redefinition of rights and obligations. It has a core concern for social justice, and promotes social inclusion and the fostering of an active civil society where community and state act in partnership. It seeks to revive civic culture, and looks for a synergy between public and private sectors, utilizing the dynamism of markets but with the public interests in mind. Third Way politics represent the renewal of social democracy (Giddens, 1998, p. 131).

The Emergence of the 'Active' Dimension

Protagonists of a Third Way approach argue that economic competitiveness should not be unduly hindered by the organization of welfare provision. This approach is part of a wider attempt to bring civic rights and responsibilities into a keener balance with rights to State benefits. The French social philosopher Pierre Rosanvallon delivered a specific contribution to this debate in his well-known work *nouvelle question sociale* or, in English, 'the new social question' (2000). He departs from the observation that the welfare state has come under severe pressure internationally, partly for the well-known reasons of slowing economic growth and declining confidence in the public sector. He cites a deeper and less familiar reason for the crisis of the welfare state. He argues that a fundamental practical and philosophical justification for traditional welfare policies – that all citizens share equal risks – has been undermined by social and intellectual change. If we wish to achieve the goals of social solidarity and civic equality for which the welfare state was founded, we must radically rethink social programs.

Rosanvallon begins by tracing the history of the welfare state and its founding premise that risks, especially the risks of illness and unemployment, are equally distributed and unpredictable. He shows that this idea has become untenable because of economic diversification and advances in statistical risk analysis. It is truer than ever before – and far more susceptible to analysis – that some individuals will face much greater risks than others because of their jobs and lifestyle choices. Rosanvallon argues that social policies must be more narrowly targeted. He draws on evidence from around the world, in particular France and the United States, to show that such programs as unemployment insurance and workfare could better reflect individual needs by, for example, making more explicit use of contracts between the providers and receivers of benefits. His arguments have broad implications for welfare programs everywhere and for our understanding of citizenship in modern democracies and economies.

Such a more individualized approach, advocated by authors of the Third Way or 'the new social question', is opposed to the so-called old-style social democracy that was inclined to treat welfare rights as unconditional claims. The new style social democracy emphasizes obligations as well and therefore wants the citizens to be 'active' in exercising these, as if they were moral duties. The example that has predominated in this book is that people on employment benefits should carry the obligation to look actively for work. In the UK, the phrase, 'welfare to work', borrowed from the USA, guides specific policies targeting the unemployed, amongst which young people are included and expected to be 'active'. Therefore, European governments now assume a more central role in ensuring that welfare systems do not discourage an active search for acceptable forms of economic and social participation (Giddens, 1998). However, the Third Way allows that economic development, as Sen (1999) argues, can only progress and support human well-being *with* the support of the contributions that can be made by health, education, and civil and political freedoms.

The UK's *New Deal* program was seen as a breakthrough program that attempted to put into practice Third Way politics in ways that would benefit young unemployed people. However, as with other projects studied in our research, we notice that many such activation strategies – many of which continue to be advocated as effective solutions – still focus on the employment aspects of policy making. This is also the case in the concept of the 'active welfare state' that has found its way to recent European policy documents.

It could be that the broad perspective on the renewal of society in various domains of life is still being reduced to economic and employment strategies, thereby again reinforcing the primacy of the economic. Mizen argues, in his recent analysis of the Third Way and youth policy in the UK:

> In this world view, the quality of the nation's capital is held to be *the* decisive source of investment over money capital, plant or materials, and as one of the few assets still nationally anchored, is amenable to direct government control. By manipulating the supply of (youth) labour, the prospect of greater inward international investment can be increased and, by extending the process of learning, creating flexible and more 'relevant' forms of education and by training workers to effectively learn to learn, the competitive edge offered by new technology and the 'knowledge economy' can be harnessed to progressive ends (Mizen, 2003, p. 468; see also Thompson, 2002).

This definition of the Third Way shows clearly how the notion of 'active' has become integral to politics and policy discourse, and how it aims to be responsive to reform for 'progressive ends' that serve modernization and the needs of global employers. In other words, this new approach is opposed to the so-called old-style social democracy that was inclined to treat welfare rights as unconditional claims.

Policy Frameworks to Combat Youth Unemployment

Social exclusion is especially dramatic when it concerns young people. The experience, in the beginning of their adult life, that they are not legitimate members of society in general and the labor market in particular, can influence them negatively in the long run. On the one hand, the EU and its member states have demonstrated awareness of such a consequence, making youth a central issue for the future of the Union. A European Observatory on Policies to Combat Social Exclusion was set up in 1990. Leney (1999) argues how the Observatory helped to establish the EU's longer-term commitments:

> Over the course of three years or so...the European Commission's policy became to integrate the earlier distributional approaches to poverty with a broader approach that emphasized the relational aspects of social exclusion... Even at this early stage, the main policy emphasis of the Commission was on combating unemployment and promoting employability, as part of a package of policies geared to improving competitiveness and growth (Leney, 1999, p. 40; see also Room, 1995).

These beginnings led social exclusion to being perceived as a multi-dimensional phenomenon. It was also accepted that mostly women, discriminated groups, ethnic minorities, handicapped, and young people are affected by growing market competitiveness and economic globalization processes. More and more the EU recognizes that these groups need specific policies to support their social integration. Moreover, it is well known that high levels of youth unemployment have been a long-standing problem all over the EU. Political and technical initiatives have been taken in order to set up programs, and stimulate reflection and debates aiming at enhancing the opportunities of young people throughout Europe. The key policy strands in this field are education and employment.

For example, the 1995 White Paper on Education and Training (European Commission, 1995) both implicitly and explicitly concerned itself with unemployment and social exclusion. It expresses a major need for a generation of skilled young people, with a sense of European identity: autonomous, enterprising, adaptable, flexible, and capable of taking the responsibility for the EU consolidation and development in the future. A wide range of strategies for formal, informal, and non-formal learning are proposed with attention to creating an *inclusive learning society*. But, until more recent years, Leney argues that actions beyond the policy rhetoric have been largely concentrated on encouraging and funding:

> training in the member states designed to counter unemployment and to improve the employability of marginalized groups due to restrictions imposed by the subsidiarity principle with regard to both funding and policy interventions (Leney, 1999, p. 38).

We see a turn, however, after the Luxembourg presidency, and conference when there was an attempt to develop a framework:

> in which some convergence of the national employment policies could occur, without negating the particular circumstances, structures and traditions of member states...

Emphasis was to be placed on the strategies needed to reduce youth unemployment and on developing and funding activity that involves developing *employability, rather than passive support for the unemployed* (Leney, 1999, p. 40).

This is when the activation discourse and more linear top driven performance managed strategies begin to wield their effects on local initiatives. Greater standardization begins to be hailed as a success story. Policy makers are patting themselves on the back for at last getting some control over disparate policies, through more explicit policy guidelines, action plans, and pre-specified performance criteria. However, what starts to be *less and less visible* from the top, is that:

> Member states are finding it difficult to develop policies that achieve an appropriate balance between reinserting the excluded into employment, and preventing the new groups in the population from drifting into long-term unemployment. The emphasis in most of the plans is on the former (ibid, p. 40).

So on the one hand, what we continue to see is the strength of an ideology that makes economic productivity the base for social integration and perceives employment as the result of a better and more adequate education for everyone. On the other hand, there is awareness that new technologies of communication and information and their constant evolution require a permanent process of learning and self-actualization. The White Paper, *Teaching and Learning: Towards the Learning Society*, expressed the danger that Europe will get divided between the ones who:

> can interpret, the ones who can solely use and the ones who stay marginalized in a society that assists them: in other words, between the ones who know and the ones who do not know (1995, p. 14).

This new kind of social exclusion is often referred to as 'info-exclusion'. It is recognized that individuals who cannot handle these new technologies will increasingly become marginalized from the worldwide process of information exchange and knowledge development. On the other hand, young adults are becoming highly qualified in fields with increasingly no correspondence to the labor market needs: they have the knowledge, the technical skills, but no room to perform their activity. This can also be a new form of exclusion.

This policy perspective influences member states to put a lot of emphasis on vocational training, not only as initial training, but also in a lifelong perspective. Concerning youth, the initial vocational training plays a major role and is defined by the European Council (1994) as:

> any form of initial vocational training, including technical and vocational training and systems of apprenticeship, which enables young people to gain a vocational qualification recognized by the competent authorities of the member state in which it is obtained (ibid).

The EU further strengthens its influence as a key actor through trying to implement a system of accreditation and organization of vocational training equivalent for all member states. Apart from being preoccupied with instrumental competencies, the EU has demonstrated increasing concern with the development of social and biographical competencies. In this regard the European Council writes that:

> in the society of the future, Education, Training and Guidance would not just be required to find solutions to the problems of integrating young people into working life; they will have an increasingly central role to play in every aspect of personal development, in social integration and in the awareness of shared values, in handing on the cultural heritage and in developing individual self-reliance (1996, p. 2).

These documents show also how European policy makers increasingly frame the process of education, training, employment, and guidance in terms of an individualized, personal trajectory towards employment. The young people are expected to become active and assume responsibility themselves for taking their own employability seriously. Ferrera et al. (2000) speak about the 'increasing use of activation policy and tightening eligibility for unemployment benefits' as essential ingredients in effective EU driven policy mixes and institutional reforms.

It is also recognized by the Commission that youth, as well as other 'vulnerable groups', need support on levels not commonly addressed by the formal educational systems: the acquisition of social skills required at the workplace, information about career opportunities according to specific motivations and interests and real experience at different work settings in order to avoid what the Commission calls the 'no experience, no job trap' (European Commission, 2000, p. 12). Following this line, in the Employment Guidelines for 2001, the Council recommends that young Europeans should be offered some form of training, job experience or 'employability measure' before they have been unemployed six months.

This trend towards the strengthening of the self-training attitude reflects not only a political, but also a cultural change. However, the present tendency of exploring one's own labor identity in order to discover new trajectories does not always match the real conditions of the labor market. To a certain degree, this still prefers the 'robot' worker to the 'reflective' worker (Van Hootegem, 2000), except for the privileged few. Moreover, as Furlong and Cartmel, (1997) argue in the context of young unemployed:

> underlying social changes, the powerful chains for human interdependence which produce and reproduce inequalities are kept intact, while the actors, believing themselves to be responsible for and in control of their destinies, attempt to cope individually rather than collectively, with problems which are socially generated and largely outside the control of individuals (p. 131).

Non-neutral Discourses

This simplified outline of a range of European policy developments and trends helps to draw our attention to how paradoxes and contradictions on the ground are 'bred' at higher levels of the system. The discourse promising opportunities for all can be understood as anything but neutral:

> it is presented as if it were value free and merely technical. Its implementation is often informed by the ideology of technical rationality with its stress on value-neutrality...
> [It] is motivated by ideological rather than educational intentions...pedagogical practices are [being] profoundly influenced by political/economic theories (Tabulawa 2003, p. 11).

He suggests that such policies may signify to professionals on the ground some form of escape from restrictive educational structures and pedagogies which have often failed these young people in the past (Tabulawa, 2003). Professionals, politicians, and young people alike can be seduced by the promise of a greater emphasis on activity, on learner centeredness, practical learning, and notions of social constructionism (as if all involved were powerful agents of change who can take responsibility for reconstructing their world).

Tabulawa (2003) suggests a direct link to the current wave of globalization, which is attempting to imbue education with corporate and managerial discourses that in turn can alter modes of thought and practice. Like Edwards et al. (2001), he suggests that we adopt a critical stance towards these methodologies, which can also be seen as an attempt to bring:

> those on the periphery into line and that this is being accelerated by the current wave of globalization, which is a carrier of conservative neo-liberal ideology...as the dominant theory of development in the 1980's (Tabulawa, 2003, p. 15).

Tabulawa adopts a world systems view to argue that the USA, Western Europe and Japan operate socially and economically as if they were 'core' and less industrialized nations merely peripheral: a tension that is characterized by economic and power relations that are anything but equal. We would suggest that a similar tension is at play within Europe. On the one hand, there is the constant economic pressure to compete with the major and emerging powers that are irrevocably subject to forces of globalization. On the other hand, the core–peripheral dynamic becomes reproduced in the specific field of Europe. In this case the 'poor unemployable' are seen as at risk to a competitive Europe and are then made subject to practices that maintain them as peripheral.

To return to Edwards et al. (2001) on a similar concern, with respect to discourses about social (ex)(in)clusion:

> it may not be entirely surprising the concern for inclusion has become a dimension of national policy [UK] at just that point at which globalising processes are subjecting the nation to ever increasing strains and when there is a crisis discourse over society 'falling apart' (p. 417; see also Edwards and Usher, 2000).

Yet the margins between 'mainstream' and 'perhipheral' are continually being redrawn, as the boundaries themselves become subjected to globalization forces. As Sennet (1999) and Chomsky (1996) argue, there are few employees today who can consider themselves exempt from practices that can marginalize them in a matter of minutes.

Giddens (1991) argues that the time–space compression, and the mobility of capital flowing around the world, is increasingly being disconnected from the social relationships in which money and wealth were previously embedded. These processes of 'disembedment' put compromises between labor and capital in previous welfare societies under new pressure. These aspects of globalization also re-define divisions of labor and core–periphery relationships. The periphery, which used to be clearly located in Third World countries, is now becoming a feature of (the so-called) First World countries. We increasingly find Fourth World poverty in the former First, Second and Third Worlds (Castells, 1993).

Many people in our case studies would not see themselves as part of this emerging Fourth World. However, there is a danger that the clients of the projects which we have studied are being 'trained' to become members of the reserve army of labor upon which corporate profit depends. Their only choice is to receive benefit through participation in legitimated activation schemes or drop out completely and survive on the streets. In Part I we spoke of being prepared only for 'jobettes', and what others have referred to as the McDonaldization of the labor market.

> Democracy and a commitment to human rights are key defining features of the European Union. Nevertheless, the inhabitants of Europe, living their local realities sometimes based in poverty and unemployment, and subject to racism, inadequate housing and high levels of crime, may not recognize that the European project is, in its intention, inclusive, since an inclusive society is far removed from their experience. (Osler and Starkey, 1999, p. 214).

The increasingly hegemonic pull of particular ideological and economic stances can blur and blot out the stark realities that confront socially excluded and unemployed young adults. The EU functions as a key actor by legitimating and standardizing such modes of thought across member states. We envisage serious consequences of these current trends in policy and practice within the EU (economically and socially). These are likely to impact unproductively on the lives of many more young adults than the ones who participated in our study. Behrens and Evans (2002), in their study of *New Deal*, point to the deep undertow of tensions that have been so evident in our own research:

> Exercising proactive behaviours against the odds is one way for young people in precarious positions to break through the barriers, but policies based on this amount to making the strongest demands on those who are in the positions of least power. For the policy communities, the most significant challenge is to move away from deficit approaches, which start with the assumption that agency is lacking, and therefore needs to be developed, and towards *policies* which assume that agency is present but will be channelled in different directions (Behrens and Evans, 2002, p. 36).

It is within this context that we can still imagine possibilities in this moment for Europe to resist the growing global emphasis on the economic at the expense of the social. But we suggest that such possibilities must make the recognition and exploration of paradox and contradiction central to their expression in specific contexts of practice. We pursue such notions of activation in this different key in the chapter that follows.

Chapter 11

Restrictive and Reflexive Activation Discourses Explored

'Activation' Re-visited

Empowering and Disciplining Dimensions of Activation

'Activation' is increasingly becoming 'a magic word' (Kazepov, 2002). We have shown how this discourse is giving direction to policy and practice in many European countries, especially the ones with a social democratic tradition. This is the case in most of the Western European countries and applies to all countries included in the research that underpins this book.

In various policy and research documents, further to our discussion in the previous chapter, 'activation' is being explicitly formulated as a strategy to demonstrate that social initiatives need not foster dependency. Sometimes it is also described as a specific form of empowerment targeted at particular groups. The Third Way approach focuses on empowering individuals, families, and communities to move out of poverty, unemployment, and social exclusion through a combination of initiatives that emphasize individual responsibility, social support, education, and 'welfare to work' initiatives (Gamarnikow and Green, 1999, p. 50). In the Netherlands, which in many respects has taken a lead in the development of activation policies, the definition is as follows:

> Activation is the enhancement of social participation and the breaking or prevention of social isolation by means of meaningful activities that can be a first step towards paid work (Centrum Sociaal Beleid).

Also the Finnish government makes the notion of activation central to its social policy strategy up until 2010. This policy stresses the importance of gearing social and health policy towards improving people's ability to enter the labor market and to remain in it longer before retirement. As such, activation is seen as a strategy that will enable the government to cope with a wide variety of challenges such as the ageing of the population, the improving of the effectiveness of the social services, the struggle against poverty, and so on. In some cases, the Finnish included, activation is predominantly connected to labor market participation, whereas in other cases, it has a broader orientation towards different kinds of participation in society.

At this point, we wish to reinforce the distinction made by Kazepov (2002, p. 22), between 'social activation' and 'labor activation'. On the one hand, he argues that policy makers are conceiving *social activation strategies* as relevant for those people whose degree of autonomy is perceived to be so badly compromised that they have no sustainable future in the labor market nor little chance of achieving self-reliability. On the other hand, *labor activation strategies* tend to be targeted at recipients of social benefits whose personal capabilities are perceived as sufficient to labor market placement. In the context of the latter, activation programs are meant to develop the technical competencies that will equip them to get a job.

In many of the projects we visited in our research, labor activation was the principle objective, while elements of social activation also played an important complementary role. The intertwining of strategies was especially evident in the projects that we typified as the 'informing and helping' culture of learning in Chapter 5. These targeted the so called 'destabilized'. In other projects, we saw many different attempts to balance labor and social activation, but this dual strategy always carried with it pressures to 'discipline' the participants. These pressures are rooted within a set of discursive practices that legitimate an external authoritative push to make young adults act as more responsible job seekers and citizens.

Similarly, genuine efforts to increase young unemployed Europeans' self-expression and personal development also seemed equally disciplining: 'emotional pawing', as the Danish researcher described it and 'officials wanting to know your business too much', as young people often put it.

This tension is consistent with the way in which Kazepov (2002) describes current activation policies on the broader European scene. His analysis of 'Social Assistance and Activation Measures in Europe' describes two distinct goals of activation:

- getting people off-the-payrolls by cutting down public expenditure for social assistance and employment measures, reducing the social costs of poverty and unemployment;

- empowering people who are out of work by improving their life conditions and increasing their opportunities by giving wide social support through *ad hoc* designed accompanying measures (ibid., p. 20-22).

Two narratives can be related to these two goals. One concerns the 'duties' of the beneficiaries. The other focuses on the right of the beneficiary to obtain support to prevent or overcome marginalization. These distinct narratives, in their turn, give rise to two very different 'logics of activation':

- a 'stick and carrot' logic, whereby high levels of discretional power are given over to the professionals to evaluate a 'beneficiary's' commitment, and to introduce the threat of reducing, suspending or terminating income support;

- an empowerment logic, which conceives of professionals and the 'beneficiary' as mutually involved in the same program, yet the beneficiary is expected to participate actively, while the professional commits himself to providing tools for 're-insertion' of the person into the labor market.

The language whereby young unemployed people become constructed as 'beneficiaries' of activation itself indicates a significant ideological turn. Moreover, the notion of empowerment itself shifts from something that in radical education terms has been enacted as something which educators support people in *doing for themselves*, to that which people in power *do for or to them*.

These reconstructions of notions of 'disciplining' and 'empowerment' objectives and these logics of activation help to give further strength to our focus in this book on 'paradoxes of activation'. Activation *inevitably is double edged*.

We have encountered this paradox in most of the projects that we investigated. We found that the young people, who are the most successful in the education, training, employment, and guidance projects, are the ones who can find an adequate balance in this tension. In the first part of this book we have emphasized that an either/or opposition in this respect seems no longer fruitful: something that continues to be borne out by research in this area (for example, Behrens and Evans, 2002). We have therefore suggested that the professional needs to remain reflexively concerned with creating opportunities for the participants to empower themselves, while simultaneously limiting these very opportunities. However, in this chapter we shall go further than this, in our exploration of paradoxes and possibilities for 'activation'.

What we see as key is what has recently been described in various studies as the 'pedagogical paradox' (Depaepe, 1998). This is inevitable and un-resolvable. Any relevant pedagogical intervention will always be double edged: it will enable people, while at the same time it will reduce their options and limit their freedom. Interventions that only give freedom, while at same time refusing or neglecting to give direction, can give rise to disorientation among participants. Interventions which over-accentuate control, while leaving little room for experimentation and agency, can generate insecurity and neurotic reactions when the subject is confronted with difficult choices.

Since the paradox cannot be resolved, finding a good balance between empowerment and control becomes an important matter. However, as our analysis of the interpretive professional made clear, no equilibrium is available. Given the complexity and unpredictability of the situations in which professionals and unemployed young adults find themselves, the balance has to be reflexively invented and reinvented and renegotiated time and again.

In the projects we researched, we observed that professionals and policy makers often have great difficulty in coping with this tension. Too often, the exertion of 'control' takes precedence over empowerment. As we have also observed, 'schemes' that are conceptualized and presented as individualized 'packages' of generic skills and knowledge to be 'delivered' can become ends in themselves, offering little of value in shifting these young adults' opportunities.

What we remain interested in is how to create environments that activate young adults' imaginations and sense of possibility, promote new forms of social and economic engagement, and develop functional abilities that align to wider practices of labor and social participation.

Returning to the Three Lenses

We shall open up our interest in these paradoxes from two different perspectives, with reference to the three basic lenses that have given direction to previous observations in this book. Firstly, we posit the notion of restrictive activation, and extend our analysis of the discourse that we perceive to be dominant, or at least, in ascendance throughout Europe. We then suggest an alternative discourse: that of reflexive activation. This, we believe, in its different constructions and assumptions, has the potential to open up alternative choices for policy makers and practitioners.

- *'Shifting labor identities'* will be considered firstly, from the perspective of a critique on identity construction of the socially excluded in particular activation discourses. We shall then consider an alternative perspective, whereby we problematise the very notion of 'exclusion'.

- *'Transforming competences'* will be discussed firstly with reference to the phenomenon of 'limiting responsibilities' – a prominent feature in quite a few of the observed projects, that links to recent work on 'bounded agency' as a feature of activation initiatives in England and Germany (Behrens and Evans, 2002; Evans, 2002).

- *'Shifting pedagogies'* will be analyzed in terms of tendencies to 'decontextualise' activation strategies that we found across our empirical research. We shall consider the alternative of situated activation practices: strongly contextualized learning strategies that are disconnected neither from young peoples' biographies nor social situations, nor the labor market and socio-economic processes. These are always simultaneously impacting on professionals' attempts to develop opportunities and capability for participation.

The following table summarizes the key tensions we see operating with regard to these paradoxes of activation (Table 11.1). In other words, we develop our notion of 'paradoxes of activation' as a function of quite complex interactions across the above three dimensions, education, training, employment, and guidance practices, and the wider economic and political context. The very act of naming key tensions in dominant discursive practices, as suggested by our research, itself suggests possibilities for alternative ways of working. Reflexive activation will build on this discussion. Explored from the perspective of practices and principles whereby conditions for different forms of learning and activation might be jointly conceived between young people and professionals in ways that relate to the very conditions of uncertainty and disadvantage that sustain their situation. We will explore the notion of reflexive activation as itself a social learning process.

Table 11.1 Basic Lenses

Basic Lenses	Restrictive Activation	Reflexive Activation
Shifting labor identities	*Problematizing the excluded*	*Problematizing exclusion*
Transforming competences	*Limited responsibilities*	*Extending responsibilities*
Shifting pedagogies	*De-contextualized practices*	*Contextualizing practices*

It is our hope that this chapter will offer readers both summative and formative support at this stage in the book, and fresh ways of perceiving, reflecting upon, and enacting activation practices and/or strategies with unemployed young adults. In the final chapter, we shall pay attention to processes of systemic learning in the EU that we believe are equally critical to opening up and sustaining more diverse situated alternatives at local levels.

Restrictive Activation

The Problem with Problematizing the Socially Excluded

We have found, somewhat contrary to our expectations, that in all of the activation practices which we studied, a great deal of attention is paid to issues of identity. Although there were some marked differences across the different cultures of learning we distinguished in Part II, all four cultures give biographical and social competencies a prominent place. We have found how important it was to create opportunities for the young adults to learn to make sense of and navigate various options and orientations in relation to the labor market and to integrate these navigations into their biographical and social stories.

What struck us was the extent to which education, training, employment, and guidance practices have integrated intuitively or reflexively recent sociological insights concerning the emergence of biographical reflexivity as an overall adaptation strategy in late modern societies. The social changes that have had a strong impact on the development of identity have been described and documented in detail during the last decade. For example, Ulrich Beck (1986, 1992) introduced the concept of the 'risk society' in which:

> social institutions once thought to ensure our safety also exercise excessive power over our time. Rather than unequivocally conforming to traditional social norms, contemporary individuals opt instead for alternative more fluid and entrepreneurial lifestyles. These are perceived to offer greater individual freedom from canonical time structures (Herkenhoff et al., 2002, p. 3).

The notion 'reflexive biography' clarifies the extent to which traditional identities are under pressure nowadays. The development of identities and biographies is increasingly disconnected from traditional social and cultural bonds, and from classical social class distinctions. The nature and pace of technological, social and economic change in present-day society make the image of who one is, where one comes from and what one wishes to achieve in life, a necessary subject for ongoing self-reflection. Biographies become 'self-reflexive':

> In the individualized society, individual people have to learn, under the threat of permanent discrimination, to behave as the center of action, as planning bureaus with respect to their own life courses, their competencies, their orientations, their partnerships and so on (Beck, 1986, p. 217; translation by the authors).

However, we have also found that attention to biographical reflexivity in projects often suffered from tendencies of 'economicization'. In other words, they become mired in the 'stick and carrot' rationale of activation. We have seen how attempts to foster biographical and social reflexivity often become instrumentalized to fit into the disciplining goals of activation. Both professionals and participants are increasingly compelled to operate within highly standardized and regulated limitations, guided by external pre-defined 'success criteria' that are meant to be achieved in tightly bounded time limits.

This disciplining character of project practices implied in many cases a negative valuation of the identities of the participants. We have called this elsewhere the 'discourse of deficiency' (Jansen and Wildemeersch, 1996). This discourse constructs the identities of so-called disadvantaged groups, such as young unemployed adults, in such a way that the deficits are accentuated. This negative valuation becomes the basis for legitimizing restrictive activation practices. In other words, the 'problem' of social exclusion is increasingly attributed to the so-called deficiency of individuals, groups, and communities.

This discourse is often posited as 'neutral', or as 'common sense'. There are two main reasons that we wish to challenge the espoused 'neutrality' of this discourse: First, it tends to essentialize and 'psychologize' the characteristics of dependency. This means that deficits become diagnosed as deficient attributes of individuals, families, or communities (Young, 1999). They begin to be perceived as lacking in the skills, cognitions and values which are perceived as necessary to participate adequately in the present day 'information society', 'knowledge-based society', or 'post-industrial' society.

This discourse further implies that the cause of the problem is located in the more or less constant features of the 'deficient' target group. Statements such as the following are being heard more frequently, seem less and less open to question, and are increasingly accepted as 'common sense':

> *There are many opportunities open for Them, if They could take advantage of all the education and training opportunities on offer, and overcome for example, their laziness, victimhood, addictions, and preferences for easy rides at tax payers expense.*

As such discourses take hold, the 'deficient group' is constructed as the Other in the media and in everyday conversation. The underlying mechanisms that have contributed to social exclusion – such as poverty, multi-generational unemployment, racism, and immigration – remain unproblematized and pushed to the margins of thought and action.

In other words, in restrictive expressions of the activation discourse, we do not see mechanisms of social exclusion defined as the problem, but the socially excluded themselves become problematized.

Of course it cannot be denied that there are individuals who are lacking in the confidence, capacity, skills and inclination to participate in particular segments of the labor market. Yet, we suggest that these deficits could simultaneously be construed as manifestations of the transforming conditions of society, present day capitalism, and the labor market. The latter stance would imply that 'responsibility' for the problem of social exclusion and unemployment cannot exclusively be attributed to the individuals who are perceived as 'unable to cope' with the present day context.

This brings us to the second reason why activation strategies cannot be treated as neutral activities. As mentioned above, activation strategies always reflect particular relations of power between different groups, categories, and classes in society. Some groups are defined as 'socially excluded' or 'at risk of exclusion', and in need of being activated and included, while others escape such negative definitions and consequent strategies of activation and inclusion. Who is perceived to be in which category, what is perceived to be the normative 'center' and what is constructed as the unacceptable periphery, is in constant flux. This is influenced by dominant power relations and power mechanisms, shifting discourses, and also acts of creative agency and reflexive re-authorship.

Michael Young (1999), with reference to Giddens (1998), astutely observes that social exclusion in our advanced societies today is a dual process. By this, he implies that not only are people at the bottom of the social ladder becoming detached from mainstream society. People at the top also increasingly and willingly detach themselves from social solidarity mechanisms. The latter are increasingly resisting taking responsibility for their own complicity in maintaining patterns of advantage and disadvantage. There are strong moves against participating in a society where it is acceptable that wealth is distributed to reduce inequalities (Chomsky, 1995).

This resistance, as we have seen in the previous chapter in the discussion of the European welfare state, arises out of an ideology that sees welfare provision organized by the state as counterproductive, expensive, and inhibitive of the entrepreneurial climate. It is perceived to infringe on personal profits and advantages. The advantaged come to feel that they can rationalize paying less tax for the 'deficient' group, from whose situation they feel increasingly disconnected. At corporate levels, whole companies are relocating their services, such as call centers, to countries where there is less regulation and the opportunity of higher profits for reduced taxes.

However, it is those at the 'bottom' of the social fabric who are treated as irresponsible and who are assumed to take advantage of the social security system. Paradoxically, those in the upper categories, who could equally be accused of irresponsibility, are mostly treated with respect and esteem. Their choices can be regarded as acts of creative entrepreneurship.

Yet middle class people who construct themselves as anything but the 'deficient other' are themselves beginning to discover the illusory security that such polarized positions seem to offer. As downsizing, redundancies, globalization of the labor force and the erosion of permanent contracts become the norm, and employment become more and more difficult to find and to sustain, the dominant discourse can quickly extend to construct them too as deficient and as failures (Sennett, 1998).

Transforming Competences: Managing the 'Entrepreneurial Self'

The 'problematization of the socially excluded' is, according to Mitchell Dean (1995), part of a new 'politics of identity'. He argues that this has arisen in Europe, towards the end of the 1980s, out of OECD think tanks and has since spread into many of the member states over the course of the 1990s. Dean links his observations on the 'politics of identity' to the framework of 'governmentality'.

Our research helped us to understand how this politics of identity formation operates in practice. Particular groups of people, such as the unemployed young adults, are diagnosed as dependent on the social security system. In response to this dependency, activation practices are initiated. Benefits are withdrawn if young adults' participation is not seen as acceptable.

Dean suggests that 'activation' is now being interpreted and enacted as a kind of 'governmental-ethical practice'. Such practices, and their related techniques become reconstructed as justified by the fact that related procedures are in place to achieve particular ends: in this case, the 'insertion' of the lowly skilled (and the recalcitrant) into the labor market. But these very procedures are themselves constructing particular versions of: 'what it is to be a human being, the moral or governable material from which that being is made, the form into which it is to be cast and the world in which it is to live' (Dean, 1995, p. 566). As a response to discourses which focus on the deficits of the welfare state, OECD think tanks perpetuate the discourse of an 'active society'. The language shifts, and we begin to see identity itself becoming problematized. We hear about how the 'beneficiaries' of welfare need to engage in 'practices of self-formation'. These practices are meant to 'teach' them to operate as active subjects: 'The active subject is to take an active role in the management and presentation of the self, to undertake a systematic approach to the search for a job, and, ultimately, if possible, to participate in the labor force' (Dean, 1995, p. 576).

Thus, former procedures whereby social security benefits were merely managed, now become part of a larger 'identity politics' aimed at creating 'entrepreneurial selves':

> They assess each individual as a case to be managed, they supervise the individual's relation with him or herself, they neutralize dependency by identifying certain risks in his or her relation to self and they seek to promote the various qualities encapsulated in the notion of 'job readiness' (ibid., p. 576).

Dean's analysis brings the ethical dimension to the fore, in describing how technical procedures become interwoven with activities of identity formation. It thus becomes more and more clear that these practices cannot be understood as value neutral, merely technical operations – however progressive the language in which activation projects are dressed.

Dean offers us an interesting explanation of the reason why, contrary to our original research expectations, the development of biographical and social competencies was now in the foreground, not the background, in the projects we have studied. This shift is perfectly in line with the OECD emphasis on creating active, entrepreneurial subjects, who become better equipped through activation to take responsibility for their own 'employability'.

Until recently, notions such as 'identity politics' and 'labor market politics' were worlds apart. This is why we felt we could assume that mainstream activation practices would be mainly geared towards the acquisition of instrumental competences. Our research revealed, however, the extent to which identity issues and employment issues were increasingly being dialectically interwoven. Individual development and social integration were increasingly defined strictly in terms of labor market effectiveness.

The economic and labor market orientation of the activation programs thus becomes the prevailing ground for the variety of efforts undertaken. We have noticed that in many cases, 'social activation' was being legitimized by claims that it is in the service of 'labor activation'. Increasingly, also, accountability for such outputs becomes a condition of funding.

So what we are looking at here is an assumption that entry into the labor market can be considered to be the central medium of social integration (or participation). The ultimate criterion for the effectiveness of activation becomes the extent to which it contributes to this objective.

This is also confirmed by Dean (1995) who finds that in many schemes for the unemployed, broader orientations than just labor market orientations are welcomed, as long as they are 'useful in promoting job re-entry'. He offers the example of a wide variety of subjects such as English language courses, linguistic and numeracy competency courses, short courses on particular skills, participation in 'Job Clubs', on-the-job training and training courses, part-time or short-term work, courses and counseling. As long as they are seen to improve confidence, motivation and presentation, and participation in voluntary work if none other is available, they are seen as acceptable forms of activation (Dean, 1995, p. 574).

Inclusion in this approach thus becomes equated either directly or indirectly oriented with inclusion in the labor market. The labor market as it functions nowadays is not subject to the same forms of scrutiny and reformation effort. Being part of it, as it currently exists, sooner or later, in one way or another, even if only for '30 Days Max' such as in Belgium, is what now counts.

De-contextualized Practices: Social Responsibility as Individual Integrity

Our suggestion above that activation practices mainly focus on inclusion in the labor market may seem to downplay our observation that learning for social responsibility was also an important issue in many projects. We have repeatedly expressed our surprise about the espoused importance attached to 'social competencies' and to 'socially responsible behavior' in the activation practices we studied.

Yet, interestingly, we did not find many direct references to the notion of developing 'social capital' in documents on activation. It perhaps goes without saying that many architects of various education, training, employment, and guidance schemes for young unemployed adults, would argue that the building of social capital is an important objective of their enterprise. They would not accept that their efforts were limited merely to the increase of economic capital, be it on an institutional level or individual level. They would definitely, and rightly, claim that their efforts were also directed towards the enhancement of civic competence and responsibility.

However, in line with our observations above concerning the 'management of the entrepreneurial self', we would argue that a social capital orientation in the context of restrictive activation policies and practices puts an emphasis on 'individual integrity' as the means to building social capital. This in turn becomes operationalized in highly normative and disciplining – and individualized – ways.

The notion of social capital has become very popular in recent years. As often is the case, a particular phenomenon attracts our attention, not so much when it is a common feature in everyday life, but more so when it threatens to vanish. This would seem to be the case with practices that are increasingly accounted for in social capital terms.

Linking back to our previous discussion on the consequences of individualization, the notion of 'social capital' is often being used to signify the imminent disappearance of important aspects of the social fabric. We draw here on the thinking of two authors who write about this issue. On the one hand, there is Coleman, who has developed the concept of 'social capital' as complementary to 'human capital'. He understands this as a set of resources that adhere in family relations and in community social organization and that constitute an important advantage for children and adolescents in the development of their human capital (Coleman, 1988-1989).

Coleman's formulation represents an attempt to explain how actors rationally make use of their social networks as resources, which help them to improve their living conditions. In other words, social capital is seen to adhere in the structure of relations between actors and among actors. Coleman identifies three elements as playing a central role in the constitution of social capital: obligations, expectations, and trustworthiness with respect to structures, networks and information channels, and norms. On the other hand, Putnam has developed a fairly similar concept of social capital, which relates to the features of social organization such as trust, norms, and networks that can improve the efficiency of society by facilitating coordinated actions (Putnam, 2000). Contrary to Coleman's conception, however, which is posited as technically value-neutral, Putnam's concept is highly normative. He distinguishes between vertical–hierarchical and horizontal–egalitarian social networks. The vertical ones are exclusive, whereas the horizontal ones are inclusive. He argues that it is especially the 'horizontal networks, or networks of civic engagement, which tend to foster trust and reciprocity. Societies and communities with dense horizontal social networks can draw on trust and reciprocity to develop more successful political and economic outcomes' (Gamarnikow and Green, ibid., p. 48). Linked to this distinction between horizontal and vertical networks, Putnam has also introduced the distinction between bonding and bridging types of social capital. He suggests that bridging social capital brings people together across diverse social divisions and reinforces heterogeneity, whereas social bonding capital reinforces homogeneity and emphasizes exclusive identities.

A constitutive element of social capital is 'trust'. When people have a sense of belonging and when there is an experience of support by their social network, they have trust to engage with the insecurities of daily life:

> The key social locations for its development are in the interconnected social institutions of: families, particularly in parent-child relations; communities with strong norms, values and sanctions; generalized cultural norms of reliability, reciprocity and accountability; dense social networks; and civic engagement (Gamarnikow and Green, 1999, p. 49).

Gamarnikow and Green bring the reflection on social capital one step further, when introducing the distinction between different models of social capital. This distinction makes clear that the formation of social capital can be understood as the result of either individual action or of collective action. In line with this distinction, they also open up perspectives on different strategies of rebuilding social capital. They distinguish between two dominant models and propose a third one. We will introduce the two basic models here and return to the third model later in this chapter, as integral to our exploration of reflexive activation practices. The first model they call the 'individual integrity for collective goods' model.

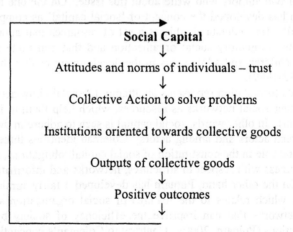

Social Capital
↓
Attitudes and norms of individuals – trust
↓
Collective Action to solve problems
↓
Institutions oriented towards collective goods
↓
Outputs of collective goods
↓
Positive outcomes
↓

Figure 11.1   Social capital: Attitudes and norms of individuals – trust (based on Gamarnikow and Green, 1999, p. 53)

This model has a strong individual bias. It puts individual integrity at the center of the social fabric, which in its turn creates the conditions for a comfortable and trustful life. It could be called a 'voluntaristic' model. Responsible social practices are basically the result of the actions of responsible individuals who engage in collective actions and thereby create institutions that contribute to the creation of collective goods. Thus, the model presents a fairly linear understanding of the construction of social capital. Building social capital is, in the first place, based on strong, trustful individuals. The trust is mainly assumed to arise from particular attitudes of integrity that exist among these individuals. This basis of trust is perceived to enable, in the second place, collective action to solve problems. Trustful individuals take responsibility for aspects of community life. This has, in the third place, positive effects on the functioning of institutions that are oriented towards the production of collective goods (such as social or public services). In the fourth place, these institutions produce outputs of collective goods (for example, social work, cultural productions or educational provision). And finally, the entire cycle is meant to lead to positive outcomes both for individuals and society.

Gamarnikow and Green call their second model, 'institutional action for collective goods'. In other words, the basis for the effective social fabric is situated in institutions that are oriented towards generating collective goods.

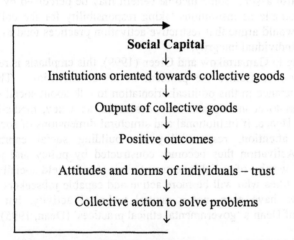

Social Capital
↓
Institutions oriented towards collective goods
↓
Outputs of collective goods
↓
Positive outcomes
↓
Attitudes and norms of individuals – trust
↓
Collective action to solve problems
↓

Figure 11.2   Social capital: Institutions oriented towards collective goods (based on Gamarnikow and Green, 1999, p. 53)

This second model works the other way round. The presence of collective goods (such as social or public services) is regarded as a precondition for the creation of basic trust in society at large and among individuals. Positive attitudes and norms are perceived to be the result of the existence of institutions that take care of people. Individual integrity is seen as dependent on an atmosphere of collective responsibility. This in turn is assumed to generate more collective action to solve problems.

These two models have the same constituting elements. In both cases they operate on the basis of a unidirectional trajectory. Yet, the basic difference between the two is that the one is emphasizing the role of the individual as the base for creating social capital, whereas the other one stresses the importance of institutions to create social capital.

We have argued that current activation discourses often take the deficient identities of their participants as the main point of departure. Projects are meant to transform these identities with the intention of turning participants into responsible people. Responsible people are presumed to be those who cannot only claim their rights to social benefits, but who also know their duties as active, entrepreneurial individuals. They are expected to take their own trajectory towards the labor market into their own hands. This emphasis on individuals 'taking responsibility' is very much in line with the first model that presumes individual integrity as the basis for generating collective goods.

We suggest that dominant activation discourses implicitly conceive of social responsibility in terms of individual integrity. The individual is vested with having the main leverage to produce social capital. An emphasis on institutional responsibilities in creating social capital was less apparent in the activation schemes that we researched. This does not mean that institutional approaches were not there or perceived to be irrelevant. The very fact of there being an activation program that also assures some income benefit may be perceived by some people as itself an example of institutions taking responsibility for the collective good. However, we would argue that restrictive activation practices tend to privilege the first model of individual integrity.

According to Gamarnikow and Green (1999), this emphasis is related to how Third Way politics frames the problem of social exclusion. They notice a significant reluctance in this political orientation to talk about social exclusion 'in terms of access to economic and other resources, as a key, mediating variable' (ibid., p. 50). Hence, if institutional and structural dimensions of social exclusion receive little attention, responsibility for building social capital shifts to individuals. Activation thus becomes constructed by policy and practice as a process that is worthy of social investment since it will yield socially responsible individual identities who will be more active and capable jobseekers and citizens. This is, as we have seen, not a neutral technical activity, but a particular manifestation of Dean's 'governmental ethical practices' (Dean, 1995).

The Imbalances of Restrictive Activation

Throughout this book, we have treated the paradox of activation as an inevitable phenomenon. Furthermore, we have argued that there can be value derived from learning from the experience of boundaries and limitations. However, if we look at the way negative identities are constructed, and additionally at the extent to which practices of personal *self-formation* become over-accentuated, we fear that activation as currently understood and practiced will have mainly disciplining rather than empowering effects.

How can a project be constructively 'activating' if it begins with a deficiency orientation that presupposes young adults enter only on the basis of negative, and not also positive competences? What kind of empowerment can result from the other competences and characteristics that young people bring to their experience of a project being put merely 'between brackets' and actively discounted?

Behrens and Evans (2002) finding that young unemployed adults in all three localities of their research in Germany and England reported 'a richer experience *outside their schemes*' is of particular relevance here:

> Respondents in the unemployed samples also had lower mean scores on indices of fulfillment in both work and personal life than their employed and higher education counterparts. The group interviews were indicative of collective feelings and expressions of frustration, stress with their situation and the limits that unemployment placed on their personal lives, although there were exceptions to this (Behrens and Evans, 2002, p. 203).

This research, as with our own, also indicates the extent to which young adults internalize covert messages signaling that an appropriate social identity cannot be formulated in positive terms until they have acquired the proper qualifications through institutionalized education, training, employment, and guidance practices. This condition begins to be constructed as the only route towards full social and economic participation, despite transformations in the labor market that may belie these assumptions.

To characterize the situation that we suggest is operating beneath the surface of many well meant practices and interventions, participants are compelled first to imbibe a self-image of a 'deficient identity' attributed to them by others. They then must make themselves dependent on externally defined norms of useful competences and strategies for achieving the intended new norm. And if they fail, they have only themselves to blame for not seizing the opportunities on offer.

Therefore, paradoxically the self same strategies that are meant to promote inclusion, simultaneously exclude those who fail to satisfy these requirements. We theorize, on the basis of our research, that the complex interaction of these various dimensions of 'restrictive' activation discourses – the problematization of the excluded, the de-limiting of responsibilities, and de-contextualized practices whereby the 'entrepreneurial self' is meant to develop – will continue to produce and legitimize conditions of social inequality.

The individual's self-responsibility for his personal well-being not only becomes *the* vehicle for social integration (Van Onna, 1990), but at the same time it pushes questions concerning the significance of social responsibilities well into the background. All responsibility is loaded onto the people who are most disadvantaged, yet paradoxically it is they whom such projects are meant to be empowering!

In this context, attention to 'tailor-made', individualized learning paths and 'self-directed learning projects' cannot be interpreted unequivocally in terms of 'progressive practice' *as if* such strategies will automatically contribute to the learner's increased empowerment. When these practices of restrictive activation are accompanied by a shift in pedagogical orientations that increasingly define social responsibility in terms of individual integrity, attention to the complex interaction of social (power) relations and structures and their impact on social opportunities disappears. Taking responsibility at this level of society goes missing from the discourse altogether. All emphasis shifts onto people's will and the quality of their efforts to qualify for a higher social status. In the long-term, in an expanded and increasingly diverse Europe, what might be the social and economic consequences of such practices?

Reflexive Activation

We will now develop an alternative discourse of 'reflexive activation'. We will argue that the notion of reflexive activation presupposes a problematizing of processes of social exclusion as integral to any education, training, employment, and guidance strategy, but in ways that do not exclude individual responsibilities. We will furthermore emphasize the need to *extend* the responsibilities of all actors involved in education, training, employment, and guidance practices. Further, a discourse of reflexive activation attends to processes of 'contextualization' and to the many meanings and possibilities with respect to strengthening the social capital of individuals and communities.

Problematizing Social Exclusion

In order to develop an alternative perspective on activation, we will make further use of the notion of 'reflexivity' as interpreted by authors such as Beck and Giddens. It was again Michael Young (1999) who has suggested the concept of 'reflexive modernization' as an alternative discourse to counterbalance the shortcomings of Third Way politics in the fields of education and employment. In the previous section, we suggested that current political solutions to social exclusion are targeted at people who are perceived to be in socially disadvantaged categories. Young argues that the architects of Third Way politics (see for example Giddens, 1998; Rosanvallon, 2000) have developed a new approach to social policy, without developing a new approach to political economy. The new social policy orientations treat 'activation' as an essential component in any attempt to re-formulate the welfare state. To reiterate points made earlier, people are thus no longer automatically entitled to social benefits. They now have the 'duty' to be active, or to engage in practices of 'self-formation' in order deserve their 'allowances' rather than to count on automatic 'social benefits' in the case of misfortune (Dean, 1995).

The problem with this approach is that it presents only a limited answer to a problematic which, like Young, we have found to be much more complex than is suggested by the Third Way architects. Young's way of re-interpreting these complexities is with the help of the theory of the 'risk society' and the related notion of 'reflexivity'. The concept of the risk society draws attention to society as presenting problems and challenges that are quite different from what we were used to in the context of classical modernization. In the risk society we are confronted with so-called 'manufactured risks', which are the (unintended) outcomes of modernization itself (Giddens, 1991.) Changes are proposed, with the argument that they are essential to improving life conditions with the help of science and (human) technology: for example, through the 'modernization' of public services, instead these so-called improvements can generate quite perverse social, economic, and cultural effects.

Dealing with the outcomes of manufactured risks demands other strategies than those developed in previous eras. In this respect, the distinction between 'reflectivity' and 'reflexivity', made by Beck, is relevant and useful. He argues that particular forms of scientific and technological 'reflectivity' were at the base of classical modernization processes. These modernization processes unquestionably produced unequalized comfort, development, and wealth. However, these processes simultaneously produced unintended risks, which cannot be countered with classical forms of 'reflectivity'. They need new forms of knowledge and systemic thinking that can be framed under the heading of 'reflexivity'. This involves 'the self confrontation with the effects of risk society and its autonomous modernization processes which are blind and deaf to their own effects and threats' (Beck, 1992, p. 202).

Young (1999) argues that we need to consider social exclusion not only in its classical form, but also as a manufactured risk. In other words, it is *also* an unintended outcome of attempts to improve the situation of multiply disadvantaged and unemployed young Europeans. This shifts the emphasis from the dominant focus on the 'socially excluded' and enables us to consider social exclusion more reflexively against the backdrop of – and as an unintended consequence of – broader changes in the existing social, political and economic context of 'reflexive modernization'. This means that the unintended outcomes of simple solutions, such as disciplining the excluded to become more active and personally accountable, or enforcing stricter performance/output management processes for activation schemes (such as in terms of successful transfers to the labor market) themselves become problematized. So, for example here, we have discovered how such measures often turn out to be counterproductive since they only further emphasize the negative identity of the excluded. Other analyses, beyond the scope of this book, point to the growing gap between rich and poor, as a result of the introduction of neo-liberal economic policies in the United States and now in Europe. Moreover, Young argues, that the simple introduction of all kinds of measures of attainment in order to raise national standards of education and training, based on external monitoring and ranking, may have the perverse effect of further polarizing the distinction between the 'excluded' and the 'included' rather than promoting social integration.

Young refers to this ensemble of measures of control as 'technocratic modernization' as opposed to 'reflexive modernization'. He asserts that they represent a 'reflective' rather than a 'reflexive' approach to accountability and effectiveness. He furthermore suggests that 'the uncritical application of quantitative procedures to human affairs should be challenged. This does not imply the outright rejection of needs for accountability, but rather the adoption of new ways of making schools and colleges accountable that involve both their staff and the communities which they serve' (ibid., p. 219). We shall return to such issues (that we refer to as multi-faceted accountability) in the final chapter.

Extending Responsibilities in Negotiated Action Spaces

Linking the problem of social exclusion to the broader context of reflexive modernity challenges us to find more sophisticated answers than those that seem to be offered by the technocratic solutions. These, we discovered, are increasingly prominent in relation to activation policy and practice across Europe. However, these sophisticated answers are not just simply available. Nor can they be formulized and turned into protocols (a further tendency in a technocratic, driven world), nor turned into off-the-shelf modules.

Instead, they need to be seen as the result of the *ongoing mobilization* of different forms of reflexivity in relation to paradoxes and contradictions presented by policy and in specific contexts of practice. For example, in our chapter on re-visioning professional practice, we emphasized that solutions to the dilemmas the professionals and the participants find themselves in today cannot be pre-given. Instead, they need to be negotiated through continuous and critically reflexive interpretations of, on the one hand, the structural and socio-political demands that direct the activities of the actors involved and, on the other hand, the social and biographical dynamics that come into play when professionals and participants meet each other in the context of specific activation programs.

We have described this encounter of structures and dynamics previously in this book in terms of 'a communicative action space'. An 'action space' can be conceived systemically as always in dynamic tension. The possibility of restrictive and reflexive activation is always present.

To illustrate, the introduction of modular, flexible, accessible courses online may work for many who are sufficiently privileged to participate actively in the information society. Such approaches may be highly efficient and effective for certain kinds of learning. But at what cost are such technical–rational solutions assumed to work for everybody? For young adults such as those we encountered in our study, these approaches to learning have no meaning or impact whatsoever. As they become more and more dominant, the discourses of pedagogy fundamentally shift. Possibilities for relational, contextualized and reflexive learning that might support the development of alternative biographical and social stories in actual communities can become severely fractured and slowly eradicated. Non-technologically based pedagogy can begin to be treated by funding bodies and by politicians as indulgent, not efficient enough, and a waste of taxpayers money. But the further 'solution' of subjecting such strategies to tighter time scales and pre-determined output criteria only further compounds the problem. So too does the reductionism of complex problems to more simple formats to suit technological formats. A host of unintended effects arise from each so-called 'solution', but in ways that often remain invisible to the 'system as a whole'.

Our interest, at European, national, regional and local levels, is in alternative ways of understanding and learning from such tensions at the interface of policy and practice and in the context of aspirations to support economic and social empowerment.

- How can more creative action, experimentation, and new forms of authorship be supported?

- How can possibilities for learning from paradoxes and contradictions, from diverse re-framings of 'problems', be sustained?

In our earlier development of the notion of action space, we have suggested that professionals and unemployed are equally restricted by the structures within which they operate (see also Behrens and Evans, 2002; Evans, 2002). Following the insights of the structuration theory, we have suggested that both groups of actors simultaneously (re)produce the structural context in which their meeting takes place, while also attempting to (re)create the conditions of their encounter. This observation is reminiscent of other considerations in literature that emphasize that, because of the unpredictability and insecurity of the conditions in which professionals operate today, 'engagement with contradictions and paradoxes' has become an inevitable feature of professional action. They therefore have to commit themselves to: 'an ongoing negotiation of the complexity and ambivalence of lifelong learning policies and practices and their effects' (Edwards et al., 2001, p. 427).

In line with this, we would argue that the creation of a 'critically reflexive and negotiated action space' becomes a key dimension of any practice that would seek to identify itself with reflexive activation (see also Weil, 1998; Percy-Smith and Weil, 2002, 2003).

Extending Responsibilities: From Protocols to Practice Principles

We now wish to offer some principles to guide the development of alternative theories of practice that spring from both the theoretical and empirical explorations we have offered thus far. We see the diverse and specifically contextualized enactment of these as holding potential for more empowering forms of activation. Their relevance and potential applicability at a more systemic level will be further developed in the final chapter.

The first principle is that of *valuing competence and diversity*. Above, we have argued that the participants in activation projects tend to be defined as deficient or deviant. In doing this, very often implicit standards of normality are being constructed and maintained. This has a disciplinary character in and of itself. What is invisible, what is visible? What is allowed to be expressed? What is not?

The valuing of competence and diversity implies that these standards of so-called 'normality' cannot be taken for granted, but are subjected to constant questioning. Survival in any work environment entails this as a matter of course, but less familiar are those processes that support new forms of critical scrutiny into the value frameworks that marginalize and discount certain groups at the expense of others. When exclusion is at stake, as it always is, it is important to legitimate ongoing inquiry into mechanisms of inclusion/exclusion as they operate in specific contexts of practice (see also Edwards et al., 2001, p. 425).

It is also vital that activation processes pay attention to and value qualities and capabilities with which participants begin a project, and which may play a role with respect to encouraging new forms of social and economic participation. Equally, what survival skills do the young professionals bring with them? What experiences of inventiveness, self-will, perseverance, and courage may open up very different forms of dialogue and practice relating to social and economic participation? The acknowledgement of these as creative positives, rather than as deficiencies and differences that 'do not fit' unexplored new norms can offer a wellspring of learning material for raising awareness of the socially constructed and debatable character of the negative identities ascribed to the unemployed in today's society.

This kind of stance on the part of the professional may support a process whereby options for self-help and personal development can be weighed more consciously against the significance of the social and economic integration that activation projects are meant to achieve. It opens up other critical and creative inquiry spaces for reflecting on the (im)possibilities of coupling self-realization to socially responsible action. Moreover, how might we connect these insights to the contexts that encourage this to a greater or smaller degree: labor organizations, living and housing conditions, (voluntary) work in community organizations, community self-help, social movements, and so on (see also Burns et al., 2004; Taylor, 2003).

Connective inquiry is the second principle that we associate with the extension of responsibility. This principle emanates from the complexity, the unpredictability, the messiness, and the political and value-laden character of the activation process. It entails the continuous involvement of the different partners, both external and internal to the project, in re-definitions of 'the problem', in the formulation of objectives and in the design and follow-up of trajectories. It entails a dialogical attitude that enables co-inquiry and co-learning and the negotiation and exploration of different meanings and interpretations. It implies the valuing of reflection-in-action which, in turn, can create new capacities for dealing with instability and complexity.

For example, enacting the above principle of valuing diversity and competence shifts the focus to the social relationships and rationalities that for these diverse young adults are integral to their own experience, knowledge, and sense of identity. These can then be made the focus for both critically and creatively reflexive co-inquiry within the projects: in other words, we are speaking about jointly developing learning cultures – cultures of inquiry – where nothing is taken as given. Moreover, differences can be explored not only in terms of dominant power relations, but also in terms of socio-cultural and individual tendencies to deny, dismiss, and fear difference. For example, we can choose in society, to construct the 'Other' as the problem, or to look also at how we too are implicated in this construction and maintenance of the Other as a way of paradoxically, *not* taking active responsibility for our own part in this.

We suggest that such approaches – as evidenced by the *Cultural Mediators* project and the *Bridging the Gap* work with homeless and multiple disadvantaged groups – had greater scope for fostering capacity (and indeed competence) for learning from experience, from uncertainty and from complexity, and for negotiating and transforming changing conditions and situations.

Emphases such as these may be seen to present professionals with a bewildering range of choices. But we contend that current technocratic demands and the standardization of de-contextualized notions of competence, are giving rise to the de-motivation and de-activation of professionals. At the same time, it is too demanding and too ambitious to expect that all of the above roles can ever be embodied into one individual professional. In an interpretive and co-inquirying practice therefore, we suggest that flexibility needs to be understood not as an attitude of individual professionals but as a function of distributed leadership through which different functions and roles are balanced yet enacted fluidly by participants in response to learning in action from specific challenges and contradictions. We include the young adults as members of such a team.

The fostering of teamwork is not necessarily at odds with specialized action of the professionals nor with the establishment of links with the external world. On the contrary, activation teams can attempt to realize what Michael Young (1999, p. 221) calls 'connective specialization': in other words, new kinds of links between specialized partners and processes both within and outside the learning institutions – or in this case, the specific activation projects.

The third principle to support extended responsibility is that of *relational social capital orientation.* As mentioned before, social capital is a concept that highlights the importance of connectedness and trust among people on the level of social institutions such as families, social networks, associations, communities and labor organizations. However, although this notion may have arisen in recognition of the disappearance of the social, the generation of social capital likewise cannot be formulized as a technical means to an end. This very colonization of such a concept by the forces of economic rationality and neo-liberal individualism may be generating significant social consequences. A relational orientation emphasizes how these understandings need to be understood as jointly and continually constructed, negotiated, and discovered.

As discussed in our chapter on agency and empowerment, activation practices offer the possibility of belonging to a community of practice. Meaning making, practice development and identity construction are not seen as modules or as separate activities. They are integral to the very act of sustaining one's participation in a community of practice and jointly creating a context that supports individual and collective thriving. But this is not achieved without active engagement and co inquiry around tension, differences, contradictions, power, and issues of individual and collective action and choice.

Integrating socially excluded and unemployed young adults into such practices may generate a sense of trust and possibility with respect not only to their lives, but also to wider societal issues, even in conditions that we described before as insecure and unpredictable. Activation projects that focus merely on building individual integrity among their participants as a means to an end, may be failing in what they may offer to alternative visions of economic and social participation.

It is in this context that we return to Gamarnikov and Green's social capital models. Their first model made individual responsibility the starting point for the creation of trust on an institutional level. The second one accentuated the institutional pre-conditions for the building of social capital, while pointing to the importance of the institutional action for collective goods.

We have found that the projects which were the most effective in creating an atmosphere of connectedness and hence, of trust among the participants and the professionals, were the ones that had a manifest ambition to embed their education, training, employment, and guidance activities in the context of a wider institutional action for community building or community development.

Examples of this include the *Cultural Mediators* project in Lisbon and the *Bridging the Gap* project in Northampton. Projects that were rather weak in this respect were initiatives that put an exclusive emphasis on individual competency development without paying much attention to the social fabric in which these young adults were embedded. These orientations had a powerful impact on the enhancement and delimitation of trust and confidence amongst the participants.

Those that undermined trust and confidence included the *Flexijob* initiative in Belgium, the Danish *House of Projects* and *New Deal* in the UK. This does of course not mean that the fostering of individual integrity should be neglected. We found much evidence that, especially in the case of young adolescents, strong support for this aspect is still very important. Our conclusion therefore is, that also in view of the development of social capital in activation projects, attention to a project as itself an institutional action for generating outcomes that have collective value and simultaneously enhance individual integrity should be balanced carefully.

Contextualized Activation Practices and Multiple Intervention Strategies

In traditional pedagogical conceptions, the learning of different kinds of competencies is exclusively located in the individual. Little attention is paid, both in theory and in practice, to how learning can be focused on social or collective value.

When an individual learning trajectory is overemphasized, we see the disappearance of conceptual notions and practices that contribute to the social dimension of learning in the activation projects. We have noticed that 'schemeland' often lacks the capacity to support relevant theory–practice connections. The focus is mainly on individualized packages and counseling/guidance aimed at fostering the development of an entrepreneurial self. In short, the learning often takes place in the context of 'de-contextualized activation practices' that have no perceived links to the social or economic worlds these young adults inhabit outside the projects.

In opposition to this, recent research on learning brings to the fore the importance of 'situated learning' embedded in 'communities of practice' (Lave and Wenger, 1991; Wenger, 1998). As explored in Part II, these orientations draw attention to the active participation of workers in social learning through everyday practices. We have used such social theories of learning as a point of departure for ourselves, suggesting how activation practices can hold more relevance for participation and learning when embedding in contexts which are closely linked to real life situations *as understood by those participating*.

The activation project that we value most in this respect continues to be the *Cultural Mediators* project in Lisbon. But as importantly, we are inspired by other innovative initiatives that are nowadays being developed in the 'social economy' such as in the French *Services de Proximité* (Gilain et al., 2001). This concept covers an ensemble of provisions operational on a community level and delivering a variety of services to community dwellers or to external clients such as home support for old aged people, kindergarten services, environmental management of public spaces, social restaurants, and so on.

The development of these services has in the past been closely linked to the creation of employment for people who have difficulty finding jobs in the regular labor market. However, in an interesting critique on the narrow economic focus to which such initiatives are geared nowadays, Gilain et al. (2001), present a multidimensional concept of activation (and 'labor market insertion') through community services. This works innovatively to reconcile ambitions for 'labor activation' and for 'social activation'. More than this, they are attempting to engage in 'institutional action' to generate outcomes that have collective value and thereby (re)build social capital, while engaging in 'situated activation practices' such as those which we have explored above.

In the first place, this initiative around community services establishes a relevant connection with the socio-economic environment while offering particular services that have both an economic and social function. In the second place they create a relevant 'community of practice' that brings together workers/trainees, volunteers and clients of the services. This is the context of a situated practice, which is part of an institutional action aimed at integrating labor market functions (employment and training), social functions (integration of volunteers), and consumption functions (clients using the services). Thirdly, the community services integrate their activation strategies – and systemic learning from these – on three different levels: vocational integration through employment activities, social integration through embedment in social networks, and civic integration through the participatory engagement in projects of societal relevance. The framework of community services itself helps us to consider activation policies and practices on multiple levels, in ways that involve a plurality of actors and aim at a plurality of effects. Although it is not applicable in all circumstances where education, training, employment, and guidance practices are developed, it may be inspiring to consider the quality of the embeddedness of different activation practices.

Such strategies locate solutions to problems of social exclusion not exclusively on the level of the individual unemployed person, but rather equally on the level of collective and innovative action and of public responsibility. These forms of collective action demonstrate the potential for triggering social learning processes that are having a profound impact on social exclusion and activation, and the communities in which they occur.

Gamarnikov and Green (1999) have also pointed to the relevance of engaging different actors, both from the public sector and from civil society, in the context of a third model that they argue may be more relevant in today's society for working towards the (re)building of social capital. This is their so-called multiple interventions model. In the two other models of social capital elaborated before (the individual integrity model and the collective action model), the process of activation is described in linear terms. Either one starts with influencing individual attitudes and norms to achieve positive outcomes on a collective level, or one starts with influencing institutions to be oriented towards the production of collective goods and collective action to solve problems. These linear processes are intended to realize some 'step by step' intermediate achievements, such as changed attitudes and norms, as clarified in the previous diagrams in this chapter.

In the 'multiple intervention model', the idea of step-by-step, cause–effect linearity is relinquished. It is replaced by the idea of non-linear sequencing, whereby all elements are interconnected and mutually constitutive. The linearity which was implied in the first two models is thus replaced by a relationship which privileges not one single element, but relates them to each other in an interactive and multi-causal way with following result.

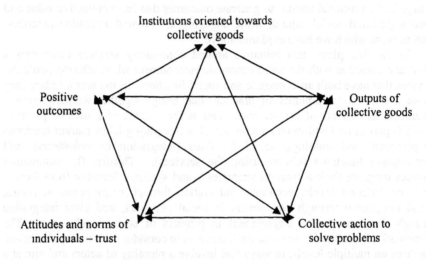

Figure 11.3 The model of multiple interventions (based on Gamarnikow and Green, 1999, p. 54)

The model of multiple interventions supports a form of theoretical pragmatism rather than causal dogmatism. This pragmatism requires professionals and young adults to remain constantly attuned to the complex reality in which they are situated. What is suggested here, both for policy strategy and practice intervention is that the actors involved reflexively consider all aspects simultaneously and try to act upon them in an integrated way.

This more systemic approach suggests possibilities for social and public learning that may be more appropriate for 'reflexive modernity' and our need to understand and cope with the risks we ourselves manufacture through, especially, adopting largely technocratic strategies to socially and economically complex situations.

Our notion of contextualized practices therefore attends to needs for integration between 'inner' project activities and the world 'out there'. Projects as a whole need to be meaningfully linked to the environment. This intention itself needs to be approached reflexively, at different levels, and in ways that work actively, yet critically and creatively through connective inquiry. In this way, we see some potential for activation projects to transcend the limitations of Rob McDonald's (1998) isolated and isolating 'schemeland'.

Secondly, we suggest that there should be an integration of different actors involved, both within and outside the project, jointly engaged in developing solutions to social exclusion as a shared and community-situated responsibility. As the projects are primarily about finding and creating employment for those who are currently excluded from the labor market, various actors can be empowered to influence the conditions of employment in differential ways. These strategies can engage those both within the project and beyond in joint processes of critically and creatively reflexive co-inquiry. Since the projects are also geared towards 'social integration', the exclusion of other actors from civil society is itself problematic. Their participation could prove highly relevant in creating integrative initiatives.

Thirdly, we suggest that there needs to be ongoing attention to how to integrate the different competences needed with respect to such enlarged activation projects. Since the very beginning of our research, the idea of integrating and balancing competencies has been a central idea. We have come back to this idea in various ways in the course of this book and consider it to still have robustness and relevance. Linking it again to Lave and Wenger's (1991) work, we conclude that balancing competences implies that participants are encouraged to explore the meaning of the knowledge, skills and practices they learn with respect to their personal life course – in the short- and in the long-term, in order to look at both the present dreams and future options (imagination). Furthermore, their commitment can be evoked by situating learning in a joint practice of common goals and shared responsibilities, and embedded in a safe and supportive atmosphere (engagement). Finally, they should be provided with the relevant know-how, skills, and hands-on experiences to give them an adequate sense of taking part in the wider world of real life labor (alignment).

Conclusion

In this chapter, we have explored reflexive activation – as an alternative discourse to restrictive activation – and as a strategy that can be jointly created between professionals, young adults, and wider communities. It is important however, to consider that these two forms of activation which are theoretical constructions, based on empirical observations, are not binary opposites. In practice, they are not always either/or positions. Inevitably, practitioners will have to balance between the two forms of activation and will have to take the ambivalence and the paradoxical character of their actions into consideration. The reference to the two forms of activation may help professionals to be more reflexive about their practice and to improve their decision-making.

Our task is almost finished now. Yet, we will not end our story without some ultimate considerations. In the next and last chapter of this book, we will investigate what has to change at other levels of the system of the EU to make developments such as 'reflexive activation' possible.

Chapter 12

Learning and Improvisation at the Policy-practice Interface

Review

Throughout this book, we have explored specific education, training, employment, and guidance practices as manifestations of increasingly dominant European policies and discourses relating to 'activation'. These have as their espoused purpose that of better integrating unemployed and socially excluded young adults into the social and economic fabric of society. However, the complex ways in which these largely instrumental and economically derived policy discourses operate at the micro level of everyday practice and impact on young adults' processes of identity formation and participation, remain largely invisible to the system as a whole.

On the macro-level, we have considered why policy makers have become so obsessed over the last decade with policies of 'activation'. We have argued that this trend is indicative of various strategies devised by social democratic governments in various European countries to resist neo-liberal challenges to the Welfare State. As discussed in Chapter 10, from the 1980s onward, welfare provision has been attacked for costing too much, and for turning our European economy into a highly uncompetitive system. Europe is compared to other systems and nation states that do not carry the 'heavy burden' of public expenditure, with respect to health, education, unemployment and other benefits. Those assuming neo-liberal positions claim that welfare provision turns people into dependent, inactive subjects who lack the personal initiative to break through cycles of dependency and disadvantage.

The European social democratic answer to such arguments is that the welfare state can continue to be retained as the backbone for the relative stability and prosperity of many members of society, and in particular for lower income and multiply disadvantaged groups. However, at the same time, they have taken these critiques seriously. Therefore, while trying to preserve the values behind welfare states, they have also allowed the introduction of new instruments. These find their origin in neo-liberal economic and management strategies.

As discussed in Chapter 10, these shifts have been framed as the so-called Third Way perspective. This has become influential in different national and European policy agendas from the second half of the 1990s onwards. The argument behind the Third Way is that it is possible to sustain welfare provision, if, at the same time, those eligible for benefit earn this right. This stance gives rise to strategies that require potential beneficiaries to demonstrate that they are actively participating in finding solutions to the problems that they encounter.

This has especially been seen to be the case for unemployed young adults. They are expected now to show in many ways that they have turned themselves into active entrepreneurs on the job market. Sadly, for many, this requirement to demonstrate 'active commitment' means that they become compelled to attend one activation scheme after another, lest they lose their right to benefits.

We have indicated the extent to which the exploration of alternative visions for reconciling social and economic tensions is becoming increasingly curtailed across Europe as these mainstream discourses become institutionalized through a variety of mechanisms. Although there is less and less 'discursive space' and funding for alternatives, we have offered some examples from our own research and elsewhere, such as from France, which challenges existing modes of practice. We suggested that these examples may be more attuned to enhancing individual and collective capacities for living, learning, and working in changing social and economic conditions. We have also considered 'reflexive activation' as an alternative discourse to 'restrictive activation' and as a strategy that can be mutually created between professionals, young adults, and wider communities. A discourse of 'reflexive activation' makes co-inquiry and situated experimentation around the social and economic paradoxes and contradictions that young adults experience in their lifeworlds central to any meaningful notion of activation. It reframes and challenges current dominant understandings of, for example, notions of labor identity, competence, and pedagogy.

In this chapter, we focus in particular on how state and EU-funded activation practices might be given greater freedom to be more diverse in their local responsiveness and expression. Put another way, we concern ourselves with how the wider system, and in particular the EU, can support new forms of policy and practice into what 'learning for inclusion' could mean in different communities and cultures. Some questions that guide us in this chapter are:

- What, and where is the space for 'policy learning' in the EU – and why might this matter?

- How are opportunities for policy and practice learning from paradoxes and contradictions arising at the policy–practice interface, and from alternative formations of the 'discursive space' around activation currently being curtailed?

- How could the EU become more effective in encouraging the development of less standardized and more pioneering 'activation' initiatives that do not rely on merely 'inserting' young adults into labor markets as given?

- How might the inquiry processes that have guided our own research at the policy practice interface be extended to support policy and practice learning from diversity and new forms of connective inquiry across an expanding EU?

- At what cost are current top down strategies of control restricting opportunities for developing new ecologies of governance around unemployment and exclusion?

- How might unemployed young adults across Europe, contribute actively to such initiatives, and what barriers and issues would need to be addressed to support their participation in such systemic learning and inquiry processes?

Throughout, we actively engage with principles explored in Chapter 11: those of valuing competence and diversity, connective inquiry, and relational social capital building. We relate these to our core concern that failures in policy learning, combined with strategies that manage and standardize processes of activation, may not only be masking, but indeed contributing to the growth of poverty, social exclusion, and labor market alienation across the EU. Need dominant practices that purport to support 'learning for inclusion' remain thus?

Policy Learning: A Contradiction in Terms?

We observed, across the six participating countries, that a growing number of private and voluntary sector providers were entering the 'activation field'. We expected to find significant differences across these more varied providers. Instead, we discovered that the nature of the provider was not in itself problematic, in terms of 'restrictive activation'. All providers of 'activation projects' were equally enjoined to realize public policy aims related to EU objectives to reduce youth unemployment while simultaneously reducing social exclusion. What seemed to make the critical difference was the extent to which they were subject to externally defined 'activation' success criteria. These would be exerted through, for example, tendering processes, contract specifications, funding criteria, or obligations to comply with particular kinds of performance management and accountability processes that were, and that are still in ascendance throughout Western Europe.

On the strength of our research, we would argue, drawing on Schön (1979) that policy makers tend to see those organizations that they select as vehicles for public policy as merely 'implementers' of policy. In turn they dismiss the tensions and complexities that arise at the interface of policy intentions and policy implementation as failures on the ground to 'get it right': in other words, as failures to 'implement' policy correctly.

Schön (ibid) invites us to question this familiar scenario. He encourages us to treat the notion of 'policy implementation' more lightly. He suggests that the minute we try to realize policy intentions in real communities, gaps are revealed between public policy aspirations, and what is possible in actual contexts of practice: what he famously has referred to as the 'swamp' (Schön, 1983). Instead, he urges use to re-frame such situations not as policy implementation failures, but rather as opportunities for learning. Instead of seeing things thus, across Europe, social democratic governments are increasingly setting in place more managerial cultures in their attempts to assure and 'modernize' processes of public policy implementation (Ferlie, 1999). This can be interpreted as an attempt to make sure that organizations functioning as public service 'vehicles' get it 'more right': that they act more rationally and therefore in harmony with politicians' agendas. It is as if all that is required to make things happen, as politicians wish is more effective and efficient management.

But how do we command and control changes in communities and in people's lives within a democracy? The familiar response now, when policy initiatives are seen to fail 'on the ground' is – as we shall explore further below – to further increase technocratic control and regulation. This is often combined with attempts to standardize understandings of best practice and then 'performance manage' their emergence through the setting of targets: as if diversity too were merely something to be controlled more effectively, rather than be seen as a source of learning.

- But what if policy makers treated the many and diverse practice wisdoms embedded within local attempts to realize policy intentions as invaluable learning resources?

- What if, rather than homogenizing standards and exerting more and more strategies of centralized control, local improvisation and learning from difference were actively encouraged as a basis for essential policy learning?

- What if such processes were seen as key to generating relational social capital, and new ecologies of governance within diverse EU communities struggling to create locally meaningful notions of social and economic empowerment in a context of globalization?

- And what if young adults themselves were active contributors to such developments?

These questions subsume a very different discourse that acknowledges the importance and possibility of iterative processes of systemic learning as integral to public policy development and implementation. Public policy implementation thus becomes 're-framed' as a process of experimentation from which 'the system' can learn.

Schön and Rein (1994) spoke about impediments to such ideas of public learning becoming normative: namely, 'pre-existing antagonism, institutionalized distrust, and limited capability for inquiry' (p. 200). Yet the overriding passion and concern that dominated Schön's working life was that of how to promote learning within systems in ways that remained dialectic rather than linear, and that *welcomed* opportunities to learn from uncertainty, complexity, paradox, and contradiction.

Schön and Rein (1994), when working together on such issues, called for new forms of 'frame-reflective' inquiry between policy makers, researchers and practitioners 'in situations of controversy' (p. 209). This is their response to the core tension that is reproduced again and again in the space between the triad made up of policy makers, researchers, and practitioners: a tension that was so evident in our research:

> Within the triad, each actor gives priority to a different field of constraints: for policy makers, it is the political environment; for researchers, peer review and funding; and for practitioners, the clienteles they directly serve. But as each actor addresses the problems *internal to its own practice*, it alters the environment of other actors and the story looks different depending on whose point of view one takes. The triadic model surfaces issues that must be addressed if we are to develop a collaborative framework that permits the three types of actors to reflect on their own practice and recognize their transactional effects on one another (Schön and Rein, 1994, p. 198).

Schön and Rein speak of this as representing a giant leap from current public policy implementation norms. We too want to initiate such a giant leap here.

> the balance of social responsibility with rights sought within meta-policy narratives about active citizenship, have yet to make a real mark in the way they are translated into professional practice. Shifts in policy rhetoric in response to social change have been slow in giving rise to corresponding learning and change in organizations, partnerships, and systems. So often, responses to youth issues focus attention on young people themselves, and how they need to behave, change or act, with insufficient consideration of how society and systems might be failing young people, and therefore how systems need to learn and change... Policy alone cannot bring about social change (Percy-Smith and Weil, 2003, p. 82).

Learning from the Past

Schön's thinking about policy learning was developed largely outside the current economic and socio-political context of Europe and at a time when the forces of globalization and neo-liberal economics were less apparent and far-reaching. However, he uses, as a high impact case study of public learning, the example of the Works Projects Administration (WPA). This was an unemployment initiative set up after the Depression in America. We wish to use this example to stretch the imaginary but also to challenge existing mindsets, and focus on what would need to change if such initiatives were to be introduced in Europe.

Similar to the neo-liberal critique impacting today, then too in the USA there was widespread political concern not to give out handouts, on the assumption that this would encourage passive dependency on the state.

President Roosevelt brought fresh thinking to this challenge, initially as governor of the state of New York. He set up the WPA based on the key principle of providing relief in 'the form of paid work, useful, dignified and *free of stigma; and that the ultimate responsibility for providing work relief lay squarely with the federal government*' (Schön, PSO's, p. 687; emphasis added). What, Schön argues, made this initiative different from many others was its fundamental 'commitment to learning about the policy problems associated with the fundamental task of providing relief to the unemployed' (1999, p. 688-689). This large scale, federally funded public works program was vested, through its leadership, in:

> an extraordinary flexibility in the design of policy and programs, an openness to *ideas from many sources, a preference for improvisation* rather than for long range planning, and *a reliance upon the delegation of responsibility and initiative to local units of operation.* Hopkins [the Director of this initiative for many years] recognized that the long-run was tenuous and uncertain, whereas hunger and suffering were immediate, that the pressures for massive performance in the face of great uncertainties meant that *agencies had to learn through doing,* and that *central administration could not hope to know as well as local officials what the problems were and what it was best to do about them* (1979, p. 688-89; emphases added).

Schön cites the extraordinary range of diversified projects developed under the auspices of the WPA, guided by a constant legitimation of these values through action. These projects not only provided work relief, but also made creative use of a wide range of existing skills within communities that simultaneously developed skills and employment that benefited individuals *and* communities. Hopkins encouraged very varied projects, in recognition of the huge variations in the situations of both unemployed people and communities hard hit by the Depression. Moreover, he welcomed innovative responses to discovered needs, special interests (such as working in collaboration with artists) and projects that could generate deeper insights into regenerating work in partnership with very different kinds of unemployed people. The question which guided this initiative was essentially, what range of strategies was possible in providing useful and dignified work that was free of stigma?

As possibilities for re-framing problems and taking action around unemployment proliferated through the WPA, so in turn the discourse changed. For example, people who had become constructed as 'tramps and bums' began to be seen as *displaced employable people.* Projects were not responding to centralized strategy directives and protocols, nor forced to conform to performance criteria that were overly standardized and far removed from the situations in which unemployed people found themselves. These projects sowed the seeds for many later initiatives, such as:

the early development of driver-testing and licensing, nursery schools, state record-keeping and statistical research, community histories, local theatres and the like. Increasingly, central administrators played the role of learning about and transmitting the project-inventions undertaken by local communities...the repertoire ranged from construction and engineering...projects in public health services, libraries, recreational services, research and records projects and the support of the arts (1979, p. 689).

We are citing this work at some length since what Schön helps us to hone in on so brilliantly in the context of activation are *the core dynamics of a large scale public policy initiative to activate unemployed that placed emphasis on*: 'improvisation, decentralization, local initiative, flexibility of response, and openness to many sources of ideas' (1979, p. 689).

We can glimpse in this case study expression at a systemic policy level of the principles we suggested in the previous chapter that can support reflexive activation: valuing competence and diversity, relational social capital building and connective inquiry.

Technocratic and Reflexive Understandings of Policy Implementation?

Relevant to our concerns here with the current context for activation, is that Schön does not gloss over the many problems of administration and the tensions that such diversity and non-technocratic leadership behavior created! For example, he offers illustrations of how the organization had to learn to improve itself in response to the myriad of problems that were discovered daily, in order to develop its actual capacity to learn from diversity and in order to maintain a flexible responsiveness to developments and trends as they arose within specific communities and local circumstances.

The pressures from above to adopt long-term planning strategies, and to assure local compliance with well worked-out, centrally-determined strategies and criteria, were difficult to resist. To maintain a broadly conceived 'tension–possibility creative action space' Hopkins had to persuade powerful people not to fall into the trap of assuming that greater certainty and control would result in more and better 'outputs'. He admonished against the unintended consequences of more hierarchical forms of governance and control. He was confident that this would lead to the generation of opportunities for social and economic participation and the preservation of human dignity that were the very intentions behind this initiative.

The leadership and management challenges for Hopkins were considerable. On the one hand, he tried to maintain a loose, flexible, responsive organization to support those upon whom success in policy 'delivery' and connective learning depended. At the same time, he had to justify public expenditure on this program through results. Concerns for financial probity and fraud, at a time of scarce resources, ran high. However, instead of over-controlling peoples' actions at local levels, he required accountability to shared values, without over-determining the various ways in which these might be given expression actively across varying local contexts and with highly diverse unemployed people.

Interestingly, according to Schön's account, Hopkins seemed to be enacting well ahead of his time novel forms of distributed leadership that are strongly emerging in the 21st century as key to successful and resilient organizations, as influenced by insights from complexity theory (for example, Wheatley, 1994; Shaw, 1997; Stacey et al., 2000; Stacey, 2001). Explicit values, multi-directional information flows, and opportunities for expressive identification with strategic objectives through diverse forms of action, as opposed to technical–rational control, become alternative means of maintaining coherence in dispersed networks of policy action.

The strategic intelligence held within such a dynamic field can then be tapped continually, in a variety of ways, and diverse forms of relational and reflexive self-monitoring and accountability can emerge. Rather than uni-linear accountability, we begin to work with notions of multi-directional responsibility. Fresh ideas for engaging with the challenges of activation could inspire others to remain creative in how they interpreted policy under different conditions. There was no coercion, through funding contracts or tightly defined performance targets, to fit a pre-determined mold.

Ultimately, this bold policy implementation experiment, despite its success in turning policy intentions into new realities for unemployed people, was eventually perceived by politicians and others in positions of power as far too amorphous and ill planned. Hopkins was eventually subjected to, and in turn had to subject his networked workforce to comply with more and more safeguards and controls. He was forced to demonstrate more explicit accountability through more closely prescribed forward planning. Increasingly, those with project ideas had to pre-specify how financial inputs would lead to the outputs being demanded. Time scales and funding were tightened up.

This shift was to prove the downfall of the WPA. This previously, highly responsive, networked structure became compelled to provide greater evidence of clear line management accountability. This greater rigidification of the organization had expected consequences. The pace of activities reduced, the formation of creative partnerships waned, and the range of new and diversified projects shrunk. Moreover, whereas before, notions of accountability worked fluidly with the concept of 'multiple bottom lines' (Weil, 1998), the single bottom line of efficiency had now taken over. Imposed criteria for success narrowed what was possible on the ground. The quality of agency and collective responsibility that had enabled the WPA to flourish for over a decade was eradicated.

What may seem extraordinary today is that this rise and fall took place over a decade! This can seem almost inconceivable in today's world. The time scales, during which significant policy change is meant to have an impact, have been shortened by the discursive practices of turbo-capitalism. Yet are the highly controlled technocratic approaches to so-called 'modernization' really so efficient and effective in relation to what we are concerned with here – activation? Whose interests are they serving? Might their uni-linear and controlling nature be their very downfall? Is this example of policy learning from the past impossible to contemplate, much less experiment with in today's Europe?

Limitations to Policy Learning in Europe

New Public Management Strategies

This book has revealed the complex ways in which young people and professionals in Europe are being defined simultaneously as both 'subjects of' and 'subjects to' the practices in which they are participating. We have demonstrated the extent to which young people and professionals are being restricted in their agency. We contend that the unintended social and economic consequences of how this is happening at this moment through activation projects are being insufficiently explored in the EU.

All agencies that receive state funding for activation projects in effect serve as vehicles for 'public policy delivery'. This places them on the receiving end of dramatic shifts within Europe away from the former light-touch regulation of public administration and largely bureaucratic models of regulation towards the tight hold control of 'the new public management' or, in the words of Young (1999), technocratic modernization strategies. These new forms of governance have been injected into Europe now for over two decades (for example, Hood, 1991; Ferlie et al., 1996).

Further to our consideration of ideologies in Chapter 9, this development has also emerged in response to the New Right's criticism. In other words, bureaucracies and European welfare states were attacked not just for their expense and other factors explored earlier in Part III, but also for their under performance, over extension, low effort and so called problem-sustaining characteristics.

Ferlie (1999) suggests that within Europe, the UK offers a high impact example of such developments and in our research this remained the case in comparison to the other five countries. It is for this reason that we use the UK in this chapter to foreground tensions that were becoming so apparent across all countries participating in our study:

It was the radical Conservative government, elected under Thatcher in 1979, that initially set out to downsize, re-structure, and 'reform' – or 'modernize' – the public sector. This was through the introduction of, for example, internal markets, whereby 'service commissioning' and 'service delivery' processes became separated and regulated by contracts, often fragmenting the same agency. There was also increased privatization, and contracting out to tender, services that were previously 'delivered' by public agencies. Such structural changes were accompanied by severe reductions in public sector funding, and legislation that entailed 'a rebalancing of the industrial relations framework to reduce the power of unions and increase that of management with the slogan that 'management must manage' (Ferlie, 1999, p. 3). At the same time, more elaborate and far reaching systems of performance management and regulation were set in place, often ensuring that strategic and often operational control was retained by policy makers through the publication of national service frameworks, guidance protocols, targets, and 'league tables' that compared outputs across agencies. This remains the case, despite ever-stronger rhetoric about the devolution of control to communities or agencies, such as schools or hospitals. At the local level, we see further fragmentation of regional and other agencies that previously, helped to support some forms of 'connective inquiry' around policy and practice tensions and that assured some form of reflexive dialogue about the unintended consequences of restricting discourses being imposed 'from the top'.

This steady but dramatic culture shift has been captured in Strathern (2000) through the term 'audit culture': a culture from which virtually no 'agency' across the world, that has been given public funding to 'deliver' public policy, is now immune. She describes the new 'audit culture' as:

> one kind of culture on the make. It is informed by practices confined to no single set of institutions and to no one part of the world. Recognizable in the most diverse places, these practices also drive very local concerns. They determine the allocation of resources and can seem crucial to the credibility of enterprises; people become devoted to their implementation; they evoke a common language of aspiration... They also evoke anxiety and small resistances, are held to be deleterious to certain goals, and as over-demanding if not outright damaging. An old name is used for the new phenomenon: accountability. Its dual credentials in moral reasoning and in the methods and precepts of financial accounting go back a long way. But over the last two decades, and in numerous contexts, it has acquired a social presence of a new kind (Strathern, 2000, p. 1).

Young (1999) points to the perverse effects of such practices on schools. They are likewise so subjected to extensive audits guided by top down prescribed success criteria, despite policy rhetoric about school 'independence', autonomy, and 'freedom of choice'. He considers how locally defined goals soon become swept off the agenda, since the sheer enormity of the demands to meet externally defined criteria for audit and 'effective and efficient' performance (and therefore continued funding) leave little time for anything else. Government-set targets become the priority that drives everything else. He notes how the displacement of attention and energy actually supports the protection of vested interests. Information flows become increasingly uni-linear and top down (1999, p 220). Nick Cohen captured the tension that the case study of Britain continues to illustrate so sharply: that of local institutions being forced to hit government targets but in ways that keep 'missing the point' (2000).

In our research, we saw the extent to which such performance management strategies produce a decreased motivation on the part of professionals when specified targets cannot be met, and are perceived as meaningless in the first place: both in terms of the espoused purposes of a specific particular policy, and also in terms of what it means to realize these in relation to the lifeworlds of actual participants, communities, and the labor market as given. Consider the following illustration of Cohen's (2000) argument that 'hitting the target may be missing the point': Given the multiple disadvantages faced by many young people in the projects we studied, and the complexities of their biographies, just to persuade them to participate in a project at all can represent a major achievement. In the same way that research has demonstrated how the role of money in motivating employees remains subservient to other factors in staying with a job, this seems also to be the case with unemployed young adults. The threat of their benefit being withdrawn is not necessarily enough to assure their participation. Professionals and young people often spoke about small but highly significant achievements that made the difference to a young person staying with a project or dropping out. For one person, getting up in the morning on time to get to a project and being addiction free for one day is a huge step. Getting to this point signifies a great deal of energy, effort, and skill on the part of professionals, in terms of building sufficient relationships and trust. This can then be built upon to extend this quality of participation. But such participation cannot be commanded. For another young adult, motivating them to learn something at the computer other than indulge in computer games can signify another major accomplishment on the part of the project and the professionals. However, when blunt output statistics are demanded, such as how many were 'inserted' into the labor market, the value of such shifts become discounted, indeed annihilated from view. The individual and collective journeys that are so germane to activation with unemployed and socially excluded young adults cannot be simplistically quantified in terms of labor market 'insertion' or economic and social participation. Yet such small steps do represent new forms of participation that differ from those that the young people might have engaged with in the past.

As target assessment increasingly becomes the tail that wags the dog, yet is increasingly disconnected from the complex realities with which young adults and professionals are grappling, some kind of manipulation of target meanings and statistics becomes inevitable – if continuing funding is to be assured. Yet drop out remains the responsibility of the organizers and becomes perceived as a symptom of their failure to make 'these young people' active responsible citizens. Young adults and professionals are further stigmatized as being 'deficient' in some way. A vicious cycle is being maintained: a single loop system where no significant learning at other levels can occur.

The perverse and wide-ranging, systemic and local effects of these practices can often be difficult to grasp, when immersed in them. Yet, our research gradually revealed the extent of the normative pulls that new management practices exerted on local projects, in the name of both increasing effectivity and efficiency, and improving the quality of activation practices. It did not seem to matter whether projects were being 'delivered' by a public sector, voluntary or private provider, nor whether they were located in the Netherlands, Denmark, or the UK. Everywhere, we saw how increasingly new practices of facilitation and support were emerging, which could be described as 'governmentality practices'. Authors such as Dean (1999) and Rose (1996, 1999), who build on Foucault, argue that governmentality is about the governing of mentalities, and especially about the self-governance of people's lives. According to new principles of governance, a shift is taking place from practices emphasizing an external locus of control (pastoral practices of governance) towards practices emphasizing an internal locus of control (advanced neo-liberal practices of governance). The subject today is expected to develop the will to mobilize the self as an entrepreneurial self who constantly tries to develop his or her life as a capitalization project, in search of 'added value'.

An important finding of our research is that in various types of projects – both alternative and mainstream – we observed that not only instrumental but also social and biographical competences were at stake. This indicates to us that also in mainstream projects, new practices are perceived as necessary in order to be successful. For young adults to be 'employable' today, it is perceived as crucial by employers and government that they are able not only to turn their instrumental skills into projects of learning and development to be worked upon. They must also include in this entrepreneurial activity the permanent (re-)construction of their own biographies, and the continuous (re-)shaping of their social networks.

So, paradoxically, progressive notions such as autonomy, self-directedness, ownership, and empowerment, which have inspired emancipatory educational and social change practices in the last decades, are now being manipulated to govern the minds and the souls of the subjects in what Dean (1999) and Rose (1999) refer to as the 'advanced neo-liberal' societies in which we live today. This exertion of new discourses at both individual and project level is one of the major findings of our research and definitely deserves a deeper understanding through additional research.

Example of New Management's 'Anti-learning' Effects

Interestingly, at the time of our study, Portugal was still operating under the older public administration model, and was less subject to the centralizing and controlling influences that were so much more predominant in Northern Europe. The *Cultural Mediators* project was freer to remain alert to 'success criteria' for cultural mediation that emerged from community critiques, rather than those imposed by external standardized and de-contextualized discourses.   Novel constructions of social and economic empowerment could be the focus for ongoing local experimentation and co-interpretation, in ways that were not confined to the project alone.   Moreover, the notion of 'cultural mediator' could be jointly constructed out of the living realities of the young adults and that community as a possible focus for 'activation funding'.

At the same time, the project's EU funding constrained the 'production' of meaningful 'outputs' to a mere eight months. There was no chance for review or extension, based on the project's or the community's insights from the project. Unlike many stand-alone projects competing for shrinking funds, this project was cushioned to some extent by the well-embedded and trusted Community Association that had 'midwifed' this project into being in the first place. This Association was continually seeking diverse sources of funding to assure more freedom in its own creative and collective agency and expressions of community partnerships. We cannot help but wonder whether others such as this Portuguese project could flourish in Northern Europe as technocratic conditions of funding continue to multiply.

Similarly, we have referred earlier to the situation of the *Bridging the Gap* project. This was initiated with funding raised by the YMCA, a voluntary organization with charitable status. However, over the course of our research, it was offered additional funding by the local Chamber of Commerce which itself had been delegated to carry out public policy relating to unemployment. This extra funding was made available *because* of the success and strength of this 'alternative project'. However, almost immediately, supposedly benign and 'innovative technologies of control' intruded. Examples of accountability requirements under the new funding contract included the production of action plans and the documentation of competency development. This undermined and fragmented the many ways in which this project had given lived meaning to the principles of valuing competence and diversity, building relational social capital and sustaining processes of connective inquiry, between staff and the young adults, and the project and the world beyond.

Similarly, competence frameworks which are increasingly standardized and prescribed from outside a local context, are rooted in status quo notions of particular jobs and professionals, as defined by employers and then often formalized into inventories and specified outputs. A progressive spin may be brought to such technologies, such as accrediting learning from 'real life' through portfolios, and such like. However, the vagueness and de-contextualized quality of these criteria against which performance is to be measured also further deflects energy and attention away from engaging with, for example, the impact of material conditions of poverty and the gap between de-contextualized competences and the changing world of labor.

Hoggett (1991, p. 249), amongst many others, argues, that increasingly mechanistic forms of policy thinking and managing performance are ill-suited to learning from paradox, contradiction, and conflict. Moreover, he points to the further paradox whereby Western capitalist countries assert the decentralization of operational control yet all the while are governing through tightly prescribed management contracts. When such strategies are combined with the further centralization of strategic command, it becomes ever more risky to challenge the status quo. Whereas in traditional welfare states, the emphasis was on public administration via formalized processes and procedures, the new dilemma that emerges, in what he refers to as post-bureaucratic systems, is:

> If an organisation simply devolves financial control whilst retaining tight centralized control over policy making then it may certainly achieve greater control over costs and encourage innovation in the use of resources at operational levels, but it may have done nothing to improve *the degree of responsiveness or local accountability of services* (Hoggett, 1991, p. 253 emphasis added).

The seeming neutrality of such strategies (in other words, in merely assuring value for money invested by tax payers, relevance to employment), sets up very contradictory pressures. On the one hand, these strategies seem to constitute learners and professionals as active, responsible, rational, and competent subjects, who know how and why to act in specific ways. It is assumed, however, that the actions and choices that will serve their best interest can be pre-defined and in turn, monitored and evaluated. So, at the same time, they are being turned into objects of power, since they are neither free to define the problem of social and economic participation on their own terms nor to evolve solutions in partnership with communities.

Techno-rational Evaluation?

The deeply embedded errors (Chambers, 1997) that are perpetuated by such strategies are further exacerbated by new management trends extending themselves to public policy evaluation and research. There is a growing body of evidence that commissioned public policy research and evaluation studies are increasingly subject to the same technocratic tendencies. The study of whether and how projects serve pre-determined ends is taking precedence over whether the underlying discourses, assumptions, and problem framings might themselves be in error (Martin and Sanderson, 1999; Herbert, 2000; Sanderson 2004). Returning to trends in the UK that we saw spreading across the EU, Sanderson (2004) cites the now even firmer hold of evidence-based, instrumental rationality on current processes of policy evaluation and research. He cites the extensive and increasingly unexplored unintended effects of dominant mantras: 'what matters is what works'.

Schön and Rein (1994) argue that there is *no* arena of public policy implementation that does not reveal problems as insufficiently defined or understood; that is not characterized by many diverse and conflicting ways of defining or responding to the problems 'on the ground' – all of which scream out for attention at the same time. There is no such thing as a 'problem free state' that can be assured through new management strategies.

We would conclude our review of the perverse effects and 'anti-learning consequences' of new management strategies with the following hypothesis. Namely, the current obsession with standardized and quantifiable strategies and outputs across Europe, juxtaposed with policy rhetorics that emphasize higher levels of individualized responsibility for economic participation, is not just limiting the responsibility of the actors involved. Perhaps one of the most potent paradoxes of all is that a rhetoric of self-governance, responsibility, ownership, and participation is being combined with practices of control and standardization which effectively limit possibilities for self-governance, responsibility, ownership, and participation – thereby having limited learning effects.

This current state of affairs in Europe could not contrast more sharply with the story of the WPA set out earlier, at least, before its demise that came with the external imposition of similar techno-rational governance strategies.

At the same time, we do not wish to appear naïve about the extent to which the rationalities and practices which resist learning at different levels of the system simultaneously serve other interests. This dilemma is captured aptly by Midgley (2000):

> There is a conflict in many Western societies between the liberal discourses of citizenship (where all people are seen as having equal value because of their status as rational beings) and the capitalist discourses of good employment practice (which limit the responsibility of organizations to their employees alone). This conflict is not

stabilized by either the inclusion or exclusion of the unemployed, but by their marginalization. If unemployed people were to be fully included along with employees in the primary boundary of industrial organization, 'good employment practice' (indeed the whole capitalist system of organization) would become untenable. However, if they were fully excluded, the liberal ideal of equal citizenship would become untenable instead... While on the whole the two discourses are mutually supportive, there are still significant tensions, and the phenomenon of unemployment points to one of them. The key to understanding the status of the unemployed is to realize that it is only possible to maintain the dual commitment to liberalism and capitalism if people who are unemployed are neither fully included nor excluded (p. 203).

Learning for Inclusion across the EU?

What we are concerned with here are more socially robust and expansive understandings of policy: its formation, implementation, and its monitoring. A fundamental question is '*who* measures what kinds of change and *who* benefits from learning about these changes' (Estrella, 2000, p. 6) and indeed, what kind of learning – if any – is going on, for whom and what purposes? Where is the space for improvisation, and learning from diversity? Where is the connective inquiry, and capacity building across member states that might generate, rather than further erode, social capital in Europe? The more techno-rational governance practices, which we have been considering in this chapter, presume a project-based approach. As Cleaver (2002) argues, this fails to recognize the distinctly un-project like nature of young adults' lives and the extent to which individualized strategies become severed from community regeneration.

We argue that policy making needs to be, and can be, more firmly rooted in learning that grapples with the inherent contradictions and paradoxes that reside in the very discourse of activation and social inclusion and exclusion. Drawing on Taylor (2003), there is scope for learning more about how people in communities and activation projects 'actually engage with each other and with the outside world in different political and economic circumstances'. About how a discourse of systemic and policy learning and inquiry might 'bring on board the discourses of power and exclusion'. About how we might 'learn more about how effective infrastructural and institutional capacity can be built' (ibid, pp. 227-28). More fundamentality, what are the 'participatory and communicative structures, including new forms of social partnership, through which a shared sense of public good is created and debated?' (IILS/UNDP, 1997).

Returning to our notions of relational social capital building from the previous chapter, one way of understanding what we are opening up here is through Gamarnikow and Green's multi-intervention model (1999). In essence, in this chapter we are extending these ideas to embrace notions of systemic and policy learning and inquiry. In such an extended model, we do indeed need to let go of the idea of step-by-step, cause-effect linearity and therefore technocratic measurability and control. Through such a model, we begin to see all elements in a complex system as interconnected and mutually constitutive. Traditional forms of research and policy debate fail to tap into the possibilities for generating new forms of reflexive dialogue and learning at and beyond the policy–practice interface. Unlike the social capital models of Putnam (2000) and Coleman (1998-99), here we are exploring notions of systemic and policy learning that privilege learning not about one single element, but rather from mutually influencing relationships.

Scope for EU Leadership: A Challenge and an Example?

We are confident that there are still many people 'out there' across Europe who are seeking and locating funding that can support non-oppressive participatory approaches to redressing social exclusion and unemployment that take account of concerns addressed throughout this book. Social and political systems are complex and dynamic, and even more so in the context of globalization. Well-meaning intentions and practices often have shadow sides that require 'a hundred pairs of eyes' to stay attuned to forces that seek to instrumentalize, appropriate, and exploit. Policy objectives cannot be evaluated on the basis of crude performance indicators, as simple successes or failures, when processes of measurement and evaluation become divorced from the politics of everyday action and choice, from young people and professionals' lifeworlds, and from the social and economic processes and power relations that shape policy and practice discourses.

If social and economic empowerment, rather than technical instrumentality is the aim, we suggest that policy intentions and practices must remain the focus of ongoing critical and dialogic inquiry, using multiple forms of knowing. This must have as its aim not merely learning from policy as given, but from alternatives that have the potential to transform existing discourses and policy assumptions.

This research suggests the potential value of new policy learning and systemic inquiry initiatives being pioneered within the EU (See Percy-Smith and Weil, 2002, 2003; Weil et al., 2002; Burns, 2003). Guided by such work, an EU funded initiative could be set up initially to inquire into the very issue of performance management and accountability, and their intended and unintended consequences when a host of predetermined conditions become a condition of 'activation' funding. 'Activation project' representatives who have been in receipt of mainstream funding, and have some lived experience to offer to systemic dialogue and inquiry around such matters, could be funded to participate. Further, at this historical moment soon after the expansion of Europe on May 1st, 2004, there is a further opportunity to also include in this experiment, others from across the newer member states of Europe who have also been attempting to engage the social and economic participation of young adults in ways that go beyond individualized labor market insertion models, such as through community-based approaches.

- What if the EU were to hunt actively and creatively for those who are doing this with some degree of success, without overly defining what is meant: in other words, to conduct a search for experiments that would stretch the current imaginary, and that could challenge existing discourses about how to reconcile social and economic tensions?

Our hypothesis that there is value in doing this derives from our Portuguese and Northampton case studies. Although each has different funding histories, both projects were able to develop their approaches with the support of funding that, in comparison with other projects studied, had relatively few strings attached. Therefore, we suggest that valuable experience may reside within new member states from which policy makers and other diverse stakeholders in the EU might usefully learn. Of particular value to such a policy and practice learning initiative will be those initiatives that are entangled in restrictive, externally imposed, management practices and the stranglehold of the dominant EU activation discourse. Put another way, rather than exporting existing EU models, as if they are the 'correct' way to proceed, why not import relational, social capital as a basis for alternative kinds of critically and creatively reflexive dialogue and inquiry?

Even the act of publicizing such an initiative would itself stretch existing influential networks in the EU beyond the usual suspects. It would require different concepts of time and communication that challenged the status quo, and extended well beyond academic networks into the informal 'activation' economy. This is often supported by poorly funded community development oriented initiatives and tireless fire souls who resist compromising their practices and values by going for mainstream funding and becoming locked into restricting discourses and governance practices. Communication and funding criteria would need to persuade those who choose to work *outside* the boundaries of restrictive norms that it is worthwhile to participate in such a venture. If techno-rational goals are imposed upon such an initiative, these would only drive away those people who have immense practice-based wisdom to offer to current EU thinking, but have no time to spare if their diversity and competence is seen to be devalued or subjugated to dominant models. If dialogue and learning are held as valuable in themselves, and such processes are facilitated and supported effectively, surprises and changes can emerge and be supported in forms that further empower those participating, and build relational social capital of a very different order to that which currently obtains in the 'activation' arena. Such an initiative could reveal possibilities that are currently not envisaged and are themselves being restricted from coming into view by virtue of the hold of dominating discourses of activation and management, and patterns of funding that favor those who are willing to conform.

Such an initiative would require facilitators accustomed to working with large scale dialogic and co-inquiry processes. It would necessitate politicians and others 'holding open the program action inquiry space' in ways that support the emergence (and further funding) of multi-stranded developments that unfreeze existing thinking and practice. Different seed dialogues, within and across member states, could slowly build participation, momentum, and insight, if those responsible are legitimated in drawing on diverse players with experience in social and economic inclusion/exclusion and empowerment practices. The call for participants and initial dialogues could be further strengthened by research that was legitimated in pursuing potential strands of inquiry that track, and 'played back' emerging insights into the connective inquiry process. As such, rather than a tightly formulated design, the intention in such complementary work would be to create a rich learning history that itself could support and stimulate new forms of policy–practice dialogue and inquiry:

- What are the different process and outcome success criteria being adopted in different communities of practice trying to generate new forms of social and economic participation and indeed empowerment within the conditions of global capitalism?

- What diverse values, assumptions and intentions guide such practices and why? Based on what prior experience, analysis and learning? Are there alternative discourses of 'activation' processes and outcomes at play in these alternatives and what can be learned from these?

- What kinds of external funding, governance, and accountability processes and economic trends are impacting upon these initiatives at present, or are likely to do so in the near future? What other forms of support and accountability might help to sustain the energy and quality of more reflexive activation processes in response to the challenges being faced in communities with large numbers of excluded and unemployed young adults?

- What questions and values, what tensions and possibilities are most worth exploring at this historical moment in the EU? What paradoxes and contradictions do we most need to gain a deeper understanding of, in terms of their unintended effects?

Cycles of such cross-cultural exchange would need to be supported by ongoing reflexive 'boundary critique' about who and what is being excluded from the ongoing inquiry, thereby enabling sufficient engagement with difference and 'discordant pluralism' (Gregory, 1996) in order to sustain such an initiative. The idea at its simplest is that of an ever-expanding, ever-deepening, cross-European critically and creatively reflexive conversation. We envisage this drawing in policy makers, practitioners, and young adults who are willing to challenge and change existing assumptions of success and at the same time, to themselves be challenged and changed by this experience. With sufficient support for ongoing action research by participants and others attached to such an initiative, many outcomes to guide and inform policy and practice development would ensue. This would enable the gathering and tracking of data that could bring into view stories and narratives from communities and local initiatives, as well as patterns and questions arising from these. It would also enable the formation of learning histories (see for example Kleiner and Roth, 2000) and polyphonic texts that tracked multiple strands of inquiry and challenge over time. These could be created throughout the life of the initiative, such as through the use of videos, storyboards, pamphlets, and so on, and which could travel from inquiry to inquiry, and be widely disseminated, both electronically and through other means.

The worst scenario would be for these initiatives to be formulated as a series of country based pilots, subjected to the usual new management practices, and required to produce best practice 'outputs' to be 'rolled out across Europe', and then disseminated as formulas, fashions, and prescriptions to which others must subscribe, if they were to receive activation related funding. Instead, we suggest that there is considerable scope to model alternative systemic learning dynamics while simultaneously supporting a reflexive critique and development supported by a rich base of living knowledge into social and economic exclusion/inclusion.

In the context of our discussion on the unintended consequences of the new public management, and prevailing practices of governance, it would seem important that such an initiative stayed focused throughout on notions of multi-dimensional accountability and responsibility rather than uni-linear, top down forms. Drawing on principles from complexity theory, what we are acknowledging here is the power of reflexive conversations that iteratively deepen and extend over time to support ongoing critiques combined with new forms of action, at and beyond the current 'activation' policy and practice boundary. EU conversations over, a three to five year period held within and across countries at established intervals, supported by a growing database of insights, case studies, emerging questions and connected research projects, could have a non-linear but radical long term effect on shifting and shaping new EU discourses about reconciling social and economic tensions. Moreover, it might spur experiments with new and more collaborative ecologies of governance that went far beyond responding merely to the demands of technocratic modernization, and free market capitalism.

Such a stretching of the current imaginary is not without precedence. On the one hand, we are encouraged by examples of systemic inquiry and networked policy learning in the UK (Midgley, 2000; Percy-Smith and Weil, 2002, 2003; Weil, 2002; Burns, 2003; Percy-Smith et al., 2003), and by critiques of and experiments with large system participatory monitoring and evaluation processes (see for example Cooke and Kothari, 2002; Estrella et al., 2000). But this is not a formulaic process. As with reflexive activation, we are speaking here about an ongoing social learning process that engages directly with complexity and issues of power, and goes beyond mere descriptions of experience. At the same time, Gaventa and Blauert (2002) caution us to remember that,

> The possibilities are not without pitfalls... [They can be] both a 'dream and a nightmare.' As with any approach, participatory processes can be misused, subject to further control that serves broader power and economic interests, become rigid and flat... [This] is a social and a political process, in which conflict and disagreements amongst stakeholders (over methods as well as broader interests) can easily take over. Disagreements may exist over indicators of success, appropriate levels of rigor, the purposes of the...process and the uses of its results...there is still much to be done – to strengthen the conceptual and methodological base...to build human and institutional capacity for [their] use, to learn to negotiate the conflicts towards building collaborative action, and to apply it on a larger scale to issues of governance and institutional learning (p. 243).

Involving Young People in Policy-practice Learning

This study has revealed the value of research and inquiry, which focuses on young people's lived realities. We welcome new policy emphases on giving young people a voice and enhancing their participation in decision making processes and research (see for example Coles, 2000). Yet, there are many barriers which undermine possibilities for involving young adults in initiatives such as we have described above, despite a greater emphasis in policy rhetoric across Europe about their enhanced participation in policy development and service design and delivery.

Barriers to and Possibilities for Participation

Percy-Smith and Weil (2003, pp. 82-83) analyze some of these barriers. For example, the structures, functioning, and priorities of government bodies often assume that experts can best serve young peoples' best interests by working on their behalf. Yet, we have seen how this can lead to overly simplistic and mechanistically conceived responses to youth problems. Further, young people tend to be treated by academics and policy makers and some professionals as lacking the capacity to participate in decisions that affect their own lives. We have also witnessed the extent to which adults' resist such participation, because of their anxieties about young people's capacity to de-stabilize the status quo. But the status quo does not necessarily serve them well and this needs to be open to critical questioning in which they too are a part. Finally, the separation of research and inquiry from policy and practice development, and the strongly differentiated roles that such separations support, gives rise to merely tokenistic involvement of young people.

What we would therefore like to do in this section is to offer insights into tensions and possibilities around involving young people in research and policy–practice dialogues and inquiry, based on our experience of projects and related research that have influenced the development of this book:

- *Voicefulness, voicelessness, and identities*: What never goes away is the tension between young people wanting a voice but at the same time not wanting to have their own cultural practices and identities usurped to serve adults' pre-determined ends. If we wish to involve young people in new forms of policy–practice learning, we need to remain open to learning from their diverse values, interests, perspectives, and cultural practices of their lifeworlds. As importantly, they need to sense that professionals and policy makers are willing to accommodate more differentiated cultural standpoints. In this way, we can avoid complacency about merely involving young people, and be stretched to think how they become integral to, and active contributors within, a dynamic and evolving system of inquiry.

- *Whose spaces and places:* Too often, we expect young adults to come to spaces and places that suit professionals and policy makers, as if this were a kind of privilege. Young people who operate at the fringes of mainstream society often do not see such invitations as providing opportunities. Instead, they can be seen merely to reinforce power differences and inequalities, and stir up memories and resentments that have contributed to their marginalized situation. For example, in this project, researchers from some participating countries invited young people to come to university buildings and talk about things in the same ways that adults participating in typical focus group sessions might be expected to do. Other researchers who went to community centers and brought in beer and pizza, and just chatted were more successful in building, over time, relationships that enabled young people to influence our thinking, and learning from, this research. Still others went into communities and mingled with networks of young people, and were in turn invited to their places, such as youth centers and so on. Over two years, a number of the research teams slowly built up youth networks, nurturing processes of participation in what we were doing.

- *Alternative time frames and styles of knowing:* Young people may not wish to participate in the entirety of a project. Instead, different youth may wish to move in and out of the process at different times. We learned neither to expect nor insist on constant commitment. We found that if young people felt valued in their coming and going, this in turn supported an ongoing connection with the project. Moreover, there are various ways in which they could be inspired to participate. Some researchers concentrated on dialogue as the primary way of engaging with the young people, with limited success. Others were more creative, using photos and questions with which the young adults could identify, to open up dialogue. Drama, video work, and peer led inquiry around issues that emerged as important are possibilities that, within the limitations of this project's funding and time scales, could not be fully realized. But the scope for such forms of participation in initiatives envisaged in the previous section was glimpsed, and deserves further attention. What struck us was how young adults could feel challenged and excited about the possibilities of drawing on the power of their experience to influence others in Europe. But they needed to feel confident that there was an audience for others to really engage with the passions, tensions, and conflicts that they considered important.

- *Relevance to whom and for what?* Attention needs to be paid to whether and how research initiatives (and various forms of participation therein) feel alive and relevant to young people. 'What's in it for me/us?' is a constant mantra when trying to involve young adults in research. The possibility of influencing adults and decision-making can be a powerful motivator. We found that there is value in challenging young people around their resistances to opportunities presented to influence their world. If such experiences also enabled young people to meet with others in similar situations across Europe, the scope becomes quite considerable. For example, in the *Bridging the Gap* project, young people chose to meet with our team of European researchers. But this visit took place on their territory. They planned the food, the formal, and the informal input. Yet, the different ways this played out in reality, and how they chose to participate (once they were *actually* confronted with these stranger adults!), took many complex forms over the few hours allocated. Little happened as planned, yet a number of the young people felt empowered by taking this space and commanding respect and attention. If it had been possible to bring not just the researchers, but different groups of youth from across the six participating countries together, we feel confident that much more could have been gained from this project, despite the many complexities and challenges of doing this. The key for initiatives is to have the capacity in terms of time, funding, and facilities for learning continually, and listening closely always, for how commitments and capacities for participation can be worked with, not worked against.

• *Relational practices:* How can young adults and professionals better understand how they are mutually intertwined in resolving difficult tensions and dilemmas around social and economic participation? Whether dialogues are initiated by young people, researchers, policy makers, or practitioners is not the point. What matters is that young people have the opportunity to challenge and change the questions being asked, to influence the direction of their lives, and to participate in creating alternatives. Reflexive activation is a jointly created process of social learning that challenges professionals and young adults to engage differently. The outcomes of such inquiry cannot be neatly predicted nor fitted into boxes. But narratives, and systematic tracking (using a variety of creative forms) of how the young adults and professionals have been challenged and changed along the way, and have jointly created alternatives that could not have been envisaged at the outset, can be equally robust. However, this requires the wider system to become committed to new ecologies of governance and participative monitoring that empower rather than dis-empower those upon whom success depends.

• *Recognizing the costs of involvement:* The involvement of young people is too often seen as an add-on to a research project, in terms of time and costs. In many ways, the limitations of funding and time, and the pressures of regular deliverables can reduce opportunities for meaningfully engaging young people. In this project there were many genuine questions within the team about what the meaningful participation of 'turned off', 'tuned out', and multiply challenged young adults might really look and feel like. We need examples of alternatives that stretch the imaginary and erode the all too easy resistance that kicks in when the involvement of young people is proposed. We need stories that challenge us to move from 'Yes but' to 'Maybe...' (see for example Percy-Smith et al., 2003). Funders too need to take responsibility for subsidizing the time and space that is needed to build relationships and to spark the involvement of young people in ways that feel worthwhile and empowering for all, and not merely instrumental, for another's ends.

- *Diversified youth:* To a large extent this research has concentrated on the lives of white European youth. Yet we are all too aware of the disproportionate representation of young people from ethnic minorities in unemployment figures. There is significant learning to be gained from policy and practice learning and accompanying research that deepens and widens understanding of stories of working effectively with young adults whose individual and collective identities are actively influenced by experiences that are connected to, for example, race, religion, and ethnicity, and how these play out in diverse community and cultural contexts across Europe.

- *Learning from the margins:* For many young people whose lives are lived largely at the margins of mainstream society, many current interventions appear to have limited impact. Youth policy may thus unintentionally reinforce the further marginalization of many so called socially excluded young adults. Further insight is required into the attitudes and orientations of young people who were often referred to in our research as the 'hardcore' of the hard to help young adults. More needs to be understood about how these young people conceptualize their own lives and life chances; how they construct their identities in relation to dominant social norms and values about social and economic commitment. What do notions such as 'socially excluded' mean to them? We might recall Martin, in Chapter 1, who was being given the choice of the environmental task force, yet resisted this, because he had learned that this was where the 'losers' were placed. We continue to believe in the potential for supported peer led research and collaborative and action research in pursuing such questions (Percy Smith et al., 2003).

Policy and Practice Learning in a Different Key: Including Young Adults in Systemic Inquiry

We would like to offer here a brief illustration of how we might relate the involvement of young people to the kind of systemic inquiry we proposed in the previous section. For example, core funding might facilitate within and across member-state, youth-led inquiry into diverse activation experiments. As integral to processes of reflexive activation, before such visits took place, there could be considerable dialogue about what questions each visiting team of young people would want to ask of the project being visited, and vice-versa. The experience of being critical peer assessors, supported by translators, would itself open up, and could support, dimensions of biographical, social, and instrumental competence that stayed dialectically related to a context that was both familiar and not. Before such a visit, project participants or communities might be asked to prepare storyboards, dramas, videos, poetry, collages, and other artifacts that for them communicated the nature of their experience of social exclusion and unemployment. Non-verbal forms of communication and expression could be privileged, given the challenge of different languages.

These teams could return and 'travel' about their own country, involving other young adults in reflections on their experience, and in a consideration of their own choices for influencing their situation. Those who have been in various 'activation schemes' could offer insights into how these have influenced their own sense of social and economic empowerment, in the context of their wider life stories. Such processes could involve policy makers and professionals, compelling them to listen and inquire into that with which they are involved from very different perspectives. Regional and national processes of connective inquiry that entail diverse stakeholders could be grown slowly over time, supported by processes of tracking and research that help to 'hold' and play back possibilities and the living knowledge that is emerging from this complex 'whole'.

Cross-European forums could be focus for further experiment and ongoing learning, as to how such processes could be supported, and how the stories of those involved could be made available face-to-face and through different media. We could envisage all sorts of learning materials emerging from such processes that could 'travel' questions and insights across different communities in Europe. Websites could be developed to support further exchanges about what different young people were learning, about what they could do in partnership with others. Emerging questions and challenges posed from such developments for participating professionals, policy makers, and academics could likewise be exchanged, in both electronic and other forms that remained accessible to diverse others elsewhere in Europe in different language.

Funding would have to support the emergence of the unpredictable, the 'unknown', that could only be created through lived encounters. For example, twinning schemes might be a start. These could then extend outwards both nationally and across Europe. Such an initiative could be designed to support processes of divergence and convergence, such as around particular themes, paradoxes, and challenging issues. Participating schemes could also host co-inquiry forums that were guided by one powerful dilemma or question around which all involved could prepare and engage using diverse and creative forms for expressing what seemed to matter.

What we are thus arguing for here is alternative forms of funding and space to support learning and improvisation at the policy–practice interface. We suggest that such ongoing processes of knowledge and practice co-generation will be more socially robust by virtue of the young adults' participation. Such initiatives would require considerably flexible infrastructure and financial support to facilitate strands of inquiry and possibilities for connective inquiry, as they emerged from the joint creation of relational social capital that these networks stimulated. Such strategies could create significantly new narratives of expertise that had the potential to open up new learning and action territory for policy makers, academics, practitioners, and young adults and their communities. Further, in and of themselves such processes would provide another form of activation that focused on new possibilities for economic and social empowerment in which active participation was made central.

There is a growing body of literature to show that the more young people become engaged the more empowered they can feel to expect and influence changes in their own and others lives (for example, Kirby, 1999; Coles, 2000; Percy-Smith et al., 2003).

Imagining these new ecologies of possibility and governance across Europe is a far cry from how one worker described the activation scheme in which he was involved:

It is as if we are just there to keep them in the holding pen

Final Reflections

In our research project and through this book, we have come to recognize how policy analysis documents and a great deal of research can (so/too) easily reduce young people and professionals' efforts to mere unemployment or employment improvement statistics. Both groups are often pushed into, and accounted for, within standardized categories that are meant to be meaningful yet often convey little. Buried deep and well hidden by neat charts and diagrams are many stories: contradictory, fragmented, always in motion.

There is no doubt that there are the 'lucky few' young Europeans for whom activation programs have offered valuable opportunities for skills development, confidence-building, and relevant, option widening, experiences of employment. There are those who have been able to re-author their lives, through 'insertion' into the labor market. However, in this study, as in other research, positive narratives of activation and opportunity remain most prevalent amongst those who have significant cultural capital to bring to their education, training, employment, or guidance scheme in the first place.

But how do we 'count' amongst the 'positive outcomes' those who have succeeded on terms that remain invisible, when measured by blunt-edged performance indicators? For example, what about Frieda who, through her activation project, was able to join a keyboard course for women? The long lists of atomized skills were little different in her project from those facing other 'Friedas' in other European countries. Frieda felt motivated and performed well on her course, despite a previous history of school failure. But then she rejected the job offer that would allow her to use these skills. The reason for this was because her most significant learning from her course was not keyboard skills. Instead, it was that she need not tolerate any longer the violence that she and her children were suffering from her husband. Frieda decided to invest her energies in moving to a safe house and to make a different life for herself and her family. She was empowered, and she empowered herself, to participate in society on terms that had new meaning for her, and her family. This would not have happened, had it not been for the conversations she had with other women on that course. But what of the project professionals who were unable to include Frieda amongst the statistics required of that project: that counted success only in terms of employment or movement to another activation scheme? Frieda may have been unemployed that year, but what of the next year? What about the significant impact that this experience might have had on her being able to take subsequent advantage of other choices? And the experience her stories may have had on others that heard it, just as others' stories influenced her? Those stories will remain invisible to the 'system' that determines the criteria by which success will be measured.

And what of Rashid, who came with his parents to Holland but after five years still could not speak the language. Finding a job was nigh impossible. But then he was put on an activation project for long-term unemployed that, in contrast to his previous ones, valued 'soft time'. For the first time, he started playing football – and proved brilliant at this. Suddenly, he wanted to, and did learn, Dutch. But this 'success', like many others in this scheme, could not be immediately or neatly quantified to enable funding to be renewed. Moreover, the queries come back at such projects: and how is 'playing football' relevant to labor market insertion? Is this a viable use of taxpayers' money?

In these and a myriad of other stories, we were challenged by the power of achievements and outcomes that could never have been predicted, nor easily understood when ripped out of the denser fabric of these young adults' particular stories. Stories of young adults engaging in new forms of economic and social participation emerge out of relationships, unlikely conversations, activities that suddenly matter and offer glimpses of possibility; out of surprise twists and intertwining tales that awaken the imagination and determination of not just individuals, but sometimes groups and even communities. How little is really known about such things across the EU?

At the same time, we are encouraged by other studies carried out under the 4th and 5th Framework programs that increasingly reveal complex interactions between education, inequalities, and social exclusion, and the underlying pull of other factors. These are being shown to be much broader and deeper than is often understood by policy makers and that one area of social policy is unlikely, on its own, to be able to address the problem: 'Research shows that education measures will have to be reinforced by wider social and economic reforms if social exclusion is to be seriously addressed' (PJB Associates, 2003, p. 2). European policy aspirations to balance social and economic tensions have a long way to go. Our analysis of the perverse effects of 'activation marketization', that we have found to be so prevalent across Europe, challenges us to acknowledge that there is much to be learned, if current discourses are manufacturing the very risks that activation policies set out to challenge.

The initiatives explored in this chapter, if implemented, may make some small contribution to unlocking potential at local level and within the system as a whole. They may open up some alternatives to the usual 'locked-in' perspectives. The mutually constituting actions of policy makers, academics, practitioners, and young adults are seldom brought into active dialogue. There is little to be gained however, if, for example, the perspective of policy makers remains dominated by managerial and performance concerns; if professionals are required to work within dominant discourses of activation; and academics stick to discourses of logic and rationality and to models of research that are largely retrospective and do little to create timely insight or action in young adults' conditions of unemployment and social exclusion as an existential affliction. And, if young adults are absent from the frame of connective inquiry and learning. We believe that there is a need for more 'whole system' approaches to learning, inquiry, and research within Europe. Further, as explored in this final chapter, there are many current impasses to systemic learning and dialogue that are rigidifying the whole fabric of European approaches to social exclusion and unemployment.

We have unfolded and intertwined multiple strands of inquiry throughout this book in the hope that they help to pry open new forms of conversation, and support the development of new policy learning and systemic inquiry 'engines' and infrastructures that simultaneously:

- nourish and stretch possibilities for community self help and connective inquiry across the EU;

- challenge existing views of activation and governance;

- fire up searches for new ways of bringing research, policy development, practice, research, and the lived realities of people's lives into new forms of relationship;

- support ongoing reflexive improvisation and learning from the ambivalences, paradoxes, and complexities of 'learning for inclusion';

- give rise to new ecologies of governance;

- foster possibilities for collaboration, critique, and possibility generation across Europe.

To develop and promote such notions of inquiry and learning will require a fundamental paradigm shift. Policy makers, professionals, and researchers must leave behind the dominant 'engineering' perspective and technocratic rationalities that curb local initiative and abandon the belief that failures in the system can be repaired through 'smart' technologies and elaborate performance management procedures. What we need to bring into connection with processes of policy formation, implementation, and research across Europe are more of the multi-voiced and interweaving stories of the diverse actors who are affected by what currently prevails: to build the complex narrative about the human condition of the unemployed and the socially excluded who are experiencing the dark side of globalized life in late modernity and to take more joint responsibility for creating alternatives in Europe that do not rely on maintaining social exclusion to achieve economic competitiveness.

Epilogue

Nothing counts so heavily against a government as allowing unnecessary unemployment... [Yet the] ancient pre-occupations of economic life – with equality, security, and productivity – have now narrowed down to a preoccupation with productivity and production...Why is it that as production has increased in modern times concern for production seems also to have increased?

John Kenneth Galbraith, *The Affluent Society*, p. 105

Why am I broke, why is my life a joke?
Why do people bitch because I smoke?
What don't people care what goes on?
Why is it me who's always wrong?
Why won't anyone let me smoke a bong?

Why's the earth going so bad?
Why do I feel so sad?
Why don't I speak to my dad?
Why do people always screw?
Why do I feel so blue?
Why did I go on a curfew?

What does anyone know? Not much.
But at the end of it, will anyone know the answers to these questions?
Probably not, but that's life.

William, a member on *Bridging the Gap*, shared this for the first time when our cross-European research team visited the project that offered him a community and a chance, as a homeless, unemployed and multiply disadvantaged young person.

December 10th, Notes from a researchers field diary:

The pool table got turned over last night and no one has owned up to it The question is asked 'What can we do to change the culture of "doing naughty things and running away?" If the social worker issues written warnings, this reinforces the self-fulfilling prophecy that they are naughty. It also means that if there is a threat that they will be evicted next time it happens, then if they are to be taken seriously it has to be carried out But that then undermines the whole purpose of [our] work It also doesn't help them learn respect. Besides, you wouldn't evict your own kids for a misdemeanor Instead of judging and admonishing the young person as being stupid or naughty or bad (in which case what they hear is stupid or naughty) the ethos is to address the situation in a more positive way by challenging the young person for example by saying, 'What did you do that for?' In this way, the individual is provided with the

248

opportunity to reflect on their own behavior, take responsibility for their actions and with the help of the worker, consider alternative ways of being. For example, a young girl comes into the office and sounds off to the worker. A colleague asks how can she take that. It is difficult but by reacting to her is judging here. One girl sometimes came into the office and if she couldn't have what she wanted she stormed out. This wasn't responded to then, but the incident was picked up on in the key work session, during which it emerged that she has always been told no, and because she lived in the shadow of her sister, feels rejected if she is told no. But having worked through that, she now comes in and easily sits and talks with her worker. However, as the worker suggests, 'Sometimes you feel like you're getting nowhere, for example, when individuals respond with, "What the fuck do I care?" But the verbal abuse and damage to property are not the issues. It is what underlies these that is important. Naughtiness and abuse is just an extension of these young peoples inner and outer worlds. It is not what is provided but how they deal with things. This is sometimes difficult. Like the young males who come charged up with high levels of testosterone'.

Appendix

Case Study Projects from the Six European Countries: 'Pen Portraits'[1]

Countries and Projects

Flanders, Belgium
- *Advise First*
- *FlexiJob/ The Farmhouse Shop*

Denmark
- *House of Keys*
- *House of Projects*

Germany
- *Female Electricians*
- *JobXchange*

The Netherlands
- *Community College/ Vocational College*
- *Right Match*

Portugal
- *Vocational Training School*
- *Cultural Mediators*

England, the UK
- *New Deal/Gateway*
- *Bridging the Gap*

These project names represent a mix of pseudonyms and actual ones, depending upon the contract with, and/or wishes of, each research partner regarding anonymity.

Flanders, Belgium

Case Study 1: Advise First

Advise First is an individualized guidance strategy, characteristic of the main trends in education, training, employment, and guidance practices in Flanders. It is a trajectory guidance program for unemployed, lowly qualified young adults under 25 receiving unemployment benefit, with the main objective of immediate labor market integration. Participation on this project commits the young adult to making efforts to improve his/her employment situation. The counseling offered by *Advise First* is intended as a requisite to lead to a choice between a vocational training program (1000 hrs) organized by the VDAB (Public Counseling and Training Service) and an application program (40 hours). If the person successfully completes the course and/or gets a job in the meantime, the right to further unemployment benefits is continued; if participation on the program is unsuccessful, the person may be excluded from further unemployment benefits. Access to the program is motivated by coercion, with the possibility of losing unemployment benefits if young adults don't conform. This can give rise to an authoritarian culture in which paternalism and unequal power relations lead to alienation and resistance of the young adults and an unstimulating learning atmosphere which pays little attention to individual biographies. Learning in this project means guidance and conformity with respect to the fixed procedures of the scheme and integration into the trajectories provided.

Case Study 2: FlexiJob and The Farmhouse Shop

The second Belgium case study consisted of two projects reflecting dual trends in more alternative provision: *FlexiJob* – a temporary employment agency; and HWW – a 'non-traditional' training provider in sales and distribution.

The *Farmhouse Shop* project is focused on training people to work in the service sector and emphasizes the development of work attitudes. Young women receive a practical 'one year' work-based training in sales and distribution, although the actual content of the training is considered to have less relevance than the training of work attitudes. Group processes are promoted by an equal division of responsibilities in the group. Within the context of the project the women are able to 'learn by doing' by putting their training into practice in the project's shop, despite a lack of work in the workshop. Success is defined in terms of young adults being able to find their own way, which professionals encourage by taking an active role in 'pushing' the young unemployed towards making decisions. Both young adults and professionals share the objective of immediate labor market participation. The projects main success lies in a very high rate of employment for ex-participants and the fact that many ex-participants can find work in areas other than what they have trained for, indicating a flexibility and transferability of learned skills.

FlexiJob is the first 'social' temporary employment agency in Belgium, located in an underprivileged neighborhood to enhance accessibility. This pilot-project is a collaborative initiative involving a youth organization with activities in the main cities of Flanders, the temporary employment agency of the Flemish Employment Office and a commercial temporary employment agency. The youth organization employs a youth-counselor with the responsibility of providing support for young people (under 30 years) in meeting their primary need to earn money on a short-term basis (less then a month) so that they can alternate employment and income generation with periods of leisure time. Young people encountered by youth workers through outreach are then helped locating short-term work by Consultants from the interim agencies.

Denmark

Case Study 1: The House of Keys

The House of Keys is a state financed clarification and training project situated in a suburban area. Its aim is to 'clarify' the career orientations of unemployed young adults, invited to take part in the course by the labor office: to motivate them and facilitate their passage into permanent jobs or further education. If they do not take part or don't finish the course they risk losing their unemployment benefit. The six month course is an alternation between classes in Danish, Math, psychology, basic computer skills, etc. and periods of trainee services in various fields of work. The course has a broad content of predetermined and compulsory subjects and is non-specific in vocational orientation. It is intended that the participants will be activated with this mixture of curriculum-based and experience-based learning in ways that address biographical as well as social and instrumental skills needs. There is also a counselor available on a voluntary basis. The whole concept of the course is part of a general trend towards labor market oriented initiatives in Denmark, which assume that activating the youth must be the main goal. Qualifications are not considered necessary, because the Danish labor market offers many jobs, which require only a low level of skills.

Case Study 2: The House of Projects

This is also a clarification project financed by public funds, targeted at young adults considered unfit for the labor market and with severe social problems (such as drug addiction, abuse) besides being unemployed. The explicit aim of the course is to support participants in coming to terms with their problems, and gain the confidence and skills to enter education or employment. The central elements of the *House of Projects* are the project workshops (textile, woodwork, metal, ceramic), chosen by the participants, which are primarily seen as a tool for achieving these objectives by improving social skills and behavior, developing self confidence and learning to adapt to fixed time frames and organization rules. Through a 'learning-by-doing' approach the young adults learn how to produce a product in the workshop. They experience success and become more self-confident in their abilities. The work in the workshops is accompanied by the opportunity to receive individual or collective counseling. The course does not have a formal start or ending and participation on the project, which is voluntary, is not framed by a fixed time span.

Germany

Case Study 1: Female Electricians

This project is an innovative initiative within the general framework of the regular vocational training system (the so-called 'dual system' in Germany). It is targeted at young women who were already at the beginning of this apprenticeship scheme, have stable social backgrounds, and who have already demonstrated a sense of agency in their lives. The main goal of the project is to provide a three and a half year long training course for the trade of electro-technicians for young women. Secondary goals include promoting the integration of women into a male dominated profession by helping them to build a female worker's identity and integration of ecological topics into the training. This training scheme embodies three learning sites: the workshop where participants can practice their trade, a part time vocational school which focuses on the curriculum and work placements where trainees gain first hand experience of the challenges they face in the workplace. The training curriculum hence seeks to balance theoretical knowledge and practical competence in a mutually sustaining way. Emphasis is on experiential learning in the workplace and self-directed learning in groups in the workshop so as to build confidence and self-reliance and sustain motivation. The role of the project leader is to challenge social stigmatization, and provide counseling, guidance and mediation.

Case Study 2: JobXchange

JobXchange is a scheme targeted at socially excluded young adults, often on the verge of homelessness and who have withdrawn from any kind of public support. The aim of the project is to put these people in contact with work experiences and, in a sense, with the 'real' world by providing short-term jobs and 'fast money' with no specific demands in terms of knowledge, work experience or commitment. These jobs range from a few hours to several weeks and are mostly in the lower tiers of the labor market such as working on a construction-site, cleaning, renovating, transport. The secondary objective is to help young people maintain stability and re-integrate into the labor market. There is no training offered by these projects, but there are voluntary options to get counseling, though not as structural elements of the project. Whilst some of the target group consist of young people who have partly withdrawn from public assistance and appear unable to meet the challenges of a regular employment; others makes use of the *JobXchange* as a short-term solution for earning money, but who seek to move on. Many of the participants on this project have been detrimentally effected by the upheavals related to the end of the GDR and the events after unification. The success of this projects lies in being able to establish contact with these people and to bring them in contact with the world of work.

The Netherlands

Case Study 1: The Community College and Vocational College

Community College and Vocational College are mainstream vocational training institutions – part of the Bureau of Labor, which provide full time vocational training programs for unemployed people or for those who require extra schooling to prevent their unemployment. The *Community College* project aims to meet the specific demands of employers as well as the unemployed. It provides intensive courses of several weeks as well as long-term programs of 1-2 years, leading to essential 'starting qualifications' for the labor market in particular fields such as catering, electro-technology, transport, business and administration, child care and carpentry. Both are targeted at learners who have already achieved some skills, have stable social backgrounds, high intrinsic motivation and have intentionally chosen a vocational trajectory and require professional training. As a minimum, trainees work towards a so-called 'starting qualification' (EU-level 2), which is equal to the level of a skilled worker entering employment for the first time. The training program is mainly curriculum-oriented, dictated by the skills requirements of particular professions, and delivered according to pre-defined educational routes. The educational philosophy emphasizes practicality and flexibility using practice-oriented and experiential methods suited to the trainees, which mean that the young adults have to bear an essential share of responsibility for their learning. Each student works independently at his/her own pace at the appropriate level. Young people are motivated by the knowledge that these qualifications are generally accepted and likely to lead to employment in a country where access to the labor market is very much mediated by school-based qualifications.

Case Study 2: Right Match

Right Match is a school providing an educational trajectory designed in cooperation with the regional educational center and the Bureau for Education and Employment. The explicit goal is to help trainees find a job through work placements and to be able to sustain that job. It is specifically geared towards providing 'at risk' 16 and 17 year old young people (mainly school drop-outs) with basic level training at assistant level (EU level 1) for a trade as a low-skilled or unskilled laborer. Young adults with severe problems (e.g. drug abuse, psychiatric problems) are excluded from participation in the project. The course is practice-based and consists out of an alternation between Schooling (studying for a trade or profession), Practice ('hands on' training in a simulated workplace environment giving experience of a number of trades and professions), Behavior development (life and social skills training), and Work experience in a job placement. Counseling is available as a supplementary option. The experiential learning and skills development in the classroom and work placements constitutes the core of the project with a special focus on promoting a positive work attitude. The training does not lead to a substantial qualification (in the Netherlands this qualification is below the 'starting qualifications' required for the majority of the population) and the training is less important than the work placement.

Portugal

Case Study 1: Vocational Training School

This private association offers two vocational training courses, one in the field of computing and the other in communications, public relations, publicity and marketing. The three-year modularized courses offer individually shaped learning trajectories as an alternative for young people (15-25 years) who have not achieved in school. Although the school is accredited by the Ministry of Education, the culture and approach of the organization has been developed in reaction to the regular training system in Portugal. This school is in part an extension to the general education system and in part a vocational training provider. The didactical principles are built around a strong practical focus geared towards the labor market rather than academic achievement. The school adopts an holistic perspective emphasizing learning for citizenship, empowerment and self-development (including raising of self esteem) as well as subject knowledge, with professionals acting as role models demonstrating democratic and human values. Additionally, counseling facilities are available for the trainees. The gap between the training and the labor market is narrowed by having professionals from the particular fields of work contribute to training and by encouraging trainees to 'establish a relationship with the labor market' through practice placement; with the result that almost all trainees secure a job after training.

Case Study 2: Cultural Mediators

This is a community-based, non-formal vocational training program located in an extremely deprived suburb of Lisbon with a predominantly ethnic population from Cape Verde. Faced with specific racially based problems of exclusion, residents have little chance of finding training outside of the ghetto. Young adults are trained to become 'intercultural mediators', a field not yet recognized as a professional activity. Although the course aims at securing placements for these young adults in the labor market this cannot be taken for granted. It is for those who seek employment, but not in jobs currently available to them such as construction or cleaning. Learning means acquiring competencies for a profession, although the main focus is on personal and social development of the individuals within their community. The professionals try to act as role models, as guides and as trainers. The fact that the training is community-based, means that the professionals have to be interested in the population of this suburb. Attention is paid to creating a warm atmosphere in order to stimulate the learning and personal self-development of the trainees, situated in their daily social environment. Making the young adults more self-reflective is an essential task of the whole training course. A strong focus is on raising awareness about the individuals and the position of the community in society. The course lasts for eight months and includes practice placements, mainly in schools, starting in the second month of training.

England, UK

Case Study 1: New Deal/Gateway

New Deal 18-24 is the latest youth training, guidance and employment initiative set up as part of the government's welfare to work programme designed to help unemployed young people off benefit and into work. The structure and delivery of *New Deal* is guided by principles of 'workfare' rather than 'welfare'. It is applicable to young people who have been unemployed and claiming Job Seekers Allowance (JSA) for 6 months. At this point JSA claimants are 'invited' to (compulsorily) attend an interview with a Personal Adviser. Failure to attend leads to loss of benefit. *New Deal* involves three stages: The *Gateway* period (maximum four months), The *New Deal* options and a period of follow through support. During the *Gateway* phase, clients are helped to find out what help is needed to get them into work. This may involve careers guidance or short skills courses such as confidence building, literacy or numeracy. Clients are then helped in choosing a course of action from one of four *New Deal* options: Full time work (subsidised or unsubsidised), Full time education or training (up to NVQ level II), work in the Voluntary sector or with the Environmental Task Force. These options constitute the second stage of *New Deal* and last for between six and twelve months. Follow through constitutes the third stage of *New Deal* in which individuals are provided with continued support and guidance with respect to labour market participation. The Employment Service take a lead role in the delivery of *New Deal*, but work in partnership with career services, education and training providers, voluntary sector organisations and businesses to deliver the *New Deal* options.

Case Study 2: Bridging the Gap, the YMCA Northampton

The YMCA Northampton (TYN) is a voluntary sector organisation providing Housing and Resettlement services for young people (16-25 years). TYN's *Bridging the Gap* is an in-house life and social skills training programme which is one element of a wider co-ordinated, strategic plan to provide high quality, holistic, support services to young people aged 16-25 who are socially excluded. It focuses on self-development and individual empowerment rather than immediate labour market integration. The programme enables young people to stabilise their life by emphasising learning around different elements: physical/psychological, financial, education-training-employment, substance use, life and social skills and personal relationships. Informal education techniques are used including art, poetry, recreational activities and everyday events. The objectives of the programme are to: create an active learning project, which makes learning opportunities accessible, but does not limit the potential for achievement. *Bridging the Gap* has developed from TYN's successful keyworking system and ethos of 'success through empowerment' and being non-judgemental. The project is delivered using Personal Development Plans, delivered at the speed of the individual and in a way that maximises opportunities to succeed on their own terms. The keyworking that facilitates the delivery of training takes places on a 24/7 basis. The project was initially set up as a pilot project, funded by the local Chamber of Commerce for a period of 6 months as part of a regional *Learning Gateway* programme.

---

[1] It is important to note that the following profiles, or 'pen portraits', are descriptions of the case study projects as they were at the time of the research and may have changed since the research was undertaken.

Bibliography

Ackers, H.L. (1998), *Shifting Spaces, Women, Citizenship and Migration within the EU*, Bristol, Policy Press.

Ainley, P. and Rainbird, H. (eds), (1999), *Apprenticeship· Towards a New Paradigm of Learning*, London, Kogan Page.

Andersen, J. (2000), *Køn, Klasse Og Ligestilling*, Research Paper, 7(00), Research Papers from the Department of Social Sciences, Denmark, Roskilde University.

Arnold. R. and Siebert, H. (1997), *Konstruktivistische Erwachsenenbildung, Von Der Deutung Zur Konstruktion Von Wirklichkeit*, Baltmannsweiler, Schneider Vlg.

Arnold, R. and Schüßler, I. (1998), *Wandel Der Lernkulturen, Ideen Und Bausteine Fur Ein Lebendiges Lernen*, Darmstadt, Wissenschaftliche Buchgesellschaft.

Baethge, M., Hantsche, B., Pelull, W. and Voskamp, U. (1989), *Jugend, Arbeit Und Identitat· Lebensperspektiven Und Interessensorientierungen Von Jugendlichen*, Opladen,Göttingen, Leske and Budrich, Opladen.

Banks, M. et al. (1992), *Careers and Identities*, Milton Keynes, Open University Press.

Bates, I. and Riseborough, G. (eds), (1993), *Youth and Inequality*, Buckingham, Open University Press.

Bauman, Z. (1999), *Globalisering, De Menneskelige Konsekvenser*, Hans Reitzels Forlag.

Bauman, Z. (2000), *Liquid Modernity*, Cambridge, Polity Press.

Baumann, G. (1999), *The Multicultural Riddle· Rethinking National, Ethnic, and Religious Identities*, London, Routledge.

Bean, C. (1994), 'European Unemployment: A Survey', *Journal of Economic Literature*, Vol. 32(2), pp. 573-619.

Beck, U. (1986), *Risikogesellschaft. Auf Dem Weg in Eine andere Moderne*, Frankfurt, Suhrkamp.

Beck, U. (1992), *Risk Society Towards a New Modernity*, London, Sage.

Beck, U. and Beck-Gernsheim, E. (2001), *Individualization· Institutionalised, Individualism and its Social and Political Consequences*, London, Sage.

Beck, U., Giddens, A. and Lash, S. (1994), *Reflexive Modernization: Politics Tradition and Aesthetics in the Modern Social Order*, Cambridge, Polity Press.

Beck, W., Van Der Maesen, L. and Walker, A. (eds), (1998), *The Social Quality of Europe*, Bristol, The Policy Press.

Behrens, M. and Evans, K. (2002), 'Taking Control of their Lives? A Comparison of the Experiences of Unemployed Young Adults (18-25), in England and the New Germany', *Comparative Education*, Vol. 38(1), pp. 17-37.

Bell, R. and Jones, G. (1999), *Independent Living, Income and Housing*, London, National Youth Agency.

Bennett, A., Cieslik M. and S. Miles (2003), *Researching Youth*, London, Palgrave, pp. 1-12.

Bernstein, B. (1977), 'Class and Pedagogues, Visible and Invisible', in J. Karabel and A.H. Halsey (eds), *Power and Ideology in Education*, New York, Oxford University Press, pp. 511-534.

Bernstein, B. (ed.), (1986), *The Structuring of Pedagogic Discourse: Class, Codes and Control*, Vol. 4, London, Routledge.

Bessis, B. (1995), From Social Exclusion to Social Cohesion: Towards a Political Agenda', in *Policy Paper No. 2, The Roskilde Symposium, March 2-4*, Roskilde, Denmark, UNESCO MOST/WHO/EU, http://www.unesco.org/most/besseng.htm.

Bogt, T.F.M., Ter and Meeus, W.H.J. (1997), 'Adolescentie' in J. Kooistra and I. Van Mourik, (eds), *Leefvormen, Identiteit En Socialisatie*, Utrecht, Lemma, pp. 141-172.

Bouget, D. (1998), 'The Maastricht Treaty and Social Quality: A Divorce?' in W. Beck, L. Van Der Maesen and A. Walker (eds), *The Social Quality of Europe*, London, Policy Press.

Bourdieu, P. (1985), 'The Genesis of the Concepts of "Habitus" and "Field"', *Sociocriticism*, Vol. 1(2), pp. 11-24.

Bray, J., Lee, J., Smith, L. and Yorks, L. (2000), *Collaborative Inquiry in Practice*, London, Sage.

Brine, J. (2001), 'Education, Social Exclusion and the Supranational State', *International Journal of Inclusive Education*, Vol. 5(2/3), pp. 119-131.

Brown, J. (2001), 'The World Café: Living Knowledge through Conversations that Matter', Ph.D. Dissertation, The Fielding Institute.

Buchner, P. (1990), 'Growing Up in the Eighties: Changes in the Social Biography of Childhood', in L. Chisholm, P. Buchner, H.-H. Kruger and P. Brown (eds), *Childhood, Youth and Social Change: A Comparative Perspective*, Basingstoke, Falmer Press.

Burns, D. (2003), *Whole System Action Research in Complex Governance Settings*, Keynote Address, ALARPM 6th World Congress and PAR 10th World Congress, Pretoria, September, 2003.

Burns, D., Williams, C. and Windebank, J. (2004), *Community Self-Help*, Basingstoke, Palgrave Macmillan.

Bynner, J., Chisholm, L. and Furlong, A. (eds), (1997), *Youth, Citizenship and Social Change in a European Context*, Aldershot, Ashgate.

Bynner, J.M. (1987), 'Coping with Transition, ESRC's New 16-19 Initiative', *Youth and Policy*, Vol. 22, pp. 25-28.

Calmsfors, L., Forslund, A. and Hemstrom, M. (2002), *Does Active Labour Market Policy Work? Lessons from the Swedish Experiences*, Working Paper No. 4, Uppsala, IFAU, Institute for Labour Market Policy Evaluation.

Capra F. (1996), *The Web of Life: A New Scientific Understanding of Living Systems*, New York, Anchor Books, Doubleday.

Castells, M. (1993), 'European Cities, The Informational Society, and the Global Economy', *Journal of Economic and Social Geography*, Vol. 83(4), pp. 247-257.

Castells, M. (1997), *The Power of Identity: The Information Age, Economy, Society and Culture*, 1st Ed., Vol. 2, Cambridge, Massachusetts, Blackwell Series.

CEDEFOP (2001), *Training and Learning for Competence*, Second Report on Vocational Training Research in Europe, Luxemburg, Office for Publication of the European Communities.

Centrum Sociaal Beleid, S.D, http://www.lokaalsociaalbeleid.nl.

Chambers, R. (1994), *Migrancy, Culture, Identity*, London, Routledge.

Chambers, R. (1997), *Whose Reality Counts? Putting the First Last*, London, Intermediate Technology.

Chandler, D. and Torbert, W. R. (2003), 'Transforming Inquiry and Action by Interweaving 27 Flavors of Action Research', *Action Research*, Vol. 1(2).

Chomsky, N. (1995), *The Minimalist Program*, Cambridge, Massachusetts, MIT Press.

Chomsky, N. (1996), *Class Warfare: Interviews with David Barsamian*, London, Pluto Press.

Cieslik, M. and Pollock, G. (eds), (2002), *Young People and Risk Society: The Restructuring of Youth Identities and Transitions in Late Modernity*, Aldershot, Ashgate.

Cleaver, F. (2002), 'Institutions, Agency and the Limitations of Participatory Approaches to Development', in B. Cooke and U. Kothari (eds), *Participation: The New Tyranny*, London, Zed Books.

Coffield, F. (ed.), (2000a), *Differing Visions of a Learning Society: Research Findings*, Vol. 1, Bristol, Policy Press and ESRC.

Coffield, F. (ed.), (2000b), *Differing Visions of a Learning Society: Research Findings*, Vol. 2, Bristol, Policy Press and ESRC.

Cohen, N. (2000), 'Hit the Target and Miss the Point', *New Statesman*, Vol. 13(590), 31 January, p. 10.

Cohen, P. and Ainley, P. (2000), 'In the Country of the Blind? Youth Studies and Cultural Studies in Britain', *Journal of Youth Studies*, Vol. 3(1), pp. 75-95.

Cohen, P. (2003), 'Mods and Shockers, Youth Cultural Studies in Britain' in A. Bennett, M. Cieslik, and S. Miles, (2003), *Researching Youth*, London, Palgrave, pp. 29-54.

Coleman, J.C. and Hendry L.B. (eds), (1990), *The Nature of Adolescence*, 2nd Ed., London, Routledge and Kegan Paul.

Coleman, J.S. (1988-9), 'Social Capital in the Creation of Human Capital', *American Journal of Sociology*, Vol. 94, pp. 95-120.

Coles, B. (2000), *Joined-Up Youth Research Policy and Practice: A New Agenda for Change*, Leicester, Youth Work Press and Barnardos.

Cooke, B. and Kothari, U. (2002), *Participation, The New Tyranny?* London, Zed Books.

Council of the European Union (1994), *Establishing an Action Programme for the Implementation of a European Community Vocational Training Policy*. 94/819/EC, Council Decision of 6 December 1994, Official Journal, L 340, December 29, pp. 0008-0024.

Council of the European Union (1996), Official Journal, 6802/96

Council of the European Union (2001), Official Journal, January 24

Dean, M. (1995), 'Governing the Unemployed Self in an Active Society', *Economy and Society*, Vol. 24(4), pp. 559-583.

Dean, M. (1999), *Governmentality: Power and Rule in Modern Society*, London, Sage.

de Geus, A. (2002), *The Living Company: Habits for Survival in a Turbulent Business Environment*, 1st Ed., Boston, Harvard Business School Press.

Denzin, N.K. and Lincoln, Y.S (eds), (1994), *Handbook of Qualitative Research*, 1st Ed., London, Sage.

Depaepe, M. (1998), 'De Pedagogisering Achterna, Aanzet Tot Een Genealogie Van De Pedagogische Mentaliteit In De Voorbije 250 Jaar', *in Pedagogics: Towards a Genealogy of the Pedagogical Mentality in the Past 250 Years*, Leuven, Acco.

du Bois-Reymond, M (1995), 'Future Orientations of Dutch Youth: The Emergence of a Choice Biography', in A. Cavalli and O. Galland (eds), *Youth in Europe: Social Change in Western Europe*, London, Pinter, pp. 75-95.

Dupont, S. and Hansen, L. (1997), *En Undersøgelse Af Nogle 40 – 60 Årige Mænds Motivation Og Barrierer I Forhold Til Deltagelse I Voksenuddannelse – Et Sammendrag*. Dansk, Undervisningsministeriet, http://www pub.uvm.dk/1998/4060aarige/.

Dwyer, P. (1998), 'Conditional Citizens? Welfare Rights and Responsibilities in the Late 1990s', *Critical Social Policy*, 57, Vol. 18(4), pp 493-517

Edwards, G. (1999), *Pure Bliss. The Art of Living in Soft Time*, London, Piatkus.

Edwards, R. and Usher, R (1997), 'Globalisation and a Pedagogy of (Dis)Location', in A. Armstrong, N. Miller and M. Zukas (eds), *Crossing Borders, Breaking Boundaries*.

Proceedings of the 27th Annnual SCUTREA Conference, July 1-3, University of London, SCUTREA.

Edwards, R. and Usher, R. (2000), *Globalisation and Pedagogy: Space, Place and Identity*, London, Routledge Falmer.

Edwards, R., Armstrong, P. and Miller, N. (2001), 'Include Me Out, Critical Readings of Social Exclusion, Social Inclusion and Lifelong Learning', *International Journal of Lifelong Education*, Vol. 20(5), pp. 417-428.

Elmeskov, J. (1993), *High and Persistent Unemployment: Assessment of the Problem and its Causes*, Economics Department Working Paper 132, Paris, OECD.

Engeström, Y. (1996), 'Interobjectivity, Ideality, and Dialectics', *Mind, Culture, and Activity*, Vol. 3(4), pp. 259-265.

Estrella, M. et al. (eds), (2000), *Learning from Change: Issues and Experiences in Participatory Monitoring and Evaluation*, London and Ottawa, Intermediate Technology Publications and International Development Research Center.

European Commission (1995), *White Paper on Education and Training: Teaching and Learning, Towards the Learning Society*, Brussels, Office for Official Publications of the European Communities, COM (95), p. 590.

European Commission (1997), *Agenda 2000*, Vol. 1, Office for Official Publications of the European Communities, Brussels.

European Commission (2000), *Commission Staff Working Paper: A Memorandum on Lifelong Learning*, Brussels, European Commission, SEC (2000), 1832.

European Group for Integrated Social Research (EGRIS), (2001), 'Misleading Trajectories: Transition Dilemmas of Young Adults in Europe', *Journal of Youth Studies*, Vol. 4(1), pp. 101-118.

Evans, K. (1998), *Shaping Futures: Learning for Competence and Citizenship*, Aldershot, Ashgate.

Evans, K. (2002), 'Taking Control of Their Lives? The Youth Citizenship and Social Change Project', *European Education Research Journal*, Vol. 1(3), pp. 497-521.

Evans, K. and Heinz, W R. (eds), (1994), *Becoming Adults in England and Germany*, London, Anglo-German Foundation for the Study of Industrial Society.

Evans, K. and Furlong, A. (1997), 'Metaphors of Youth Transitions, Niches, Pathways, Trajectories or Navigations' in J. Bynner, L. Chisholm and A. Furlong (eds), *Youth, Citizenship and Social Change in a European Context*, Aldershot, Avebury.

Farrell, L. (2000), 'Ways of Doing, Ways of Being: Language, Education and "Working" Identities', *Language and Education*, Vol. 14(1), pp. 18-36.

Federation of European Employers (2001), *The Future of a Social Europe*, http://www.fedee.com.

Federation of European Employers (2001), http://www.euen.co.uk/histsoc.html.

Feira Summit (2000) http://www.europarl.eu.int/conferences/euromed/instorge/feira_en.pdf.

Ferlie, E., Ashburner, L., Fitzgerald, L. and Pettigrew, A. (1996), *The New Public Management in Action*, Oxford University Press.

Ferlie, E. (1999), *Inaugural Professorial Lecture*, Unpublished Paper, Imperial College.

Ferrera, M., Hemerijck, A. and Rhodes, M. (2000), *The Future of a Social Europe. Recasting Work and Welfare in the New Economy*, Report Prepared for the Portuguese Presidency of the EU, Oeiras, Celta Editora.

Finn, D., Blackmore, M. and Nimmo, M. (1998), *Welfare to Work and the Long Term Unemployed*, London, Unemployment Unit and Youth Aid.

Finnish Government, S.D. http://www.vn.fi/stm/english/tao/strategt2010.htm.

Foucault, M. (1984), 'Nietzsche, Genealogy, History' in P. Rainbow (ed.), *The Foucault Reader*, New York, Pantheon Books, pp. 76-100.

Freire, P. (1993), *Pedagogy of the Oppressed*, New York, Continuum.

Furlong, A. and Cartmel, F. (1997), *Young People and Social Change: Individualization and Risk in Late Modernity*, Buckingham, Philadelphia, Open University Press.

Gamarnikow, E. and Green, A. (1999), 'Developing Social Capital, Dilemmas, Possibilities and Limitations in Education', in A. Hayton (ed.), *Tackling Disaffection and Social Exclusion: Education Perspectives and Policies*, London, Kogan Page, pp. 47-64.

Gaventa, J. and Blauert, J. (2000), 'Learning to Change by Learning from Change, Going to Scale with Participatory Monitoring and Evaluation', in M. Estrella et al. (eds), *Learning from Change, Issues and Experiences in Participatory Monitoring and Evaluation*, London and Ottawa, Intermediate Technology Publications and International Development Research Centre, pp. 229-243.

Gayle, V. (1998), 'Structural and Cultural Approaches to Youth: Structuration Theory and Bridging the Gap', *Youth and Policy*, Vol. 61, pp. 59-72.

Gibbons, M. et al. (1994), *The New Production of Knowledge: The Dynamics of Science and Research in Contemporary Societies*, London, Sage Publications.

Giddens, A. (1979), *Central Problems in Social Theory – Action, Structure and Contradiction in Social Analysis*, London and Basingstoke, Macmillan Press.

Giddens, A. (1984), *The Constitution of Society: Outline of the Theory of Structuration*, Cambridge, Polity Press.

Giddens, A. (1991), *Modernity and Self-Identity: Self and Society in the Late Modern Age*, Stanford University Press.

Giddens, A. (1998), *The Third Way: The Renewal of Social Democracy. Self and Society in Late Modern Age*, Cambridge, Polity Press.

Giddens, A. (2000), *Sociology*, 4th Ed., Cambridge, Polity Press.

Gilain, B., Jadoul, P., Nyssens, M. and Petrella, F. (2001), 'Les Services De Proximité, Une Pluralité d'Acteurs et d'Effets sur l'Insertion', in G. Liénard (ed.), *l'Insertion, Défi Pour l'Analyse, Enjeu Pour l'Action*, Sprimont, Mardaga, pp. 241-268.

Glaser, B.G. and Straus, A.L. (1967), *The Discovery of Grounded Theory: Strategies for Qualitative Research*, Chicago, Aldine

Gobin, C. (1997), 'Taming the Unions, The Mirage of a Social Europe', Translated from French by B. Wilson, *Le Monde Diplomatique*, November, http://www.mondediplo.com/ 1997/11/europe.

Green, A. (2002), 'The Many Faces of Lifelong Learning, Recent Educational Policy Trends in Europe', *Journal of Education Policy*, Vol. 17(6), pp. 611-626.

Green-Pedersen, C. and Van Kersbergen, K. (2001), 'The Politics of the "Third Way"· The Transformation of the Danish and Dutch Social Democrats' in *Third Ways in Europe*, Workshop 11, Paper for the ECPR Joint Session of Workshops, Grenoble, April 6-11.

Griffin, C. (1993), *Representations of Youth, The Study of Youth and Adolescence in Britain and America*, Cambridge, Polity Press.

Griffin, C. (1997), 'Troubled Teens: Managing Disorders of Transition and Consumption', *Feminist Review*, Vol. 55, pp. 4-21.

Grossberg, L. (1996), 'Identity and Cultural Studies: Is that All There Is?' in S. Hall and P. du Gay (eds), *Questions of Cultural Identity*, London, Sage, pp. 87-107.

Grubb, D. and Martin, J. (2001), *What Works and for Whom: A Review of OECD Countries' Experiences with Active Labour Market Policies*, Working Paper No. 14, Uppsala, IFAU, Institute for Labour Market Policy Evaluation.

Hake, B. (2000), 'Deelname Aan Levenslang Leren Voor Iedereen?' in F. Glastra and F. Meijers (eds), *Een Leven Lang Leren?* Den Haag, Elsevier.

Hammer, M. (1996), *Beyond Reengineering· How the Process-Centred Organisation is Changing Our Work and Our Lives*, New York, Harper Collins

Hammer, T. (2003), *Youth Unemployment and Social Exclusion in Europe*, Bristol, Policy Press.

Harrison, B. (1994), *Lean and Mean: The Changing Landscape of Corporate Power in the Age of Flexibility*, New York, Basic Books.

Henderson, P. (1997), *Social Inclusion and Citizenship in Europe: The Contribution of Community Development*, Lille, CEBSD.

Herbert, A. (2000), 'Constraints on Critical Questions', Paper Presented to the *Organisational Learning and Future of Work Stream: 5th World Congress on Action Learning*, Action Research Process Management, September, University of Ballarat.

Herkenhoff, P. (ed.), (2002), *Tempo*, Publication of the Tempo Exhibition, June 29-September 9, New York, Museum of Modern Art (Moma), Queens, New York State, http://www.moma.org/exhibitions/2002/tempo/Index.html.

Hertz, N. (2002), *The Silent Takeover, Global Capitalism and the Death of Democracy*, London, Arrow Books.

Heylen, F., Goubert, L. and Omey, E. (1996), 'Unemployment in Europe: A Problem of Relative or Aggregate Demand for Labour?' *International Labour Review*, Vol. 135(1), pp. 17-36.

Hoggett, P. (1991), 'A New Management in the Public Sector?', *Policy and Politics*, Vol. 19(4), pp. 243-256.

Hood, C. (1991), 'A Public Management for All Seasons?', *Public Administration*, Vol. 69(1), pp. 3-19.

Hutton, W. (1995), *The State We're in*, London, Jonathan Cape.

Ivanič, R. (1997), *Writing and Identity: The Discoursal Construction of Identity in Academic Writing*, Amsterdam, Philadelphia, John Benjamins Publishing Company.

Jackman, R. (2002), 'Determinants of Unemployment in Western Europe and Possible Policy Responses', *Economic Survey of Europe 2002*, No. 2.

Jackman, R., Layard, R. and Nickell, S. (1996), 'Combating Unemployment: Is Flexibility Enough?' in OECD, *Macroeconomic Policies and Structural Reform*, Paris, OECD, pp. 19-58.

Jackman, R., Layard, R., Manacorda, M. and Petrongolo, B. (1997), *European Versus US Unemployment: Different Responses to Increased Demand for Skill?* Centre for Economic Performance, Discussion Paper No. 349, June, London, CEP, http://www.cep.lse.ac.uk/pubs/download/dp0349.pdf.

Jansen, T. and Wildemeersch, D. (1996), 'Adult Education and Critical Identity Development, from a Deficiency Orientation Towards a Competency Orientation', *International Journal of Lifelong Education*, Vol. 15(5), pp. 325-340.

Jessop, B., Peck, J. and Tickell, A. (1997), 'Retooling the Machine, Economic Crisis, State Restructuring and Urban Politics', in A.E.G. Jonas and D. Wilson (eds), *The Urban Growth Machine, Critical Perspectives Twenty Years Later*, New York, State University of New York Press, pp. 141-162.

Kazepov, Y. (2002), 'Social Assistance and Activation Measures in Europe', Paper Presented at the *Cost 15 Conference*, Oslo, April 5-6, pp. 1-32.

Kemmis, S. (2001), 'Exploring the Relevance of Critical Theory for Action Research, Emancipatory Action Research in the Footsteps of Jürgen Habermas', in P. Reason and H. Bradbury (eds), *The Handbook of Action Research, Participative Inquiry and Practice*, London, Sage, pp. 91-102.

Kinder, K., Wakefield, A. and Wilkin, A. (1996), *Talking Back: Pupils Views on Disaffection*, London, NFER.

Kirby, P. (1999), *Involving Young Researchers, How to Enable Young People to Design and Conduct Research*, York Publishing and Joseph Rowntree Foundation.

Klein, H. (1990), 'Adolescence, Youth and Young Adulthood, Rethinking Current Conceptualizations of Life Stage', *Youth and Society*, Vol. 21(4), pp 446-471.

Lather, P. (1991), *Getting Smart, Feminist Research and Pedagogy with/in the Postmodern*, New York, Routledge.

Lave, J. and Wenger, E. (1991), *Situated Learning, Legitimate Peripheral Participation*, Cambridge, Cambridge University Press.

Law, B. (1996), 'A Career-Learning Theory' in A.G. Watts et al. (eds), *Rethinking Careers Education and Guidance, Theory, Policy and Practice*, London, Routledge, pp. 46-72.

Law, B., Meijers, F. and Wijers, G. (2002), 'New Perspectives on Career and Identity in the Contemporary World', *British Journal of Guidance and Counselling*, Vol. 30(4), pp. 431-449.

Lawy, R. (2002), 'Risky Stories, Youth Identities, Learning and Everyday Risk', *Journal of Youth Studies*, Vol. 5(4), pp. 407-423.

Layder, D. (1998), *Sociological Practice: Linking Theory and Social Research*, London, Sage.

Leney, T. (1999), 'European Approaches to Social Exclusion', in A. Hayton and A. Hodgson (eds), *Tackling Disaffection and Social Exclusion*, London, Kogan Page, pp. 33-45.

Lincoln, Y.S. and Guba, E.G. (1985), *Naturalistic Inquiry*, Beverly Hills, California, Sage.

Lisbon Summit (2000), http·//www.euractiv.com/cgi-bin/cgInt.exe?714and1015=9and1014 =ld_ lisbon

Luxembourg Jobs Summit (1997),
   http://www.europa.eu.Int/comm/employment_social/elm/summit /en/home.htm.

MacDonald, R. (1998), 'Youth, Transitions and Social Exclusion Some Issues for Youth Research in the UK', *Journal of Youth Studies*, Vol. 1(2), pp. 163-177.

MacDonald, R. (ed.), (1997), *Youth, the 'Underclass' and Social Exclusion*, London, Routledge.

Makepeace, G.H., Paci, P., Joshi, H. and Dolton, P.J. (1999), 'How Unequally has Equal Pay Progressed Since the 1970s? A Study of Two British Cohorts', *Journal of Human Resources*, Vol. 34(3), pp. 534-556

Marshall, J. (1995), *Women Managers Moving on*, London, Routledge.

Martin, S. and Sanderson, I. (1999), 'Evaluating Public Policy Experiments, Measuring Outcomes, Monitoring Progress or Managing Pilots?', *Evaluation*, Vol. 5(3), pp. 245-258.

Mclaughlin, M.W. and Heath, S.B. (1993), 'Casting (?) the Self· Frames for Identity and Dilemmas for Policy' in M.W. Mclaughlin and S B. Heath (eds), *Identity and Inner-City Youth, Beyond Ethnicity and Gender*, New York, Teachers College Press.

McRobbie, A (1994), *Postmodernism and Popular Culture*, London, Routledge.

Meijers, F. and Wijers, G. (1998), 'Flexibilisation Or Career Identity?' in D. Wildemeersch, M. Finger and T. Jansen (eds), *Adult Education and Social Responsibility*, 1st Ed., Frankfurt, Peter Lang, pp. 73-94.

Midgley, G. (2000), *Systemic Intervention, Philosophy, Methodology and Practice*, New York, Kluwer Academic/Plenum Publishers

Miles, S. (2000), *Youth Lifestyles in a Changing World*, Milton Keynes, Open University Press.

Mingione, E. (1994), 'Life Strategies and Social Economies in the Postfordist Age', *International Journal of Urban and Regional Research*, Vol 18(1), pp. 24-45.

Mizen, P. (2003), 'The Best Days of Your Life? Youth, Policy and Blair's New Labour', *Critical Social Policy*, Vol. 23(4), pp. 453-476.

Myles, J. (1991), 'Is There a Post-Fordist Life-Course?' in W.R Heinz (ed.), *Theoretical Advances in Life-Course Research*, Weinhem, Deutscher Studien Verlag.

Nava, M. (1992), *Changing Culture*, London, Sage Publications.

Nielsen, K. (1992), *Kultur Og Modernitet*, Aarhus, Universitetsforlag.

Nowotny, H., Scott, P. and Gibbons, M. (2001), *Re-Thinking Science, Knowledge and the Public in an Age of Uncertainty*, Cambridge, Polity Press.

Nuissl, E. (1992), 'Lernökologie', in P. Faulstich et al. (eds), *Weiterbildung Für Die 90er Jahre*, München, Weinheim.

O'Brien, M (1998), 'Theorising Modernity, Reflexivity, Environment and Identity in Giddens' Social Theory' in M. O'Brien, S. Penna and C. Hay (eds), *Reflexivity, Environment and Identity in Giddens' Social Theory*, Essex, Pearson/Longman.

OECD (2000), *Where are the Resources for Lifelong Learning?* Paris, OECD.

Osler, A. and Starkey, H. (1999), 'Rights, Identities and Inclusion, European Action Programmes as Political Education', *Oxford Review of Education*, Vol. 25(1-2), pp. 199-215.

Percy-Smith, B., Burns, D., Walsh, D. and Weil, S. (2003), *Mind the Gap: Healthy Futures for Young People in Hounslow*, Bristol, UWE and Hounslow Community Health Council.

Percy-Smith, B. (1999), *Multiple Childhood Geographies: Giving Voice to Young People's Experience of Place*, PhD Thesis, University College Northampton.

Percy-Smith, B. and Walsh, D. (2002), 'Responding to Underachievement and Disaffection: Lessons from New Start for Educational Reform' Paper presented at the *Youth 2002: Research, Practice and Policy Conference*, Keele University, July 22-24.

Percy-Smith, B. and Weil, S. (2002), 'New Deal Or Raw Deal? Dilemmas and Paradoxes of State Interventions Into the Youth Labour Market' in M. Cieslik and G. Pollock (eds), *Young People in Risk Society: The Restructuring of Youth Identities and Transitions in Late Modernity*, Aldershot, Ashgate, pp. 117-136.

Percy-Smith, B. and Weil, S. (2003), 'Practice-Based Research as Development, Innovation and Empowerment in Youth Intervention Initiatives using Collaborative Action Inquiry' in A. Bennet, M. Cieslik and S Miles (eds), *Researching Youth*, Hampshire, Palgrave Macmillan, pp. 66-84.

PJB (2003), *New Perspectives for Learning: Insights from European Union Funded Research on Education and Training*, Issue 6, September.

Power, A. (1997), *Estates on the Edge*, London, Macmillan.

Putnam, R. (2000), *Bowling Alone: The Collapse and Revival of American Community*, New York, Simon and Schuster.

Reason, P. and Bradbury, H. (2000), *The Handbook of Action Research: Participative Inquiry and Practice*, London, Sage.

Richardson, L. (1997), 'Skirting a Pleated Text, De-Disciplining an Academic Life' in *Qualitative Inquiry*, pp. 295-303.

Roberts, K. (1995), *Youth and Employment in Modern Britain*, Oxford University Press.

Room, G. (1995), 'Poverty and Social Exclusion: The New European Agenda for Policy and Research', in G. Room (ed.), *Beyond the Threshold: The Measurement and Analysis of Social Exclusion*, Bristol, The Policy Press, pp. 1-9.

Rosanvallon, P. (2000), *The New Social Question*, Princeton University Press.

Rose, N. (1996), *Inventing Our Selves: Psychology, Power, and Personhood*, Cambridge University Press.

Rose, N. (1999), *The Powers of Freedom: Reframing Political Thought*, Cambridge University Press.

Rosengard, A. (1995), 'Youth Homelessness: The Construction of a Social Issue', *Urban Studies*, Vol. 32(7), pp. 1218-1221.

Roth, G. and Kleiner, A (2000), 'Developing Organizational Memory through Learning Histories', in W. James, J. Cortada and J. Woods (eds), *The Knowledge Management Year Book 2000-2001*, Butterworth-Heinemann, pp. 123-144.

Rudd, P. and Evans, K. (1998), 'Structure and Agency in Youth Transitions, Student Experiences of Vocational Further Education', *Journal of Youth Studies*, Vol. 1(1), pp. 39-62.

Salmon, P. (1990), 'Personal Stances in Learning', in S. Warner Weil and I. McGill (eds), *Making Sense of Experiential Learning*, Buckingham, SHRE and Open University Press, pp. 230-241.

Sanderson, I. (2004), 'Is it What Works that Matters? Evaluation and Evidence-Based Policy Making', in Economic Research Institute of Northern Ireland, January 27.

Schon, D. (1983), *The Reflective Practitioner: How Professionals Think in Action*, New York, Basic Books.

Schön, D. (1979), 'Public Service Organizations and the Capacity for Public Learning', *International Social Science Journal*, Vol. 31, pp. 682-695.

Schön, D. and Rein, M. (1994), *Frame Reflection, Toward the Resolution of Intractable Controversies*, New York, Basic Books.

Schuller, T. and Field, J. (2001), 'Social Capital, Human Capital and the Learning Society', in R. Edwards et al. (eds), *Supporting Lifelong Learning, Making Policy Work*, London, Routledge Falmer, pp 76-87.

Sels, L. and Van Hootegem, G. (2001), 'Seeking the Balance Between Flexibility and Security: A Rising Issue in the Low Countries', *Work, Employment and Society*, Vol. 15(2), pp. 327-352.

Sennett, R. (1998), *The Corrosion of Character*, New York, WW Norton.

Sennett, R. (1999), *Det Fleksible Menneske, Eller Arbejdets Forvandling Og Personlighedens Nedsmeltning*, Højbjerg, Hovedland.

Shaw, P. (1997), 'Intervening in the Shadow Systems of Organizations: Consulting from a Complexity Perspective', *Journal of Organizational Change Management*, Vol. 10(3), pp. 235-250.

Siebert, H. (1991), 'Lernökologie', *Literatur- Und Forschungsreport*, Vol. 27, pp. 64-69.

Simonsen, B. and Ulriksen, L. (1998), *Universitetsstudier I Krise. Fag, Projekter Og Moderne Studenter*, Roskilde Universitetsforlag.

Skelton, T. and Valentine, G. (1998), *Cool Places, Geographies of Youth Cultures*, London, Routledge.

Smith, M. (2002), *Culture, Reinventing the Social Sciences*, Buckingham, Open University Press.

Solorzano, D. and Yosso, T. (2002), 'Critical Race Methodology: Counter Storytelling as an Analytical Framework for Education Research', *Qualitative Inquiry*, Vol. 8, pp. 23-44.

Stacey, R. (2001), *Complex Responsive Processes in Organizations: Learning and Knowledge Creation*, London, Routledge.

Stacey, R., Griffin, D and Shaw, P. (2000), *Complexity and Management*, London, Routledge.

Strathern, M. (ed.), (2000), *Audit Cultures: Anthropological Studies in Accountability, Ethics and the Academy*, London, Routledge.

Tabulawa, R. (2003), 'International Aid Agencies, Learner Centred Pedagogy and Political Democratisation: A Critique', *Comparative Education*, Vol. 39(1), pp. 7-26.

Taylor, M. (2003), *Public Policy in the Community*, New York, Palgrave Macmillan.

Thijssen, J. and Lankhuizen, E. (2000), 'Competentiemanagement En Employabilitystrategie, Een Kader Voor Beleidskeuzes' in F Glastra and F. Meijers (eds), *Een Leven Lang Leren?* Den Haag, Elsevier

Toulmin, S. and Gustavsen, B. (1996), *Beyond Theory: Changing Organisations through Participation*, Philadelphia, John Benjamins.

Ulrich, B. (1992), *Risk Society: Towards a New Modernity*, Translated from German by Mark Ritter, London, Sage [First published 1986].

UNDP (1998), *National Human Development Report 1998*, Warszawa, UNDP.

Usher, R., Bryant, I. and Johnston, R. (1997), *Adult Education and the Postmodern Challenge: Learning Beyond the Limits*, London and New York, Routledge.

Valencia, R. (ed.), (1997), *The Evolution of Deficit Thinking in Educational Thought and Practice*, New York, Falmer Press.

Van Hootegem, G. (2000), *De Draaglijke Traagheid Van Het Management* [The Bearable Slowness of Management], Leuven, Acco.

Van Manen, M. (1990), *Researching Lived Experience, Human Science for An Action Sensitive Pedagogy*, Albany, State University Press.

Van Onna, B. (1990), Individuealisering En Sociale Interventie, *Tijdschrift Voor Agologie*, Vol. 19(2), pp. 88-101.

Vandenbroucke, F. (2000), *Op Zoek Naar Een Redelijke Utopie De Actieve Welvaartstaat in Perspectief*, Leuven, Garant.

Weil, S. (1986), Non-traditional Learners within Traditional Higher Education Institutions, Discovery and Disappointment, *Studies in Higher Education*, Vol. 11(3), pp. 219-235.

Weil, S, (1988), 'From Language of Observation to a Language of Experience: Studying the Perspective of Diverse Adults in Higher Education', *Journal of Access Studies*, Vol. 3(1), pp. 17-43.

Weil, S. (1989), *Influences of Lifelong Learning on Adults Expectations and Experiences of Returning to Formal Learning Contexts*, Unpublished Phd Dissertation, University of London.

Weil, S. (1996), 'From the Other Side of Silence', *Changes*, Vol. 14(3), pp. 223-231.

Weil, S. (1998), 'Rhetorics and Realities in Public Service Organizations: Systemic Practice and Organizational Learning as Critically Reflexive Action Research (CRAR)', *Systemic Practice and Action Research*, Vol. 11(1), pp. 37-62.

Weil, S. with Annamonthodo, P., Brandt, G., Cheung, D., Douglas, C., Gunning, M., Phoenix, A., (1985), *Through a Hundred Pairs of Eyes*, London Institute of Education, CSDHE/LGTB.

Weil, S. and Frame, P. (1992), 'Capability Through Business and Management Education', in Stephenson, J. and Weil, S. (eds), *Quality in Learning*, London, Kogan Page.

Weil, S.W. and McGill, I. (eds), (1990), *Making Sense of Experiential Learning*, Buckingham, SRHE/Open University Press.

Weinberg, J. (1999), 'Lernkultur, Begriff, Geschichte, Perspektiven', in Arbeitsgemeinschaft Qualifikations-Entwicklungs-Management (ed.), *Kompetenzentwicklung '99, Aspekte Einer Neuen Lernkultur. Argumente, Erfahrungen, Konsequenzen*, Münster, Waxmann, pp. 81-143.

Wenger, E. (1998), *Communities of Practice, Learning, Meaning and Identity*, Cambridge, University Press.

Wheatley, M. (1994), *Leadership and the New Science*, San Francisco, Berrett-Koehler.

Wildemeersch, D. (2000), 'The Interpretive Professional', in K. Illeris (ed.), *Adult Education in the Perspective of the Learner*, Roskilde University Press, pp. 157-176.

Wildemeersch, D. (ed.), (2000), *Enhancing the Participation of Young Adults in Economic and Social Processes: Balancing Instrumental, Biographical and Social Competencies in Post-School Education and Training*, European Commission, Targeted Socio Economic Research, Project in the *Education, Equality, Exclusion* group, http://www.improving-ser.sti.jrc.it.

Wildemeersch, D. (ed.), (2002), *Refocusing Balancing Competencies*, Report for the European Commission – Targeted Socio-Economic Research, Leuven, Katholieke Universiteit Leuven, Centre for Social Pedagogy.

Wildemeersch, D., Jansen, T. and Finger, M. (eds), (1998), *Adult Education and Social Responsibility Reconciling the Irreconcilable?* Frankfurt, Peter Lang.

Wildemeersch, D., Jansen, T., Vandenabeele, J. and Jans, M. (1998), 'Social Learning: A New Perspective on Learning in Participatory Systems' *Studies in Continuing Education*, Vol. 20(2), pp. 251-265.

Young, M.F.D. (1999), 'Some Reflections on the Concepts of Social Exclusion and Inclusion, Beyond the Third Way', in A. Hayton (ed.), *Tackling Disaffection and Social Exclusion, Education Perspectives and Policies*, London, Kogan Page, pp. 210-223.

Ziehe, T. (1989), 'Ambivalenser Og Mangfoldighet' in J. Fornäs and O. Nielsen (eds), *En Artikkelsamling Om Ungdom, Skole, Æstetikk Og Kultur*, København, Politisk Revy.

Ziehe, T. (1992), 'Cultural Modernity and Individualization: Changed Symbolic Contexts for Young People', in J. Fornäs and G. Bolin (eds), *Moves in Modernity*, Stockholm, Almqvist and Wiksell International.

Index

For Product Safety Concerns and Information please contact our
EU representative GPSR@taylorandfrancis.com Taylor & Francis
Verlag GmbH, Kaufingerstraße 24, 80331 München, Germany